ENCODING
METHODISM

TELLING AND RETELLING
NARRATIVES OF WESLEYAN ORIGINS

TED A. CAMPBELL

NEW ROOM
B O O K S

Encoding Methodism: Telling and Retelling Narratives of Wesleyan Origins

The General Board of Higher Education and Ministry leads and serves The United Methodist Church in the recruitment, preparation, nurture, education, and support of Christian leaders—lay and clergy—for the work of making disciples of Jesus Christ for the transformation of the world. The General Board of Higher Education and Ministry of The United Methodist Church serves as an advocate for the intellectual life of the church. The board's mission embodies the Wesleyan tradition of commitment to the education of laypersons and ordained persons by providing access to higher education for all persons.

The name *New Room Books* comes from the New Room, a historic building in Bristol, England, and place of John Wesley's study. Built in 1739, it is the oldest Methodist chapel in the world.

Encoding Methodism: Telling and Retelling Narratives of Wesleyan Origins

HIGHER EDUCATION & MINISTRY
General Board of Higher Education and Ministry
THE UNITED METHODIST CHURCH

New Room Books Editorial Board

CONTENTS

to
Lydia Anne

A certain woman named Lydia,
a worshiper of God, was listening to us;
she was from the city of Thyatira
and a dealer in purple cloth.
—Acts 16:14

PREFACE

This book studies narratives of Wesleyan origins, as these narratives have been utilized to encode the identities of Wesleyan communities, including the earliest Methodist societies and subsequent Methodist churches.

In developing this work, I have benefited greatly from some previous works that offer conceptual frameworks for what follows. One is Albert C. Outler's essay "A New Future for Wesley Studies: An Agenda for 'Phase III,'" in which Outler laid out a schema of previous work in Wesley studies, identifying concerns characteristic of particular generations of Methodists in their reinterpretations of John Wesley.[1] Another helpful set of material for this study is Richard P. Heitzenrater's work "Wesley as Seen by His Contemporaries" and "Wesley in Retrospect" in his volumes on *The Elusive Mr. Wesley*.[2] These readings, Heitzenrater's introductions to them, and his comments on the later biographies of John Wesley also indicate how Wesley was perceived and appropriated in subsequent generations, and these observations have also helped form the vision of an encoded history that follows. Two articles offered in 1988 at the celebration of

---

1   Albert Outler, "A New Future for Wesley Studies: An Agenda for 'Phase III,'" in *The Future of the Methodist Theological Traditions*, ed. M. Douglas Meeks (Nashville: Abingdon Press, 1985), 34–52.

2   Richard P. Heitzenrater, *The Elusive Mr. Wesley*, 2nd. ed. (Nashville: Abingdon Press, 2003), 211–394. These materials comprised vol. 2 of the first edition of this work, which was originally issued in two volumes.

the 250th anniversary of John Wesley's Aldersgate-Street experience offered helpful perspectives on how Methodist leaders in different historical eras thought of John Wesley's Aldersgate-Street experience, one by Jean Miller Schmidt and the other by Randy L. Maddox.[3] Furthermore, two articles by Russell E. Richey have documented the role of histories published in Methodist *Disciplines* as narratives that shape Methodist identity at specific points, and these are also helpful in shaping the following account of how narratives of Wesleyan origins have evolved.[4]

This research was made possible, in part, by a Scholarly Outreach Award from Perkins School of Theology at Southern Methodist University and by an opportunity to participate in the Summer Wesley Seminar at Asbury Theological Seminary in the summer of 2015 led by Professor Kenneth J. Collins. I want to thank the administration and staff of Bridwell Library at Southern Methodist University, Dean William B. Lawrence, and Associate Dean Evelyn Parker of Perkins School of Theology. I also received assistance from the libraries of Asbury Theological Seminary and Asbury College during the summer seminar I spent in Wilmore. I am grateful for personal insights from Donald W. Dayton, especially concerning narratives of John Wesley described by advocates of the Holiness movement.

The book is dedicated to our daughter Lydia Anne. For her confirmation at Rockville United Methodist Church in Rockville, Maryland, she received a copy of *Endless Line of Splendor* by Halford Luccock and Webb Garrison, one of the narratives of John Wesley and Methodism discussed in the text following. I'm always delighted to see her signature when I open the book.

3   Jean Miller Schmidt, "'Strangely Warmed': The Place of Aldersgate in the Methodist Canon," in *Aldersgate Reconsidered,* ed. Randy L. Maddox (Nashville: Kingswood Books, 1990), 109–19; Randy L. Maddox, "Aldersgate: A Tradition History," in *Aldersgate Reconsidered,* 133–46.

4   Russell E. Richey, "History in the Discipline," in *Doctrine and Theology in The United Methodist Church,* ed. Thomas A. Langford (Nashville: Kingswood Books, 1991), 190–202; and "History as a Bearer of Denominational Identity: Methodism as a Case Study," in *Beyond Establishment: Protestant Identity in a Post-Protestant Age,* ed. Jackson Carroll and Wade Clark Roof (Louisville: Westminster/John Knox, 1993), 270–95.

INTRODUCTION

How do communities transmit their identities across generations? One way is to tell narratives of their origins. This book examines how Wesleyan and Methodist communities have told and retold narratives of their origins to encode and transmit their communal identities across generations.

Communities often encode their identities in narratives. Who are the Jewish people? One answer traditionally given in the annual Seder meal begins with this narrative statement:

> An Aramean tried to destroy my father. He went down to Egypt and sojourned there with meager numbers; but there he became a great and very populous nation.[1]

What is the Christian church? One answer might be that it is the community that solemnly recites a narrative like this:

> Christ has died; Christ is risen; Christ will come again.[2]

---

1   A midrash on Deuteronomy 26:5 in the Passover Haggadah; in Joseph Tabory, ed., *JPS Commentary on the Haggadah* (Philadelphia: Jewish Publication Society, 2008/5768), 89 and see the expansion that follows on 90–91. Although the first sentence differs from the traditional translation of the verse ("A wandering Aramean was my ancestor," NRSV), the midrash relies on a different vocalization of the Hebrew letters in which the word *oved* ("wandering") in older vocalizations was vocalized as the verb *ibed* ("destroyed"). But Laban did not succeed in destroying Jacob, hence the further understanding that "An Aramean [Laban] *tried to destroy* my father [Jacob]" (my emphasis).

2   The memorial acclamations uttered by congregations in the eucharistic prayer as it was revised in the twentieth century on the basis of ecumenical study by Catholics (in English-language contexts, though no longer in use), Methodists, Anglicans, Lutherans, and others. They are cited here from Rite II for the Holy Eucharist in *The Book of Common Prayer of the Episcopal Church in the USA* (New York: Oxford University Press, 1990), 363; cf. *The United Methodist Hymnal: Book of United Methodist Worship* (Nashville: Abingdon Press, 1989), 10, 14, 16, 18, 20, 22, 24–25.

In both cases, a community's identity is encoded in a narrative. The canons of Jewish and Christian Scripture themselves involve narratives that have defined Jewish and Christian communities, and the books of the Old Testament in Christian Bibles are ordered in such a way that they reinforce a particular narrative framework. Unlike the Jewish ordering of the *Tanach*, the Christian ordering of the Old Testament concludes with the prophets, setting up the narrative of John the Baptist and Jesus that follows in the Gospels. These uses of narratives to describe communities involve richly interwoven complexities, using historically encoded language that arose out of contested claims about the identities of these communities.

This book studies the ways in which Wesleyan communities have utilized narratives of Wesleyan origins to encode and transmit their identities. Wesleyan communities, including the earliest Methodist societies and later Methodist denominations, have described themselves by telling a story, the story about John Wesley and the communities he formed in the eighteenth century. Like the narratives that Jews and Christians used in the past to describe their communities, these are neither simple nor politically innocent stories. They are narratives woven together from previously existing and richly interwoven complexities using historically encoded language, and they arose out of contested claims about what it meant to be Wesleyan or Methodist.

The transmission of narratives is only one of the ways in which communities hand on their identities to new generations (e.g., 1 Corinthians 15:3). The transmission of common teachings (doctrine) and the transmission of common and authorized practices are also ways of handing on a communal identity to new generations. Narratives, teachings, and practices become deeply interwoven as communities transmit them to new generations: communal narratives often describe communal teachings and practices; communal practices often contain and enact communal teachings; and communal liturgies often encode historical narratives. My earlier study of *Wesleyan Beliefs: Formal and Popular Expressions of Core Teachings of Wesleyan*

Communities (2010) examined the communal transmission of beliefs in historic Wesleyan communities.[3] The present book continues this train of inquiry by considering the communal transmission of narratives in historic Wesleyan communities. Like the earlier work *Wesleyan Beliefs*, this work considers popular narratives of origins transmitted in historic Wesleyan communities as well as formal and authorized narratives of Wesleyan origins. I intend to follow these two works with a third work on the transmission of communally sanctioned practices in Wesleyan communities.

METAPHORS FOR TELLING AND RETELLING NARRATIVES OF COMMUNAL ORIGINS

A PLAY WITHIN A PLAY

My reflections on the complexities of retelling narratives began with my dissertation (1984) on John Wesley's uses of ancient Christian sources.[4] I realized in that work that I had to discern three different historical contexts in play: my own historical context in the late twentieth century, the historical context of John Wesley in the eighteenth century, and the historical context of the early Christian writings Wesley studied and used from the first through the fourth centuries CE. I began to envision a complex interlocking narrative, something like a play within a play within a play.

This work also involves three levels of historical reflection:

(1) the level of myself and contemporary readers considering these historical phenomena in our own historical contexts,

(2) the level that involves a series of individuals and communities who have told narratives of Wesleyan origins, and

---

3   Ted A. Campbell, *Wesleyan Beliefs: Formal and Popular Expressions of Core Teachings of Wesleyan Communities* (Nashville: Kingswood Books, 2010).

4   Ted A. Campbell, "John Wesley's Conceptions and Uses of Christian Antiquity" (PhD dissertation, Southern Methodist University, 1984); published as *John Wesley and Christian Antiquity: Religious Vision and Cultural Change* (Nashville: Kingswood Books, 1991).

(3) the level of the origins of Wesleyan communities in the eighteenth century.

The consistent focus of this book is on the second level (that is, the individuals and communities that have told narratives about Wesleyan origins), though one can never proceed without consciousness of our own contexts as interpreters (level 1) and the contexts and actual events involved in the eighteenth-century origins of Wesleyanism (level 3). And these levels are not discrete. Levels 2 and 3 overlap at the point where John Wesley (level 3) told narratives of his own movement (functioning at level 2). Levels 1 and 2 overlap at the point where I and some of my readers (level 3) have also functioned as narrators of the Wesleyan movement (level 2).

Recognizing these three levels, I envisioned a complex historical scenario like viewing a play within a play, like an audience (level 1) viewing Shakespeare's *A Midsummer Night's Dream* (level 2) and the play about Pyramus and Thisbe embedded within it (level 3). One advantage of the metaphor of a play within a play is that it helps understand this three-level structure of interpretation. The disadvantages are that it does not account for the multiplicity of interpreters on which this work focuses (level 2), and the metaphor of a play may suggest something entirely constructed on the part of a writer or a community.

SOCIAL CONSTRUCTIONISM

Since the mid-twentieth century scholars have spoken of the "construction" of the past or even of all reality on the part of individuals and especially of communities.[5] *Construction* in this case seems to be a metaphor, and if I were to employ this metaphor, I might say that the concern of this book is with the "social construction" of the past

---

5   The classic work of social constructionism is Peter L. Berger and Thomas Luckmann, *The Social Construction of Reality*, 2nd ed. (Garden City, NY: Anchor Books, 1967).

on the part of Methodists and other Wesleyan communities.[6] This way of speaking has its merits. It recognizes the extent to which a community's narrative of its own origins is a product of the community's habitual and occasionally creative narrative accounts of its identity.

I resist versions of social constructionism that suggest that a narration of the past is merely a construction, understood literally and not metaphorically—that is, not just a "construal" of the past on the part of narrators or of a narrative community but a construction in the sense of a fabrication with little or no relevance to what happened in the past. This outlook can fail to recognize the many ways in which the perspectives of interpreters open new ways of understanding what really happened in the past, and I am as concerned with what really happened in the past as I am with the ways in which communities and individual narrators have told and retold stories about what happened in the past.[7] Moreover, the telling and retelling of narratives are themselves part of history in the sense of what really happened in the past.

To take a specific example, the American Methodist theologian Umphrey Lee wrote a volume in 1936 entitled *John Wesley and Modern Religion*. Lee attempted to show that John Wesley was a "modern" Christian thinker in Wesley's emphasis on the central role of religious

---

6   Whether *construction* is a metaphor depends upon the literal meaning associated with the term. I take it in this context as a noun based on the verb *construct*, thus literally denoting fabrication (in the literal sense of *that* word) on the part of constructors or fabricators. If the noun is understood as being based on the verb *construe*, however, the word *construction* could carry a literal meaning, through the appropriate noun in that case really should be *construal*. As it has been used in the discussion of the "social construction of reality," the term seems overwhelmingly to denote fabrication on the part of human fabricators. In this sense, I think, it must be metaphorical. A similar phrase applied specifically to historical narratives is *invented traditions* on the part of narrators as used by Eric Hobsbawm in "Introduction: Inventing Traditions" in Eric Hobsbawm and Terence Ranger, eds., *The Invention of Tradition* (Cambridge: Cambridge University Press, 1983), 1–14.

7   Taking this point of view, I presuppose the possibility of a form of historical objectivity; not an absolute objectivity as if humans had the perspectives of gods, but at least what historian Allan Megill calls "dialectic" objectivity, implying that that our knowledge of the world arises from the interaction of our subjective interest and our willingness to consider that which presents itself as an object external to ourselves and to the cultural communities of which we are a part. *Objectivity* in this sense denotes our own vulnerability to that which stands outside of ourselves and outside of the cultures of communities of which we are a part. Cf. Allan Megill, "Introduction: Four Senses of Objectivity," in Allan Megill, ed., *Rethinking Objectivity* (Durham, NC and London: Duke University Press, 1994), 1–20.

experience.[8] This portrayal of Wesley falls in the midst of what I will call the period of Methodist "Modernism," and it provides an example of the way in which Methodists in this period had recourse to the narrative of the Wesleyan revival, a narrative of the Wesleyan movement as a harbinger of modern religious experience. Historians who point out Wesley's connections to Enlightenment thought, for example, Wesley's use of Lockean terminology to describe religious experience as conveying "simple ideas," have vindicated much of Lee's point of view.[9]

Other scholars such as D. Stephen Long have contested the modern or modernist image of John Wesley, pointing out that Wesley also reflected medieval philosophical views long out of fashion, and a traditional theology at odds with much of modern theological reflection.[10] Lee's narrative of Wesley was certainly a *construal* of the past and perhaps *constructed* in the sense that he offered a creative rereading of the Wesleyan revival and Wesleyan theology in the light of his own age and the concerns of Methodist people in his age. But even so, Lee's view of Wesley was not thoroughly constructed or fabricated, because his perspective allowed him to see some things about John Wesley that really happened and were not merely a construction or projection of an interpreter. Lee could see that the emphasis on religious experience was not a peculiar Methodist trait; it was consistent with specific modern ways of understanding Christian

---

8   Umphrey Lee, *John Wesley and Modern Religion* (Nashville: Cokesbury Press, 1936); see the discussion of Lee's work below in the chapter on Methodist Modernism.

9   Frederick Dreyer, "Faith and Experience in the Thought of John Wesley," *American Historical Review* 88 (1983): 12–30; cf. Richard E. Brantley, *Locke, Wesley, and the Method of English Romanticism* (Gainesville: University Press of Florida, 1984); Rex Dale Matthews, "'Religion and Reason Joined': A Study in the Theology of John Wesley" (PhD dissertation, Harvard University, 1986). A similar idea is expressed in the title of Henry Rack's biography of John Wesley, *Reasonable Enthusiast*, where *reasonable* expresses the Enlightenment aspect of John Wesley's thought: *Reasonable Enthusiast: John Wesley and the Rise of Methodism* (Philadelphia: Trinity Press International, 1989). See also Gregory S. Clapper, *John Wesley on Religious Affections: His Views on Experience and Emotion and Their Role in the Christian Life and Theology* (Metuchen, NJ: Scarecrow Press, 1989).

10   D. Stephen Long, *John Wesley's Moral Theology: The Quest for God and Goodness* (Nashville: Abingdon Press, 2005), stresses Wesley's use of Platonic and medieval philosophical ideas, involving the understanding of "moral theology" as contrasted with "ethics." In a very different way, the "enthusiast" side of Henry Rack's title, *Reasonable Enthusiast*, expresses the anti-Enlightenment aspect of John Wesley's thought.

faith. Lee's perspective allowed him to see some things that had been missed in traditional Methodist depictions of John Wesley. I resist the language of construction because it can be taken to denote a simple fabrication.

THE INHERITANCE OF GENETIC CODE

Beyond construction, another popular contemporary metaphor for the inheritance of cultural traditions is that of the genetic inheritance of DNA. Richard Dawkins suggested in 1976 a cultural analogy to the transmission of biological genetic code. He coined the term *meme* to denote the cultural counterpart of a biological gene and theorized that cultures transmit "memes" (cultural data) that compete for adequacy just as "selfish genes" (Dawkins's phrase) compete for dominance. Memes are cultural replicators just as genes are biological replicators.[11]

The genetic metaphor would allow us to say that Wesleyan and Methodist communities inherit certain traits, the "DNA" or memes that come from their past and include traits that identify Wesleyan communities. The Methodist DNA or memes might include specific teachings and practices as well as narratives that have been transmitted in Wesleyan communities. But a problem with the metaphor of DNA is that genetic traits are expressed and repressed randomly in biological reproduction apart from human intervention in the genetic code. The DNA metaphor places such a stress on the givenness or determination of inheritance that it minimizes the creative roles that may be played by individuals and communities in transmitting cultures.

MODULES OF REUSABLE CODE

We can also consider a set of metaphors derived from the field of computer programming, the notion of *reusable code*. The earliest

---

11   Richard Dawkins, *The Selfish Gene* (New York and Oxford: Oxford University Press, 1976), 203–15.

computer programs were linear sequences of instructions or "code." As programming advanced, programmers (coders) began to devise sections or modules of code that could be reused, and they referred to this streamlined process as *modular programming*. Reusable modules of code could be "invoked" or "called" from another part of a program. As modular programming evolved, modules could call each other many levels deep. A "control loop" of code would call a module that called various other modules, each of which in turn might call yet other modules of code. Code modules, if properly constructed, could even invoke or call themselves, thus "recursive" code. Coders develop "libraries" of code modules that can be readily reused.[12]

The invocation of reusable modules of code can serve as a contemporary metaphor for the reuse of historical narratives. Historical narratives can function as code that communities consistently reuse to define (encode) their own identities. Communities and individual narrators invoke or call these modules of historical narratives, just as computer programs invoke or call modules of computer code. That is, communities and storytellers make decisions about which elements of the past will be expressed or repressed. The metaphor of reusable code acknowledges the creative role that individuals and communities can play in shaping narratives that describe their identities, and it allows that interpreters can be gifted in such a way that they can understand what happened in the past.

Foundational narratives have a special relevance as reusable code by which communities describe their identities. But communities also alter the modules of narrative code they use and combine them in creative new ways. This metaphor helps us envision that there are specific clusters of narratives—I will call them *narrative modules*—that can be combined in various ways to produce a narrative in which communal identities are encoded.

---

12 Wolfgang Pree, *Design Patterns for Object-Oriented Software Development* (Workingham: Addison-Wesley Publishing, 1995), 3–11 for a survey of developments in modular programming including object-oriented programming as introducing abstract data structures or data types utilized in object-oriented programming.

Here's an example. Methodists in the nineteenth century liked to invoke the narrative of John Wesley's Aldersgate-Street experience, an experience that they had good reason to call Wesley's "conversion" experience (see chapter 1). But they typically invoked specific accounts of Wesley's Aldersgate-Street experience—namely, the account that Wesley himself gave in the second fascicle of his published *Journal*, or a later account of the experience given in Thomas Coke and Henry Moore's *The Life of the Rev. John Wesley, A.M.* (1792), itself based primarily on Wesley's *Journal* account.[13] Thus, a nineteenth-century account of Wesley might invoke the code of Coke and Moore's account of Aldersgate, which in turn invoked the code of the *Journal* account of Aldersgate. Each of these invocations involved reusing the code for (the narrative of) the Aldersgate-Street experience. But not all Wesleyan accounts would invoke the coded narrative of the Aldersgate-Street experience, and some that did put a very different meaning on it than Coke and Moore had done.

The metaphor of reusable code has its own problems. It may not recognize as fully as the DNA metaphor how powerful inherited narrative modules may be in shaping historical consciousness. For example, recent studies of eighteenth-century Anglicanism, in contrast to conventional Methodist ways of telling the story of John Wesley, have emphasized the vibrancy of the eighteenth-century Church of England and its successes in responding to the crises posed by the Enlightenment and the Industrial Revolution.[14] But when I present this new perspective to students who have been formed in traditional Methodist churches, they tend to have a viscerally negative initial reaction,

---

13   [Thomas] Coke and [Henry] Moore, *The Life of the Rev. John Wesley, A.M.: Including an Account of the Great Revival of Religion, in Europe and America, of which He was the First and Chief Instrument* (London: G. Paramore, 1792; hereafter referred to as "Coke and Moore, *Life of Wesley*"). Coke and Moore refer to Aldersgate as "his Conversion" in the title of book 1, chap. 4, on p. 130. The account of Aldersgate is given on 148–60.

14   Here I have reference to such works as J. C. D. Clark, *English Society, 1688-1832* (Cambridge: Cambridge University Press, 1985); John Walsh, Colin Haydon, and Stephen Taylor, eds., *The Church of England, c. 1689—c. 1833* (Cambridge: Cambridge University Press, 1993); William Gibson, *The Church of England, 1688-1832: Unity and Accord* (London: Routledge, 2001); and Jeremy Gregory, *Restoration, Reformation, and Reform, 1660–1828: The Archbishops of Canterbury and Their Diocese* (Oxford: Oxford University Press, 2000).

as if to ask, "How could this possibly be?" The narrative of Anglican declension has so framed their consciousness as Methodists that a counter-narrative seems intuitively false. This reveals a weakness in the metaphor of code modules. Programmers do reuse modules of code, sometimes in what they describe as code "libraries," and often without updating their code modules as they reuse them. But they do not ascribe the value to inherited modules of code that communities may ascribe to inherited ways of telling their foundational narratives. Score one for the DNA metaphor here, and I recognize the problems inherent in any of these metaphors. In fact, I will sometimes use the term *code* in a deliberately ambiguous way to refer to inherited modules of narrative in ways that allude both to the inherited genetic "code" of DNA and to modules of computer "code."

TYPICAL CODE MODULES UTILIZED IN THE FOUNDING NARRATIVES OF WESLEYAN COMMUNITIES

Communities that tell a narrative of Wesleyan origins as a way of accounting for their community's identity have something like a kit of narrative modules that they use and reuse to describe the origins and identity of their communities. We can envision this kit of modules as a collection of stories told by preachers and other oral narrators, or written on paper saved in file folders, or written in word-processor files on computer storage media, or saved in the cloud (that is, on someone else's servers), or perhaps published in a printed or electronically readable book. In many cases the material had been originally transmitted in the memories of the tellers of narratives, encoded memories that were repeated so many times that their accuracy seemed utterly trustworthy to the tellers. But the tellers of these narratives could still combine and recombine trusted elements or modules of the narrative together in distinctive ways.

As Wesleyan communities told and retold the narrative of their origins, they employed specific recurring elements or modules of

Wesleyan narratives. In the following tables I will identify some of these most common narrative modules to which I will return in considering particular narratives in the following chapters. The first five modules of reusable code involve descriptions of the background of the Wesleyan movement as ways of introducing the Wesleyan narrative.

NARRATIVE MODULES DESCRIBING THE BACKGROUND OF THE WESLEYAN MOVEMENT

Narrative module **AnglicanDeclension**: a narrative of Anglican declension alleging a dysfunctional state of the Church of England in the ages before Wesley and, specifically, the wickedness or at least lack of spirituality of its clergy. This module developed very soon after John Wesley's death and often functioned to justify the need for separate Wesleyan churches.

Narrative module **SocialDysfunction**: a narrative of social and moral dysfunction in the early eighteenth century, typically pointing to moral dissolution (typical of nineteenth-century narratives) and the needs of persons displaced by the Industrial Revolution (more typical of twentieth-century narratives). This module could function to build a sense of the identity of Wesleyan communities as responding constructively to moral and social conditions.

Narrative module **AnglicanVitality**: a narrative characteristic of more recent scholarship on eighteenth-century Anglicanism pointing to the strengths of the Church of England and perhaps other Protestant communities in the eighteenth century, including strong attendance at worship, comprehensive educational and pastoral activities on the part of its clergy, and their fostering new congregations to respond to social displacement in the Industrial Revolution. It remains to be seen how this narrative module might function in narratives of Wesleyan origins to build a sense of Wesleyan or Methodist identity.

Narrative module **EuropeanPietism**: a narrative module that sees European Pietistic movements as a significant factor in the background of early Methodism, often in combination with some of the other background modules described here.

Narrative module **AmericanReligion**: a narrative module favored by some American authors that offered an account of North American religion, typically beginning with New England Puritanism and continuing with the (First) Great Awakening as a preface to a narrative of American Methodism. This module functions to explain the need for Methodism in North American contexts and the distinctive gifts that Wesleyan communities offered in North America.

Beyond these beginning or background modules, narratives of Wesleyan origins could invoke specific modules of the story of the Wesleys' movement. Some of these refer to moments in the chronology of John Wesley's (and sometimes Charles Wesley's) life that would be included in any such narrative, whether told by a religious community or not. But as the following table indicates, these narrative modules usually encode clues to Methodist identity beyond the mere historical narrative.

TYPICAL NARRATIVE MODULES IN ACCOUNTS OF THE WESLEYAN MOVEMENT

Narrative module **EpworthUpbringing**: a narrative of the Wesleys' upbringing in the Epworth Rectory, and the methodical nurture provided them especially by Susanna Wesley, offering an initial clue to the meaning of *Methodist*.

Narrative module **JWInfluences**: a narrative of John Wesley's (and perhaps Charles Wesley's) readings, often construed as influences on their theology and practices, from a variety of sources that differ according to specific invocations of this module. This narrative module often serves to "locate" or identify Methodism within a spectrum of other church traditions so that the question of Methodism's ecclesial identity often lurks behind descriptions of influences on John Wesley's thought.

Narrative module **QuestForHoliness**: a narrative describing John Wesley's sense from 1725 that he was called to a life of holiness, though he struggled to find a way to it; thus, this narrative module is often tied closely to the next one. This and the next module often function as a way of preparing for the module **AldersgateExperience** (below) to describe Methodism's identity as a pietistic "religion of the heart," though this narrative module can also support the claim that the identity of Methodism is tied primarily to the cultivation of holiness.

Narrative module **SpiritualDysfunction**: a narrative of the dysfunctional state of John Wesley's spiritual experience and his failure to find the way to holiness prior to his 1738 Aldersgate-Street experience, including his questions about the relationship between justification and sanctification. This module can be tied to the narrative module **AnglicanDeclension** (above), suggesting that the root of Wesley's own spiritual dysfunction lay in the spiritual declension of Anglicanism in his day.

TYPICAL NARRATIVE MODULES IN ACCOUNTS OF THE WESLEYAN MOVEMENT (continued)

Narrative module **OxfordSociety**: a narrative of the Wesleys' Oxford religious society, often invoking the year 1729 (especially in earlier narratives) as a symbolic date for the beginning of the Methodist movement. This module often functions to build the identity of Methodism as cultivating holiness through accountability groups, thus preparing the way for module **ClassesBands** (below).

Narrative module **GeorgiaPietists**: a narrative of the Wesleys' Georgia travels and their meeting Moravians and perhaps Lutheran (Salzburg) Pietists there. This module can function to build a sense of Methodist identity as a movement for heart religion and to build a sense of Methodist identity as cultivating holiness through accountability groups such as the Moravian bands.

Narrative module **AldersgateExperience**: a narrative of the Wesleys' religious experiences of May 1738, with a variety of interpretations and weightings of these experiences, and often a more general narrative of their consistent concern with the role of religious experience in Christian life. Most often this narrative will function to build the sense of Methodist identity as a religion of the heart and often supports the teaching of the need for an experience of assurance of pardon accompanying justification.

Narrative module **WesleyDoubts**: a narrative of the Wesleys' struggles with doubts following their religious experiences of 1738, and sometimes including John Wesley's later corrections to his published *Journal* referring to his spiritual experience leading up to Aldersgate. This module can serve to moderate claims of Methodist identity as a religion of the heart and to moderate claims about the necessity of an experience of assurance for true justification.

Narrative module **FieldPreaching**: a narrative of John Wesley's earliest outdoor preaching in 1739 as a way of introducing the broader need for itinerant preaching. This narrative module can serve to build a sense of Methodist identity as an evangelistic community and as a way of explaining the eventual division of Methodist communities led by John Wesley from the Church of England.

Narrative Module **MinistryWithPoor**: a description of John Wesley's focus on ministries among the poor, often linked to the background narrative of **SocialDysfunction**. This narrative came to be favored through the twentieth century to build a sense of Methodist identity in solidarity with the poor.

TYPICAL NARRATIVE MODULES IN ACCOUNTS OF THE WESLEYAN MOVEMENT (continued)

Narrative module **WesleyCommunicator**: a description (if not a narrative) of John Wesley's skills at communication and disseminating culture, especially apparent in narratives from the late twentieth century.

Narrative module **WesleyEvangelist**: a significant extension of the module **FieldPreaching**, with the claim that the primary identity of Wesleyan communities is their identity as evangelistic communities, overshadowing the claim that the cultivation of holiness in existing Christian communities was the principal aim of the Wesleyan movement.

Narrative module **ClassesBands**: a narrative of the Wesleys' organization of classes, bands, and societies, often including the organization of the United Societies in 1739 and the regularization of these societies by the "General Rules" (1743).

Narrative module **StillnessMeans**: a narrative of the Wesleys' differences with an eccentric group of London Moravians in the 1730s and 1740s over the issue of "stillness" and the means of grace, often alleging (inappropriately) that the London Moravians of this time were representative of Moravian teachings and practice. This module can serve to moderate claims of Methodist identity as a pietistic community in suggesting that they avoided such extreme positions as this group of Moravians advocated (see also module **Tensions1760s** below). Positively, this module can serve to strengthen the traditional ecclesial identity of Wesleyan communities by showing their commitment to conventional "means of grace."

Narrative module **ArminianVsCalvinist**: a narrative about the struggle with Calvinistic Evangelical clergy and the issues of Arminian vs. Calvinistic teachings on predestination, limited atonement, and Christian perfection. This module usually served to differentiate the identity of Wesleyan communities within the scope of Evangelical communities, identifying them as Arminian communities in contrast to Calvinistic Evangelical groups.

Narrative module **MethodistPreachers**: a narrative of John Wesley's decision to employ lay preachers and his organization of them into a conference of preachers (1744) and subsequently into circuits; some versions of this module also include his designation of women as exhorters from the 1760s and as preachers from the 1770s. Like the earlier module **FieldPreaching**, this module serves to identify Wesleyan communities as evangelistic communities and prepares the way to explain division of communities (eventually churches) associated with John Wesley from the Church of England.

TYPICAL NARRATIVE MODULES IN ACCOUNTS OF THE WESLEYAN MOVEMENT (continued)

Narrative module **CWPoetry**: a narrative of Charles Wesley's poetic works and their contributions to the Wesleyan movement. A certain selection of Charles Wesley's poetry was often invoked to describe the identity of Methodism as a pietistic expression of Christian faith, though a different selection of Charles Wesley's poetry could also be utilized as a way of building the more traditionally ecclesial or "high-church" identity of Methodism as liturgically oriented communities.

Narrative module **WayOfSalvation**: a narrative about John Wesley's teaching on the way of salvation including prevenient ("preventing"), justifying, and sanctifying grace, and typically including an account of his teaching on Christian perfection. This module serves to reinforce the transmission of distinctively Wesleyan beliefs and can be utilized in a variety of ways, for example, to build the identity of Methodism as a pietistic community, to relate Methodism to other strands of Christian traditions, and to build a sense of Methodist identity as communities committed to the cultivation of holiness.

Narrative module **DoctrinalLiberality**: a narrative of John Wesley's openness regarding doctrine characteristic of Methodists from the Modernist period (early twentieth century), typically mentioning the lack of doctrinal requirements for participation in Methodist societies and interpreting "Catholic Spirit" as denoting very broad liberality in doctrine. This module can build a sense of Methodism as a more open-minded or progressive community.

Narrative module **MethodistPersecution**: a narrative of the heroic suffering of Methodist leaders and people in the early decades of the Methodist movement. This module functioned in earlier Wesleyan narratives to strengthen a sense of distinctive Methodist identity and often to justify the differentiation of Methodism and Anglicanism.

Narrative module **JohnAndMary**: a narrative about John Wesley's marriage to Mary Vazeille, often alleging her wickedness and/or instability as grounds for their separation. This module functions to defend John Wesley from critics who alleged that he was unfaithful.

Narrative module **Tensions1760s**: a narrative about tensions in the Wesleyan movement in the 1760s and beyond. Like the module **StillnessMeans** (above), this code module often functions to moderate claims to the identity of Wesleyan communities as pietistic communities by showing that they disavowed excessive or eccentric claims about religious experiences.

TYPICAL NARRATIVE MODULES IN ACCOUNTS OF THE WESLEYAN MOVEMENT (continued)

Narrative module **AnglicanWesley**: a distinct narrative from the later 1800s that emphasized Wesley's identity as an Anglican clergyman, sometimes (on the part of Anglicans) in opposition to Methodist churches, sometimes (on the part of sophisticated Victorian Methodists) as a defense of Wesleyan communities and their identities as churches.

Narrative module **MethodistDeclension**: a narrative of the falling away of Methodist people from the high standards set in the early years of the revival. This is a module initiated by John Wesley himself that functions to encode high standards of accountability as a hallmark of Wesleyan identity.

Narrative module **MethodistBenevolence**: a narrative of the Wesley's benevolent institutions. This module can function simply to build a positive image of Wesleyan communities, though it can also be linked to **SocialDysfunction** and **MinistryWithPoor** (above) to build a sense of the identity of Methodism as responding positively to social conditions.

Narrative module **AmericanOrdinations**: a narrative of John Wesley's decision to authorize the formation of a Methodist church (denomination) in North America in 1784 and his ordinations associated with this. This module functions consistently to explain the division of Methodist communities from Anglicanism, though different ways of telling this narrative can build a sense of Methodist identity as a radical Protestant community or as a more traditional church.

Narrative module **ChurchFounder**: a more elaborate narrative that explicitly claimed John Wesley as the deliberate "founder" of a distinct church (or in older terminology, "sect"). This module is more typical of American Methodist narrators with little recognition of why British Methodists wanted to downplay John Wesley's independence from Anglicanism.

Narrative module **EcumenicalWesley**: a narrative of Wesley's central teachings as being consistent with those of historic Christian churches, typical of mid-twentieth-century interpreters of John and Charles Wesley. This module thus functions to relate Methodist communities to broader Christian communities and sometimes presupposes the module **JWInfluences**.

Narrative module **OppositionToSlavery**: a narrative about John Wesley's opposition to slavery, invoking his letter to William Wilberforce and other writings against slavery. This module can function as an expression of **MethodistBenevolence** or can function in twentieth-century narratives to build a broader sense of Wesleyan communities as responding constructively to social conditions.

TYPICAL NARRATIVE MODULES IN ACCOUNTS OF THE WESLEYAN MOVEMENT (continued)
Narrative module **JWDeath**: a narrative of John Wesley's triumphant Christian death. This module generally functions to reinforce a sense of Wesley's holiness and the providential oversight of Wesleyan communities in their origins.
Narrative module **GrowthOfMethodism**: narratives of the growth and spread of Methodist societies both before and after Wesley's death, sometimes involving accounts of Methodist missions throughout the world. This can reinforce module **WesleyEvangelist** as encoding the evangelistic identity of Wesleyan communities, and it can also be tied to narratives of Methodist ecclesial expansion throughout the world.

These are typical modules that might be invoked in encoding a narrative of Wesleyan origins, though particular communities and individual coders of the narrative might also invoke other material relevant to their concerns, and each module might be given different weightings (valuations) and placements in their narratives. The list given here will serve as a checklist to test which elements or modules of the narrative of Wesleyan origins various tellers of that narrative decide to utilize or not.

In the accounts following, I will sometimes give a table showing how narrative modules were combined in specific narratives of Wesleyan origins. In other cases, though, especially in discussing narratives from the late nineteenth century to the present time, I will discuss how specific narrative modules came to be the focus of contention in Wesleyan communities. For example, there was an extended controversy over the meaning of John Wesley's Anglican identity (module **AnglicanWesley**) in the Victorian era, a controversy in the early twentieth century over the various strands of Christian tradition influencing John Wesley's "churchmanship" (module **JWInfluences**), and an exploration of (not so much a controversy over) Wesley's relevance in ecumenical contexts (module **EcumenicalWesley**) in the mid-to-late twentieth century.

The "Control Loop" or Metanarrative of Decline and Renewal

Modular computer programs typically begin by executing a "control loop," a master module of code that calls all other modules. The program continues to go through this control loop, waiting for and processing input, sending output to users, processing and storing data, until the program is terminated. Historical narratives are often set within an overarching narrative, what some interpreters have called a *metanarrative*, that frames all the narratives and sub-narratives that appear within it. A historical metanarrative, then, answers to a control loop of computer code and is critical for understanding the overall shape of narratives recited or written. Narratives of Wesleyan communities need to be understood within an overarching view of history that shaped Western consciousness until quite recently and that functions as a control loop within which Wesleyan narratives are set.

Describing the Wesleyan movement as a "revival" suggests a particular historical narrative according to which there was something wonderful in the past worthy of reclaiming, followed by a period of loss, then followed by a time in which there was a recovery of that which had been lost: a "renaissance," a "renewal," a "reformation," a "restoration," a "revival." This overarching narrative (metanarrative) can be thought of as a control loop of narrative code that "calls" or "invokes" the Wesleyan narrative of Methodist origins and that frames Wesleyan narratives in such a way that they can scarcely be understood apart from it.

In fact, a metanarrative or control loop of "Western civilization," one can argue, was a narrative that valued Greek and Roman civilizations as norms for culture, saw the Middle Ages as "dark ages" in which the cultural achievements of Greece and Rome were lost, and then saw modern European civilization as a rebirth or "renaissance" of classical culture. This narrative came into existence in the Renaissance when the term *middle age* (*media aetas*; later "Middle Ages") was encoded as a way of describing this understanding of history. A parallel narrative was applied to Christian history, which we can describe as follows:

NARRATIVE MODULES IN THE WESTERN CHRISTIAN PATTERN OF DECLINE AND RENEWAL

The glorious age of **primitive Christian simplicity and purity**, associated with the New Testament church and (possibly) the early Christian church of the first four centuries.

A middle period of **decline** in Christian morals, teachings (doctrine), and practices.

An age of **restoration**, **reformation**, **renewal**, **rebirth**, or **revival** of the primitive vision.

Writers of the European Renaissance had expressed this view of Christian history long before the Protestant reformations. Jean Gerson and other conciliarists, for example, had appealed to the "primitive church" as a basis for the reform of the papacy in the late Middle Ages.[15] Their narrative presupposed something wonderful and normative from the past (the period of the primitive church), a subsequent period of decline (especially represented in the divided papacy), and then a recovery or restoration of the primitive vision. The Protestant reformations brought a powerful reshaping of historical narratives following this general pattern, according to which the church in the period of the New Testament and perhaps the earliest Christian centuries was the norm; the Middle Ages were identified with Catholic superstition and ecclesial decline; and the Protestant reformations in their various forms were seen as heroic attempts to restore primitive Christian faith and life.

The use of the metanarrative of declension and revival as an overarching control loop has been played out time and again in subsequent

---

15   Louis B. Pascoe, *Jean Gerson: Principles of Church Reform* (Leiden: E. J. Brill, 1973), 26–27, 59–60.

Western Christian historical narratives. For example, there was the attempt of the Stone-Campbell Restoration movement to "restore" New Testament Christianity on the American frontier in the early nineteenth century[16] or the claims of Aimee Semple McPherson and other early Pentecostal leaders that the early church described in the Acts of the Apostles represented the "former rain" of the Holy Spirit, followed by a centuries-long period of spiritual drought, followed by the "latter rain" associated with the outpouring of spiritual gifts in the early Pentecostal revival.[17]

The common understanding of the Wesleyan movement as a "revival" points to this overarching historical narrative of decline and restoration. It is encoded in the inscription on John Wesley's tomb behind the City Road Chapel in London:

This Great Light Arose
by the Singular Providence of God
To Revive, Enforce and Defend
The Pure Apostolical Doctrines and Practices
of the Primitive Church[18]

Thus, the narrative of the Wesleyan revival can be seen as a module of code invoked within the larger Western control loop of origins, decline, and restoration, a sub-narrative or code loop within that larger encoding loop or framework, and each element or module of the narrative of the Wesleyan loop might be described as a sub-sub-loop recoursing back through the loop of the Wesleyan revival narrative and to larger loop or narrative of decline and revitalization in which it was

---

16 Douglas A. Foster, "The Nature of the Apostolicity of the Church: Perspectives from the Churches of Christ," in *Ancient Faith and American-Born Churches*, eds. Ted A. Campbell, Ann K. Riggs, and Gilbert W. Stafford (New York, NY and Mahwah, NJ: Paulist Press, 2006), 71–80.

17 This view of history is laid out in a sermon by McPherson entitled "Lost and Restored," in Aimee Semple McPherson, *This is That: Personal Experiences, Sermons and Writings*, repr. ed.,The Higher Christian Life: Sources for the Study of the Holiness, Pentecostal, and Keswick Movements (Los Angeles: Bridal Call Publishing, 1919; New York and London: Garland Publishing, 1985), 380–406, and esp. 385–89 (on the "former rain" of the Spirit on the day of Pentecost), 390–95 (on the dearth of the Spirit in the Middle Ages), and 395–403 (the "latter rain" of the Spirit in the Pentecostal revival).

18 Transcribed from photograph.

embedded. This is complex, but I have come to understand that it is in fact the way in which Reformation and post-Reformation Christian cultures construed and utilized such narratives to identify their own communities. What follows then will be a sketch of how one might begin to understand a set of interlocking narratives utilizing reusable code modules.

A Scheme of Wesleyan Narrative Evolution

To examine a moment in the past as it has been narrated again in sub-sequent ages involves a nonlinear approach to the telling or writing of history. It cannot proceed by simply narrating a sequence of events in chronological order since it must leave the thread of historical narra-tive consistently to consider how people in a period have had recourse to a foundational narrative or to other resources from the past of their movement or tradition. That is why the metaphor of code "loops" or modules works so well in this case. But to flatten out such a looping narrative into a linear story that can be read sequentially requires a scheme of periodization in which subjects in one historical period are understood as engaging in the valuing and sometimes the devaluing of previous historical eras as they invoke encoded modules describing the earlier periods.

In what follows I will utilize a scheme of periodization to examine how the Wesleyan past has been valued and devalued by subsequent Wesleyan Christians, involving the following five historical periods in the evolution of the Wesleyan tradition:

- The Wesleyan period itself—that is, the period in which John and Charles Wesley were active in the life of the Wesleyan movement as a movement within existing Christian communities (primarily the Church of England), from roughly 1731 (the beginnings of Method-ism in Oxford) through the founding of a Methodist church in North America in 1784.

- The period of early Methodist churches in America and Britain in the very late eighteenth century from 1784 through the middle of the nineteenth century.

- A period of Methodist flourishing or "ascendancy" in the mid-to-late nineteenth century associated with the expansion of Methodist missions beyond Britain and North America.

- A period of Methodist Modernism, from very late in the nineteenth century through the 1960s.

- A period beyond Modernism, from the late 1960s through the present time.[19]

These periods overlap each other at the boundaries, as must be the case in designating periods of cultural history. For the sake of division into chapters, chapter 1 covers the Wesleyan period, roughly the eighteenth century. Chapter 2 covers the period of early Methodist churches in the very late eighteenth century and the early nineteenth century. Chapter 3 covers a period of Methodist ascendancy in the late nineteenth century. Chapter 4 covers the age of Methodist Modernism in the early twentieth century, and chapter 5 describes Wesleyan narratives in a period beyond Methodist Modernism, comprising the later twentieth century and the beginning of the twenty-first century.

A fuller periodization scheme might be able to divide Methodist history into much finer periods that would allow more elaborate comparisons, although parallels between British and American Methodist churches as well as Methodist churches in other parts of the world might not cohere in a finer scheme of periodization. In the narrative that follows I will examine a sample of Wesleyan narratives from each of these five periods, asking how Methodists in each period encoded their own past and how, in particular, they understood the distinctive identity of Methodism based on their encodings of the Wesleyan past.

---

19   I have resisted the temptation to refer to this period "beyond Modernism" as a period of "Postmodernism," simply because of the multiple and highly contested construals of "postmodernity" and "postmodernism." See the beginning of chap. 5.

Throughout these five periods, I have examined a select number of the hundreds of works giving narratives of the origins of Wesleyan communities. It is crucial to emphasize that *what follows here is not simply an account of scholarship about John and Charles Wesley.* Such an account would involve far more than this work intends to accomplish. *This book focuses on narratives that encode the identities of Wesleyan and Methodist communities*, and it considers popular as well as scholarly books, pamphlets and tracts, and sometimes narratives embedded in other works; for example, official Methodist and Wesleyan church documents. It includes works from the lifetime of the Wesleys through recent decades. The works considered are not limited to writers who are or were members of Wesleyan or Methodist communities, but the emphasis in this study falls on narratives that function to describe the identity of Wesleyan and Methodist communities. So, in choosing the material studied in what follows, I have preferred

- narratives, that is, chronological accounts of the life of John Wesley (most typically), connected to . . .

- the founding of Methodist or Wesleyan communities (including the earliest Methodist societies), and

- indications of how these narratives encode Methodist identities.

So, simply a biography, even a theological or spiritual biography, of John Wesley not connected to the development of Wesleyan or Methodist communities falls outside of what is considered here. Likewise, a narrative of the rise of Methodist communities not connected to narratives about John and Charles Wesley would also fall outside of what this work considers. What I've tried to focus on in what follows is narratives of Wesleyan origins that function to encode the identities of Wesleyan communities.

I admit that in practice I have not consistently or strenuously applied these criteria. Sometimes, for example, a work will focus only on a specific part of the narrative of John Wesley's life; but if this account

is connected to the development of Methodist and Wesleyan communities, and if it gives indications of encoding Methodist identity, then I
might utilize it. Sometimes persons outside of Wesleyan or Methodist
communities have offered narratives that have deeply influenced Wesleyan communities or have themselves utilized Wesleyan narratives to
encode the identities of other Christian communities, such as Pentecostal churches. I have included some of these as well.

WESLEYAN NARRATIVES IN THE WESLEYAN PERIOD

EIGHTEENTH CENTURY

I n the period between roughly 1731 and 1784, Methodism functioned as a religious society or an alliance of religious societies
largely within the context of the Church of England. The earliest
Methodist accounts of their own origins used the year 1729 as a rough
designation for the beginning of the first Oxford Methodist society,
although in fact this may not have occurred until as late as 1732. A case
might also be made for the year 1739, which marked John Wesley's first
field preaching (in early April) and his reorganization of the Bristol societies that George Whitefield left in his hands. Methodism continued to
function as a religious society for British Methodists until the organization of the Wesleyan Conference as an ecclesial community in 1795 and
for those allied with Charles Wesley who continued to function within
the canonical parameters of the Church of England even through the
1820s.[1] But the Methodist movement changed very significantly from
the year 1784 when John Wesley authorized the formation of a Methodist church independent of the Church of England in North America
and performed ordinations to support the formation of the new church,

---

1   On the continuing existence of "Church Methodism," see Gareth Lloyd, *Charles Wesley and the
Struggle for Methodist Identity* (Oxford: Oxford University Press, 2007), 227–33.

so I have taken 1784 as a termination point for the Wesleyan period and the beginning of the period of early Methodist churches.

JOHN WESLEY'S OWN UNDERSTANDING OF PRIOR CHRISTIAN HISTORY

Before considering how Methodists in the Wesleyan period conceived of their own history, it might be instructive to consider how John Wesley himself appropriated narratives of prior Christian history—that is, how he appropriated the larger "control loop" of Christian history described above that would function as a metanarrative within which Wesleyan narratives were cast. Following the general Western historical perspective described above, John Wesley did think of the period of the early Christian church, the "primitive church," as a golden age. My earlier study of *John Wesley and Christian Antiquity* (1991) showed that for Wesley, this age of exemplary Christian holiness and exemplary Christian communities was not limited to the age of the New Testament. He believed the period of early Christian purity continued at least until the time of Constantine, when in his view the church had become compromised with the Roman state and Roman culture, and compromised by accepting money from Constantine and others.

Despite his belief in a "Constantinian fall" of the church, Wesley believed that there were pockets of exemplary Christian life "even in the fourth century," as he stated it on one occasion, naming St. John Chrysostom, St. Basil the Great, St. Ephraem Syrus (he said, though he referred to a document attributed to Ephraem Syrus from a different author to whom we now we refer as "Ephraem Graecus"), and St. "Macarius the Egyptian" (now referred to as "Pseudo-Macarius") as fourth-century saints.[2]

---

2   Ted. A. Campbell, *John Wesley and Christian Antiquity: Religious Vision and Cultural Change* (Nashville: Kingswood Books, 1991), 46-51. The quotation containing the phrase "even in the fourth century" is from John Wesley, "On Laying the Foundation of the New Chapel" in *The Works of John Wesley: Sermons*, vol. 3, ed. Albert C. Outler (Nashville: Abingdon Press, 1986), 586. Ephrem Lash has shown that the work to which John Wesley referred as a treatise of "Ephraem Syrus" was from another author, only available in Greek, whom Lash proposed to call "Ephrem Graecus": Ephrem Lash, "The Greek Writings Attributed to St. Ephrem the Syrian" in

Although John Wesley shared the general prejudice against the Middle Ages that characterized the typical Western interpretation of history, he valued some movements from the later medieval period, specifically, the mendicant spirituality of the Middle Ages and some of the authors we identify today as representing the *Devotio Moderna*, especially Thomas à Kempis.[3] John Wesley regarded the Protestant Reformation as a revival of true Christian teaching and seems to have valued the constitutive documents of the Elizabethan Reformation (the Prayer Book, Articles of Religion, and Homilies of the Church of England) as exemplary of true Christian doctrine and practice.[4] In this respect, he reflected the metanarrative of decline and restoration typical of Western historiographies from the time of the Renaissance. Nevertheless, John Wesley had come to view his own age as one of deterioration in Christian morals and in Christian piety, hence the need for a revival of faith and morals.[5] He himself seldom attributed that deterioration directly to the leaders of the Church of England, but his immediate followers would do so.

John Wesley, then, reflected an overarching Christian narrative involving primitive Christian purity, medieval declension, and modern reform as a broader control loop or metanarrative within which he would locate the rise of Methodism. His sense of declension in morals and spirituality in his own age shows his perception that even within a general period of reform or renewal there may be moments of decline that warrant renewed calls for reform and renewal. As we will see, he would later perceive that the Methodist movement itself had shown signs of decline and needed renewal.

John Behr, Andrew Louth, and Dimitri Conomos, eds., *Abba: The Tradition of Orthodoxy in the West* (Crestwood, New York: St. Vladimir's Seminary Press, 2003), 90–91.

3　Ted A. Campbell, "The Image of Christ in the Poor: On the Medieval Roots of the Wesleys' Ministry with the Poor"; in *The Poor and the People Called Methodists*, ed. Richard P. Heitzenrater (Nashville: Kingswood, 2002), 47–57.

4　Ted A. Campbell, "Christian Tradition, John Wesley, and Evangelicalism," *Anglican Theological Review* 74:1 (Winter 1992), 62–63.

5　For example, Wesley's notion of "extraordinary ministers" in Wesley, *The Works of John Wesley, Sermons IV*, "Prophets and Priests," vol. 4, ed. Albert C. Outler, 75–84, presupposes that the deterioration of true Christian piety in his age demanded such an "extraordinary ministry."

WESLEY'S *JOURNAL* AS PROTONARRATIVE OF THE WESLEYAN MOVEMENT

Although it might seem impossible that Methodists in the Wesleyan period should be able to conceive of their own history as Methodists, we shall see that such texts as John Wesley's *Journal,* the Minutes of the early Methodist conferences, and other early Methodist literature did offer narratives that built a sense of Methodist identity even in the Wesleyan period. Not only in transmitting such narratives, but also in his work of defining and defending distinctive Methodist teachings and practices, John Wesley would function as a culture coder, defining his movement and handing on his sense of its distinctive identity to a new generation of Methodists.

The preeminent narrative of the Methodist movement in the Wesleyan period was given by John Wesley himself in his carefully crafted and serially published work, *The Journal of the Reverend John Wesley, A.M.* Unlike his private diaries, the *Journal* was written for publication and offered his own reflections on the events of his life, designed as a narrative that supported his particular wing of the Evangelical revival. Rather than reading the *Journal* simply as an account of what happened on particular dates in Wesley's life, we must read it as apologetic and polemical literature published at very particular moments in Wesley's career. The first fascicle of the *Journal,* for instance, deals with the years between 1733 and 1738. It was not written and published until the late spring and early summer of 1740, well after Wesley's first field preaching (April 1739) and his organization (reorganization) of the Bristol and other societies. By the spring of 1740 John Wesley was in direct conflict with a peculiar group of London Moravians, and the first fascicle of the *Journal* must be understood as an apologetic and polemical document vindicating the impending separation of John Wesley's London society from the London Moravian community.[6]

---

6   Cf. the comments of Heitzenrater and Ward introducing the *The Works of John Wesley: Journals and Diaries*, vol. 18, ed. W. Reginald Ward and Richard P. Heitzenrater (Nashville: Abingdon Press, 1988ff.), 81–82.

The fascicles of the *Journal* were widely distributed through the network of Wesleyan societies, with several thousands of copies printed in the later decades of John Wesley's life. The *Journal* utilized John Wesley's considerable rhetorical skills. It grabbed the reader's attention by beginning with this excerpt from a letter:

> Sir,
> The occasion of my giving you this trouble is of a very extraordinary na-
> ture. On Sunday last I was informed (as no doubt you will be e'er long)
> that my brother and I had killed your son . . . [7]

With this arresting opening, the *Journal* followed in many respects the format of the popular travel journal of the eighteenth century designed for a broad reading public.[8]

What the *Journal* offered its readers consistently from its first pub-lication in 1740 to its last in 1790 was not only a charming narrative of travel, witty conversations, excerpted letters, attacks by ignorant mobs, and solemn conversions but also a continuous narrative of divine providence, showing how God had blessed and guided John Wesley and the Methodists associated with him. The *Journal* set a pat-tern for subsequent Methodist historical narratives that depicted the rise of Methodism as a divinely guided enterprise.[9] It is in this sense that the *Journal* reflects the control loop or metanarrative of decline and restoration described above.

Wesley's *Journal* lent itself to understanding his own life and the early life of the Wesleyan movement as divided into specific moments that gave rise to many of the reusable modules of narrative code followed by tellers and retellers of the Wesleyan narrative. The first published fascicle of the *Journal* described a dysfunctional state of

---

7   *Journal* 1, opening letter (dated 19 October 1732), *The Works of John Wesley: Journals*, vol. 18, ed. Ward and Heitzenrater, 123.

8   *The Works of John Wesley: Journals*, vol. 18, ed. Ward and Heitzenrater, 29–31.

9   Richey, "History as a Bearer of Denominational Identity," 270 passim. Richey points out that of four consistent motifs in Methodist histories, the providential guidance of the Methodist Revival was the most consistent from the eighteenth through the twentieth centuries.

Wesley's own spiritual quest prior to 1738, concluding with the following dramatic claim:

> It is now two years and almost four months since I left my native country, in order to teach the Georgian Indians the nature of Christianity: But what have I learned myself in the mean time? Why, (what I the least of all suspected,) that I who went to America to convert others, was never myself converted to God.[10]

The second fascicle followed this with Wesley's account of his Aldersgate-Street experience. Despite notes that Wesley later added to the statement above refining the senses in which he was and was not "converted" on his return to England, these two fascicles, read in sequence, built the strong impression among his readers that the Aldersgate-Street experience was the principal work of God that led to the origins of the Wesleyan movement. Following the dramatic conclusion of the first fascicle, the second fascicle was understood as describing the conversion that Wesley lacked upon his return from Georgia.

The third fascicle followed this with the narrative of John Wesley's first field preaching in Bristol (2 April 1739), and the fourth fascicle focused on Wesley's conflict with the London Moravian society over the issue of stillness and the subsequent differentiation of his London society from the Moravian society there. The first four fascicles thus offered Wesley's readers four blocks of narrative that would become critical modules in the retelling of the Wesleyan narrative:

- The dysfunctional state of John Wesley's own spiritual experience prior to 1738, the origin of the narrative module I have called **SpiritualDysfunction**;

- The Aldersgate-Street experience construed as a conversion to true Christian faith, the original account of the module **AldersgateExperience**;

---

10 Conclusion of *Journal* 1 (the first published fascicle of the *Journal*) for 29 January 1738, *The Works of John Wesley: Journals*, vol. 18, ed. Ward and Heitzenrater, 214.

- The account of Wesley's first outdoor preaching in Bristol, reused as the module **FieldPreaching**;

- The account of the division with the London Moravian society over the issue of "stillness" and the means of grace, reused as the module I have called **StillnessMeans**.

Although the fascicles themselves focus on these four cardinal events, some other material later reused as narrative modules appeared in the *Journal*; for example, the account of Wesley's meetings with Moravians and Salzburg Pietists in Georgia, the module I have called **GeorgiaPietists**.

Subsequent fascicles of the *Journal* introduced other narratives that would be used by Methodists in recounting their narrative of origins. They described:

- the development of bands, classes, and societies and the structure of the General Rules that gave rise to module **ClassesBands**;[11]

- conflicts with Calvinistic clergy that formed the basis of the module **ArminianVsCalvinist**;[12]

- Wesley's authorization of lay preachers and his organization of their work in conferences and circuits, material that would be reused as the module **MethodistPreachers**;[13]

---

11   E.g., *Journal* 4 for 24 February 1741, *The Works of John Wesley: Journals,* vol. 19, ed. Ward and Heitzenrater, 184; *Journal* 5 for 15 February and 25 March 1742 and 8 March 1743, *The Works of John Wesley: Journals,* vol. 19, ed. Ward and Heitzenrater, 251, 258, 316; *Journal* 6 for 25 June 1744, *The Works of John Wesley: Journals,* vol. 20, ed. Ward and Heitzenrater, 34; *Journal* 7 for 24 July 1748, *The Works of John Wesley: Journals,* vol. 20, ed. Ward and Heitzenrater, 235.

12   E.g., *Journal* 4 for 20 December 1740 and 1 and 22 February 1741, *The Works of John Wesley: Journals,* vol. 19, ed. Ward and Heitzenrater, 174–75, 179–80, 182–83; *Journal* 5 for 10 October 1741 and 22 August 1743, *The Works of John Wesley: Journals,* vol. 19, ed. Ward and Heitzenrater, 230–32, 332–33.

13   E.g., *Journal* 3 for 20 October 1739, *The Works of John Wesley: Journals,* vol. 19, ed. Ward and Heitzenrater, 108; *Journal* 6 for 25 June 1744 and 1 August 1745, *The Works of John Wesley: Journals,* vol. 20, ed. Ward and Heitzenrater, 34, 81; *Journal* 15 for 19 July 1768, *The Works of John Wesley: Journals,* vol. 22, ed. Ward and Heitzenrater, 148–50.

- excerpts of his brother's verse, which with his own collations of verse would give rise to the module **CWPoetry**;[14]

- attacks by mobs and sometimes the clever ways in which Methodists eluded or talked down mobs, spawning the module **Methodist-Persecution**;[15]

- Methodists who had fallen away from the strictness of the movement in its earliest decades, thus seeding the module **Methodist-Declension**;[16]

- benevolent works in which Methodists were involved, giving rise to the module **MethodistBenevolence**;[17]

- the expansion of Methodism, including expansion into the North American colonies (module **GrowthOfMethodism**);[18] and

- his 1784 ordinations for America and Scotland (module **American-Ordinations**).[19]

The Journal of the Reverend John Wesley, A.M., thus offered the first narrative of the Wesleyan movement crafted and serially published over a half century. The very genre that Wesley chose, an

---

14 E.g., *Journal* 3 for 3 June and 23 October 1739, *The Works of John Wesley: Journals*, vol. 19, ed. Ward and Heitzenrater, 63, 109; *Journal* 7 for 29 August 1748, *The Works of John Wesley: Journals*, vol. 20, ed. Ward and Heitzenrater, 246.

15 E.g. *Journal* 6 for 11 March 1745, *The Works of John Wesley: Journals*, vol. 20, ed. Ward and Heitzenrater, 56–58; *Journal* 7 for 11 January 1747, *The Works of John Wesley: Journals*, vol. 20, ed. Ward and Heitzenrater, 152–53.

16 E.g. *Journal* 13 for 18 September 1763 and 11 July 1764, *The Works of John Wesley: Journals*, vol. 21, ed. Ward and Heitzenrater, 428, 477; *Journal* 19 for 3 April 1780, *The Works of John Wesley: Journals*, vol. 23, ed. Ward and Heitzenrater, 163.

17 E.g. *Journal* 9 for 8 and 21 February 1753, *The Works of John Wesley: Journals*, vol. 20, ed. Ward and Heitzenrater, 445, 447; *Journal* 14 for 20 February 1867, *The Works of John Wesley: Journals*, vol. 22, ed. Ward and Heitzenrater, 111–13.

18 E.g. *Journal* 7 for 8 through 22 August 1747 (expansion into Ireland), *The Works of John Wesley: Journals*, vol. 20, ed. Ward and Heitzenrater, 187–89; *Journal* 8 for 24 April through 5 May 1751 (expansion into Scotland), *The Works of John Wesley: Journals*, vol. 20, ed. Ward and Heitzenrater, 385–87; *Journal* 18 for 6 August 1776 (expansion into North America), *The Works of John Wesley: Journals*, vol. 23, ed. Ward and Heitzenrater, 26; *Journal* 20 for 30 September 1784 (North America), *The Works of John Wesley: Journals*, vol. 23, ed. Ward and Heitzenrater, 332–33.

19 *Journal* 20 for 31 August through 1 September 1784 and 1 August 1785, *The Works of John Wesley: Journals*, vol. 23, ed. Ward and Heitzenrater, 329–30, 371–72.

inexpensive serial publication following the model of popular travel narratives, lent itself to popular consumption far better than works of systematic theology or polemical literature might have done. The distribution network he utilized, that of the growing nexus of Wesleyan societies and the conference of preachers in connection with him, also served to promulgate his ideas across regional and social-class barriers. The *Journal* admitted John Wesley's own spiritual dysfunction and showed how God delivered him from it. It frequently lamented the decline of morals and culture ("manners") in his age and showed how the Methodist movement offered a corrective. In short, Wesley utilized the *Journal* to build a consistent narrative of decline and renewal showcasing the divinely guided rise and progress of the Methodist movement as God's instrument for this renewal. He encoded and transmitted this sense of Methodist identity by way of a narrative that shaped the identity of Methodism for generations to come.

The History of the Wesleyan Movement in the Minutes of Conferences

John Wesley's *Journal* became the foundational narrative for subsequent Methodist reuses of the narrative of the Wesleyan movement, but we can also consider the published Minutes of early Methodist conferences for further iterations of narrative code in the Wesleyan period. The Minutes were published after 1745, and in many cases they were revised and grouped into separate printed collections after that time. John Wesley himself set the questions for discussion in these early conferences, and in all likelihood formulated the responses that were given to them, although the fact that they were agreed upon by the body of preachers in the conferences gave them the status of corporately affirmed teachings.[20] Two questions and responses to

---

20 Richard P. Heitzenrater, *Wesley and the People Called Methodists,* 2nd ed. (Nashville: Abingdon Press, 2013), 158.

them in the collection of Minutes historically described as the "Large Minutes" or "Disciplinary Minutes" are particularly relevant as they involve a recounting of earlier events in the revival movement.

> **Q.** What may we reasonably believe to be God's design in raising up the preachers called "Methodists"?
>
> **A.** To reform the nation, and in particular the Church, [and] to spread scriptural holiness over the land.
>
> **Q.** What was the rise of Methodism, so called?
>
> **A.** In 1729, two young men, reading the Bible, saw they could not be saved without holiness, followed after it, and incited others so to do. In 1737 they saw, holiness comes by faith. They saw likewise that men are justified before they are sanctified: but still holiness was their point.
>
> God then thrust them out, utterly against their will, to raise a holy people. When Satan could not otherwise hinder this, he threw *Calvinism* in the way; and then *Antinomianism*, which strikes directly at the root of all holiness.
>
> Then many of the *Methodists* growing *rich*, became lovers of the present world. Next they married unawakened or half awakened wives, and conversed with their relations. Hence worldly *prudence, maxims, customs*, crept back upon them, producing more and more *conformity to the world*.
>
> Hence followed gross neglect of *relative duties*, especially *education* of children.[21]

The response to the first question given above will be critical, as we shall see, in understanding how the narrative of the Methodist revival gave a distinctive sense of mission to early Methodists both in Britain and eventually in North America. The response to the second question evokes what would become standard modules of the Wesleyan narrative, although they are not described very accurately in this brief statement:

---

21 "Large Minutes," following the versions of 1770 and 1772, as given in *The Works of John Wesley: The Methodist Societies, The Minutes of Conference*, vol. 10, ed. Henry D. Rack, 875, and referring back to 10:845 for the text of the first question (from the 1763 edition). The word *and* appeared in the 1770 version of the second question given here but not in the 1772 version.

▦ First is the brothers' general interest in Christian holiness, which John had cultivated himself since 1725 and for which he and his brother Charles had developed a small society at Oxford by at least 1732—the date 1729 seems to have been a shorthand reference to the sequence of events that led to the development of this society.[22] The narrative of John Wesley's quest for holiness gives rise to the code module I have called **QuestForHoliness**. The narrative of his activity in Oxford had only been hinted at in the first fascicle of the *Journal* and was reused as what I have called the **OxfordSociety** code module.

▦ Second is the brothers' developing understanding of justification by faith as a necessary antecedent to Christian holiness, although 1737 is an odd date to put on this; one would have supposed it was 1738 unless John Wesley had in mind the influence of Moravian and Lutheran communities in Georgia, where he spent almost the entire year of 1737. This narrative was often reused in the code module I have called **SpiritualDysfunction**.

▦ Third is the series of conflicts with Calvinists and conflicts against "Antinomianism" more generally, which began from the early 1740s, although Wesley does not mention the conflicts with the London Moravians in this period that led to the independence of the Wesleyan societies. The debates with Calvinists would become a standard part of the retelling of the Wesleyan narrative, the code module I have called **ArminianVsCalvinist**.

▦ Finally is a reference to Methodist declension from the standards set by the Wesleys in their early societies—that is, in the references to Methodists growing rich and conformed to the world. This initiates a narrative module that I call **MethodistDeclension**.

What is particularly notable in this compact narrative is the importance John Wesley placed on holiness. Neither the Aldersgate-Street experience, important in later accounts of Methodist origins, nor an

---

22 See Heitzenrater on the development of the Oxford Methodists in *Wesley and the People Called Methodists*, 37–64.

emphasis on religious experience in general was mentioned, and even when dealing with events of the Aldersgate period, the stress was on the doctrine of justification as an "antecedent" to holiness. This reinforces the claim in the response to the first question shown above that the distinct mission of the Methodist preachers had to do with the spread of "scriptural holiness."

The Minutes were disseminated through the conference of preachers and consistently revised through Wesley's lifetime and beyond as foundational documents for Methodist identity.[23] The historical narrative given in them reinforced the narrative in the *Journal* and offered something like a "mission" or "core purpose" statement of the early Methodist movement, a mission focused on the cultivation of Christian holiness. The Minutes show how John Wesley could utilize multiple genres, or to speak in an even more contemporary way, multiple forms of media mutually reinforcing key messages that formed the identity of Wesleyan communities.

Encoded History in Longer Narratives

John Wesley eventually expanded these brief narrates into longer narratives recounting the origins and development of the Methodist movement. In 1765, he published "A Short History of Methodism," expanding the earlier narratives to explain the genesis of Methodist doctrines regarding justification and sanctification.[24] In 1781, he expanded these earlier narratives further in "A Short History of the People Called Methodists," appended to his *Concise Ecclesiastical History*.[25] In this work Wesley offered a more detailed account of

---

23 Frank Baker's *Union Catalogue of the Publications of John and Charles Wesley*, 2nd ed., (Stone Mountain, GA: George Zimmerman, 1991) lists forty-four publications of various forms of the Minutes of the Conference within the span of Wesley's lifetime (see the entries beginning "Minutes" in the index).

24 In *The Works of John Wesley: The Methodist Societies: History, Nature, and Design*, vol. 9, ed. Rupert E. Davies, 367–72.

25 Ibid., 425–503. Wesley's *Concise Ecclesiastical History* was itself based on an English translation of Johann Lorenz von Mosheim's *Ecclesiastical History*; cf. Ted A. Campbell, "John Wesley's Conceptions and Uses of Christian Antiquity" (PhD dissertation, Southern Methodist University, 1984), 131–33.

the Methodist societies, and yet neither of these longer narratives had reference to the Aldersgate experience. The period around 1738 was described as the time in which John Wesley came to recognize the importance of justification by faith as necessarily coming before Christian holiness (sanctification),[26] but the accounts focused on the teaching about holiness as the central mission of the "people called Methodists."

John Wesley's *Journal,* the brief historical accounts in the Minutes, and his subsequent expanded historical narratives thus set the precedent for the subsequent Methodist telling and retelling of the origins of Methodism in the eighteenth-century revival. The Aldersgate narrative appeared in a prominent position in the second fascicle of the *Journal*, but as John Wesley compressed and restated the narrative as it appeared in the Minutes and the later narratives, his emphasis fell on the cultivation of holiness as the principal goal of the Methodist (Wesleyan) movement. The narrative he offered did not recount the origin of a Methodist church ("Not to form any new sect. . . .") but rather of a group of preachers and societies functioning within the contexts of the British state and of the Church of England ("to reform the nation, particularly the Church"). The narratives given in the *Journal,* the Minutes, and the subsequent histories included both John and Charles Wesley as founders of the Methodist movement.

THE SHAPE OF THE WESLEYAN NARRATIVE IN THE EIGHTEENTH CENTURY

The narratives given in the *Journal*, the Minutes, and the extended narratives strongly inculcated the sense that the mission of the Wesleyan movement was a divinely inspired and divinely guided movement, thus the key question in the Minutes framed as "What may we reasonably

---

26   In "A Short History of Methodism," ¶10, *The Works of John Wesley: The Methodist Societies,* vol. 9, ed. Davies, 369; and ¶9, 430–31.

believe to be God's design in raising up the Preachers called 'Methodists'?" In these accounts, and especially in responses to the early questions in the Minutes, John Wesley functioned as the first framer of modules of narrative code that would be consistently utilized by subsequent retellers of these narratives. In forming the Minutes and submitting them for the approval of the preachers in the conferences, he had recourse to the foundational events in his own experience that led to the distinct existence of the Wesleyan movement under his leadership. This would set the pattern for subsequent Methodist reiterations of the narrative of the Evangelical Revival, though as we shall see, these subsequent reiterations would highlight distinctive aspects of that narrative as they were adapted to the evolving mission of Methodist and Wesleyan communities in later generations.

In the Wesleyan period, then, the following modules of narrative code had begun to develop:

TYPICAL NARRATIVE MODULES IN JOHN WESLEY'S *JOURNAL*, THE MINUTES OF CONFERENCES, AND IN HIS LONGER NARRATIVES
QuestForHoliness
SpiritualDysfunction
OxfordSociety
GeorgiaPietists
AldersgateExperience (only in the *Journal*)
FieldPreaching
ClassesBands
MethodistDeclension
MethodistBenevolence

Other elements of Wesleyan narrative were latent in the *Journal* and Minutes and extended narratives considered above, and we will see many of these came to prominence in later retellings of the genesis of the Wesleyan movement.

The inclusion of a narrative of Methodist declension can be and should be read as an indictment of himself and his own religious movement. Wesley's public critiques of others (beyond himself) were almost always directed towards specific public acts or specific writings that he attributed (by name) to their authors, consistent with his advice on "evil speaking."[27] Wesley's own accounts described here do not assess general blame for the social or ecclesiastical situations he faced. That is, he did not blame the Church of England in general nor English society in general for the situation out of which the Methodist societies arose. Accounts of the rise of Methodism by subsequent Methodists would stand in sharp contrast to his narratives, often beginning with deprecatory claims about the state of the Church of England or of British society in general in the age in which Methodism arose.

JOHN WESLEY AS CULTURE CODER

What stands out in all of this is John Wesley's role as a culture coder, not only in framing historical narratives in the *Journal*, the Minutes, and extended narratives but also in disseminating published sermons, catechisms, tracts, and apologetic as well as polemical literature explaining, clarifying, and defending key teachings and practices associated with the Wesleyan movement. He utilized multiple media that reinforced consistent messages, including not only published works but orally delivered sermons and his brother's verse that could be sung to a small collection of well-known tunes. His published output and that of his brother far exceeded that of other popular evangelists of their age. Thus, I would say, John Wesley not only succeeded in gathering a body of followers in his own time, he also encoded a cultural vision that he and later they transmitted successfully to future generations.

---

27   Cf. Wesley, "The Cure of Evil Speaking," *The Works of John Wesley*, vol. 2, ed. Outler, 251–62.

By the end of the Wesleyan period there had come into existence a way of being Christian that had a distinct sense of mission grounded in the Wesleyan revival of the preceding decades, a way of being Christian that focused on the cultivation of Christian holiness within a particular set of groups including band meetings and classes, with a distinctive kit of narrative modules utilized to describe the identity of the Wesleyan community, and with reinforcing multiple media that could transmit this narrative along with distinctive beliefs and practices to new generations. The next chapter will consider how the next generations of Wesleyans retold narratives of the origins of the Wesleyan movement in the early nineteenth century.

WESLEYAN NARRATIVES IN THE AGE OF EARLY METHODIST CHURCHES

EARLY NINETEENTH CENTURY

B y 1784 at least one Methodist church (denomination) had come into existence separate from the existing structures of the Church of England. This chapter examines Wesleyan narratives in the early nineteenth century, the period of early Methodist churches. Periods of cultural history have no hard boundaries. The designation is rough, but we can identify some broad cultural traits in Wesleyan communities in this period.

The period that I define as that of early Methodist churches extends from 1784, when John Wesley authorized an independent Methodist church in North America, through roughly the middle of the nineteenth century, a period that saw the formation of many Methodist churches or denominations. In addition to the Methodist Episcopal Church (1784) and the organization of the Wesleyan Conference in Britain as an ecclesial community (1795), this period includes the development of the Methodist New Connexion (1797), the Primitive Methodist Connexion (1811), the African Methodist Episcopal Church (1816), the Evangelical Association (1816), the African Methodist Episcopal Zion Church (1821), and the Methodist Protestant

Church (1830). It was a period in which Methodists in North America and in the British Isles considered themselves to be a minority religious group and a period when persons outside the movement considered them sectarian. It was also a period of remarkable Methodist growth in both places.

After the death of John Wesley, British Methodists struggled to interpret Wesley's life in the context of their ambiguous relationship to the Church of England. The main body of British Methodists, the Wesleyan Conference, functioned within a set of legal parameters established by the Disciplinary Minutes, a "Model Deed" for Wesleyan chapels (1763), and a "Deed of Declaration" (1784) that established an ongoing structure for the conference. None of these formally separated the Wesleyans from the Church of England, and even after the Wesleyan Conference began to authorize clergy in Methodist chapels to celebrate the Lord's Supper at the same time as their neighboring Anglican parish churches did (1795), the Wesleyan Conference still professed loyalty to the Church of England. Although they may have functioned *de facto* as a separate church, they would not admit formally (*de jure*) to such a break.[1] Because of this, they had to construe the narrative of John Wesley's career and of the Methodist movement in a very careful way to explain and defend their independent institutions yet not admitting to a separation with the national church establishment.

EARLY BRITISH METHODIST BIOGRAPHIES OF JOHN WESLEY

The interpretation of the Wesleyan movement was carried on in Britain immediately after John Wesley's death by a series of biographical accounts that offered significantly differing views of the contributions of John Wesley and encoded significantly differing understandings of the

---

1   This is the general conclusion of Frank Baker's study of *John Wesley and the Church of England* (Nashville: Abingdon Press, 1970), which is discussed in more detail in the chapter on the period beyond Methodist Modernism.

identity of Methodism. John Wesley's will had stipulated that Henry Moore (1751–1844), Thomas Coke (1747–1814), and John Whitehead (ca. 1740–1804) should examine Wesley's papers and decide which to keep and which to destroy. These three planned at first to write a biography of Wesley immediately after his death, and this was made more urgent when, within three months of Wesley's death, a disaffected Methodist preacher, John Hampson (1760–ca. 1817), came out with a biography of John Wesley critical of Wesley's "enthusiasm," his authoritarian control of the preachers and societies, and other aspects of his theology and practice.[2]

However, Coke and Moore had an extended conflict with Whitehead over the issue of access to Wesley's papers, and Whitehead withheld the papers from them. Coke and Moore came out with a hastily produced biography in 1792, and Whitehead followed with a two-volume biography that appeared in 1793 and 1796.[3] Each of these could claim, based on Wesley's will, to be authorized biographies that interpreted the life of John Wesley as the progenitor of Wesleyan Methodism in Great Britain. They were, however, to produce very different accounts of the life of John Wesley and to encode within them very different meanings of the Methodist movement.

The work of Coke and Moore, *Life of Wesley,* (1792), was based on published works of John Wesley and on their recollection of Wesley's manuscripts, which they had seen previously, although at the time of their writing Whitehead was keeping the manuscripts from them. Richard P. Heitzenrater describes Coke and Moore's biography as "a prolonged eulogy of Wesley" that "bears the marks of a hastily

---

2   John Hampson, *Memoirs of the Late Rev. John Wesley, A.M., with a Review of His Life and Writings, and a History of Methodism from It's Commencement in 1729 to the Present Time,* (London: James Graham, 1791). The word "It's" [sic] in the title is spelled as it appears in the title page of the book.

3   Thomas Coke and Henry Moore, *The Life of the Rev. John Wesley, A.M* (1792), as noted in the introduction is referred to as Coke and Moore, *Life of Wesley;* John Whitehead, *The Life of the Rev. John Wesley, M.A., Sometime Fellows of Lincoln College, Oxford* (London; Stephen Couchman, 1793 and 1796), hereafter referred to as Whitehead, *The Life of Rev. John Wesley* (1793) or (1796) as appropriate.

produced work and suffers from lack of substantive quotation from the manuscripts."[4] But their work set a precedent for subsequent Methodist interpretations of John Wesley, and it is a key source for understanding how Methodists of the Wesleyan Conference in Britain and beyond "traditioned" Wesley and encoded a specific understanding of Methodist identity.

Coke and Moore divided their account into three "books," the first of which recounts Wesley's life up to his Aldersgate-Street experience. Two things stand out in this first book that were to become consistent marks of Methodist interpretations of John Wesley. In the first place, their narrative began with an account of the corrupt state of religion in England prior to the time of Wesley, which involved, as they described it, a "practical atheism," "looseness of morals" and a failure on the part of clergy to preach "the great leading truths of the Gospel," namely, justification by faith alone, communion with God, the assurance of pardon, and the doctrine of original sin.[5] Thus they introduced what I have called the module **AnglicanDeclension**. Though this view of English religion in the late seventeenth and early eighteenth century has been substantially rebutted by historians in our time (including such Methodist historians as John Walsh), it became part of the standard Methodist account of their own origins and in fact deeply influenced subsequent Anglican historiography concerning the eighteenth century.[6]

The second thing that stands out in the *Life of Wesley* by Coke and Moore is the manner in which they recounted John Wesley's Aldersgate-Street experience (module **AldersgateExperience**), referring to it unambiguously as "his Conversion" and stating unequivocally that in this experience he was "brought to the birth," that is,

---

4   Heitzenrater, *Elusive Mr. Wesley* (2003), 354.
5   Coke and Moore, *Life of Wesley* (1792), 1–8, quotations on p. 7.
6   On the historiography deprecating the condition of the Church of England in the eighteenth century, see John Walsh and Stephen Taylor, "Introduction: The Church and Anglicanism in the 'Long' Eighteenth Century," in Walsh, Haydon and Taylor, eds., *The Church of England, c. 1689— c. 1883*, 29–45; the remainder of the book gives indications of the strengths of eighteenth-century Anglicanism.

to the new birth or regeneration in Christ.[7] They quoted the account of Aldersgate directly from John Wesley's *Journal* and acknowledged only in a footnote that Wesley himself had later expressed doubts about some of his own expressions in the *Journal* account, explaining in their note that Wesley "had a measure of Faith" and was even "in a state of salvation" prior to Aldersgate, but, they went on to state, this faith was "not the proper *christian* [sic] faith."[8]

The second book of Coke and Moore's *Life of Wesley* recounted the origins of such distinctive Methodist institutions as itinerant and open-air preaching (module **FieldPreaching**), the Methodist societies, classes, bands, the "General Rules" (module **ClassesBands**), love feasts, watch nights, and conferences (module **MethodistPreachers**). They also recounted the severe persecution that Wesley and other Methodists suffered in the early decades of the movement (module **MethodistPersecution**). They gave extended quotations from the Wesleyan Minutes, explaining the distinctive teachings as well as practices of the Wesleyan movement, offering a good example of how historical narrative has often functioned for Methodists, as Russell Richey has observed, as a way of teaching doctrine.[9] The second book of Coke and Moore's *Life of Wesley* concludes by explaining the Deed of Declaration (1784) as foundational for the Wesleyan Conference.[10] The second book explained and justified the distinctive practices as well as teachings of the Wesleyan movement and its relationship to the Church of England. In explaining the Deed of Declaration, Coke and Moore explained that

> Mr. Wesley's great desire to remain in union with the Church of England, so far as the work he was engaged in would permit,

---

7   Coke and Moore refer to Aldersgate as "his Conversion" in the title of book 1, chap. 4, p. 130. The account of Aldersgate is given on 148–60, and the expression quoted here is on 148 ("He was now brought to the birth"). Similarly, they wrote of the Aldersgate-Street experience, "Now that he was a child of God . . . " (159). Jean Miller Schmidt has shown that Moore's later biography of Wesley, though it borrowed heavily from Whitehead, nevertheless displayed this evangelical tendency in strongly representing Aldersgate as Wesley's experience of the new birth: Schmidt, "'Strangely Warmed,'" 111.

8   Coke and Moore, *Life of Wesley* (1792), the footnote on p. 159.

9   Richey, "History in the Discipline," 198–202.

10   Coke and Moore, *Life of Wesley* (1792), 169–360.

would not allow him to apply for a legal establishment, or for any thing which might give to the Societies under his care the form of a separate Body.[11]

At this point in their narrative, although they discussed the Deed of Declaration of 1784, they very significantly did *not* mention John Wesley's controversial ordinations of the same year.

In the third book, Coke and Moore went back to the year 1749 to offer an account of Wesley's work in Ireland, Scotland, the Isle of Man, and the Channel Isles, and then the work of the Methodist movement in North America (module **GrowthOfMethodism**). It was only at the point of discussing the Methodist work in North America that Coke and Moore described John Wesley's ordinations of 1784, and here they gave the text of Wesley's letter of September 10 of that year ("To Dr. Coke, Mr. Asbury, and our Brethren in North America") explaining the ordinations with no further comment except to note that the American Methodists implemented the plan Wesley laid out in this letter (module **AmericanOrdinations**).[12] The implication, for Coke and Moore's English readers, was that the ordinations of 1784 were to apply to America only. They did not mention the fact that Wesley later performed similar ordinations for Scotland and then for England.[13]

The third book concludes the *Life of Wesley* by recounting John Wesley's death.[14] This set a precedent for subsequent Methodist narratives of "holy dying," seeing death as the culmination of the work of grace in the life of a Christian saint (thus module **JWDeath**). Coke's and Moore's adulation for Wesley was consistent from the very beginning. They refer to him as "our venerable Father" and "our honoured Friend" (on the first page), and then through the book Wesley is described as "the wonder of these kingdoms and *America*," and the account of his saintly death culminates their depiction of Wesley as the

---

11   Ibid., 355.
12   Ibid., 458–62.
13   Baker, *John Wesley and the Church of England*, 307–08 (ordinations for Scotland), 311–12 (ordinations for England).
14   Ibid., 361–511.

one who in the providence of God was able to bring to England—and particularly to the Church of England—the revival of religion that the conditions of the church they described at the beginning of the *Life of Wesley* so direly warranted.[15]

We can summarize Coke's and Moore's utilization of coded modules to narrate the origins of Methodism as follows:

COKE AND MOORE, *LIFE OF WESLEY* (1792)
Book 1:
AnglicanDeclension
AldersgateExperience
Book 2:
FieldPreaching
ClassesBands
MethodistPreachers
MethodistPersecution
Book 3:
GrowthOfMethodism (including brief notice of **AmericanOrdinations**)
JWDeath

John Whitehead's two-volume *The Life of the Rev. John Wesley, A.M.* (1793 and 1796) was more extensive than the work of Coke and Moore and could claim to be "collected from [Wesley's] private papers and printed works," since Whitehead did have access to the papers that he had withheld from Coke and Moore. Heitzenrater describes Whitehead's volumes as being much more historically nuanced and less polemical than the work of Coke and Moore.[16] His work differed

---

15   The adulatory expressions cited here are from ibid., iii (the first page of the dedication to the Methodist preachers) and p. 169 (the beginning of book 2).

16   Heitzenrater, *Elusive Mr. Wesley* (2003), 354.

very significantly from Coke and Moore's account. In the first place, Whitehead did not begin with an account of the state of religion in England prior to Wesley, as Coke and Whitehead had done, giving only an account of Wesley's forebears and of the life of Charles Wesley before moving to describe John Wesley's life.[17]

In the second place, Whitehead's account of John Wesley's Aldersgate experience varies greatly from that of Coke and Moore. The narrative in Whitehead's work took only two pages; it involved only two paragraphs quoted from the *Journal,* and it did not make any claims about Wesley's having been "born again" or "born anew" in this experience, though he did at least suggest that this was a conversion experience by stating that Wesley "was but a new convert" when he faced doubts following the Aldersgate-Street experience. Whitehead's narrative of the Aldersgate-Street event included references to Wesley's later corrections of his language about the experience, and Whitehead placed this material in the text preceding his account of the Aldersgate experience, not in footnotes to which Coke and Moore had relegated it.[18] Whitehead's paragraphs immediately following his description of the Aldersgate-Street experience described the doubts that Wesley had afterward. Whitehead explained that this is not unusual for "a new convert," and that "doubts and fears are consistent with justifying faith."[19] Whitehead thus introduced, along with the module **AldersgateExperience**, another module grounded in Wesley's writings that was to be reused; I have called it module **WesleyDoubts**.

Whitehead did give a full accounting of the rise of distinctive Methodist institutions such as itinerant preaching (module **Field-Preaching**), the system of classes, bands, and societies (module

---

17   The entire first book of Whitehead's book is taken up with the ancestry of the Wesley family and the lives of John Wesley's brothers Samuel and Charles: Whitehead, *The Life of Rev. John Wesley* (1793), Book 1, 1–374.

18   Ibid. (1796), 59.

19   Whitehead, *The Life of Rev. John Wesley* (1796), Book 2, chap. 4, 80–81. Schmidt also notes the moderating tendencies in Whitehead's account of the Aldersgate-Street experience: Schmidt, "'Strangely Warmed': The Place of Aldersgate in the Methodist Canon," 110–11.

ClassesBands), and the conferences of itinerant preachers (module **MethodistPreachers**). He also gave accounts of Methodist teachings, offering readers lengthy quotations from various versions of the Wesleyan Minutes, as Coke and Moore had done (module **WayOfSalvation**). But unlike Coke and Moore, Whitehead showed himself willing enough to disagree with some of John Wesley's actions: he gave a long account of the ordinations of 1784 (module **AmericanOrdinations**) and the reasons why he felt that Wesley's actions were unjustifiable. Among other arguments, Whitehead maintained that the ordinations contradicted John Wesley's own consistent claims that he would not make any break with the Church of England. Whitehead concluded his discussion of the ordinations by expressing his own wish "that both the practice of ordaining among the *Methodists*, and the memory of it, were buried in oblivion."[20] This was consistent with Whitehead's own judgment that a great strength of the Wesleyan movement had been its ability to work with Christians of different church traditions and its refusal to be identified as a church in competition with any of the existing churches.[21]

WHITEHEAD, *THE LIFE OF REV. JOHN WESLEY* (1793 AND 1796)
[Account of Wesley family and ancestry]
AldersgateExperience (much briefer than Coke and Moore)
WesleyDoubts
FieldPreaching
ClassesBands
MethodistPreachers
WayOfSalvation

20 Whitehead, *The Life of Rev. John Wesley* (1796), Book 3, chap. 5, 418–39; quotation is on 438–39.
21 Ibid. (1796), Book 3, chap. 6, section 3, 496–504.

WHITEHEAD, *THE LIFE OF REV. JOHN WESLEY* (1793 AND 1796) (continued)
MethodistPersecution
GrowthOfMethodism
AmericanOrdinations (Whitehead was critical of them)
DoctrinalLiberality (adumbrated throughout)
JWDeath

The biographies written by Coke and Moore and by Whitehead claimed the authority of Wesley's will, and both biographies appealed to the Wesleyan Conference, but two very different images of John Wesley emerged from these first biographical narratives from among the ranks of the Methodist preachers. Despite his superior historical scholarship and his access to the hijacked Wesley manuscripts, Whitehead was in a far less authoritative position with respect to the Conference. Although he had been a Methodist preacher early in his life, Whitehead subsequently became a Quaker and then became a Methodist again in 1784. But as a result of his quarrel with Coke and Moore, he was denied a class ticket and removed from the list of preachers in December, 1791 and remained outside of the Wesleyan Conference while composing his *The Life of Rev. John Wesley.* He was only restored to the Conference in 1797. Thus, although Whitehead was a very close confidant of John Wesley—he was Wesley's personal physician and was asked by Wesley to give the eulogy at Wesley's funeral—his standing with the Conference was not strong, and Coke and Moore's work (and a later, expanded life by Moore) was better positioned to represent the view of the Conference.

There is a consistent note of *liberality* (the term he frequently used) in Whitehead's encoding of the narrative of John Wesley, a note that is not at all so clear among the many virtues of Wesley depicted by Coke and Moore. Whitehead adumbrated the module **DoctrinalLiberality** that would be taken up by early twentieth-century Methodist inter-preters of Wesley.[22] Whitehead emphasized what he understood to be the original nature of the Methodist movement as a spiritual move-ment, not replacing the structures of the Church of England or any other church, and as we have seen above he strongly criticized Wes-ley's ordinations of 1784 as violating this basic meaning or mission of the Methodist movement. He also criticized the points where he believed Wesley had stepped beyond the bounds of Wesley's own authority and where Wesley was influenced by others to do things that Whitehead believed he would not have otherwise done, the ordi-nations being a case in point. Not surprisingly, Whitehead's biography of Wesley was later championed by advocates of democratic reform in Methodist denominations.[23] Jean Miller Schmidt has pointed to the "moderating" tendencies in Whitehead and the "evangelical" reading of Henry Moore in recounting the Aldersgate experience.[24] The biog-raphy of Coke and Moore set the stage for an evangelical interpreta-tion of John Wesley and the Methodist movement, and Whitehead's biography set the stage for a more liberal reading of Wesley and the meaning of the Methodist movement. As we shall see, both ways of encoding the Wesleyan past and the identity of Methodism would have their followers among subsequent Methodist interpretations of the Wesleyan Revival.

---

22 For example, Whitehead wrote that John Wesley "never published any thing with a view to pro-mote a party-spirit. A great degree of candour and liberality runs through all his publications" in Whitehead's *The Life of Rev. John Wesley* (1796), Book 3, chap. 6, section 2, 486.

23 For example, Alexander McCaine's *Letters on the Organization and Early History of the Meth-odist Episcopal Church* (Boston: Thomas F. Norris, Olive Branch Office, 1850); and Edward J. Drinkhouse's *History of Methodist Reform: Synoptical of General Methodism, with Special and Comprehensive Reference to Its Most Salient Exhibition in the History of the Methodist Protes-tant Church* (Baltimore and Pittsburgh: Board of Publication of the Methodist Protestant Church, 1899); cf. the preface, vi (which refers to Whitehead and James O'Kelly as "the two men who have been most vilified and misrepresented." These books were sponsored by the Methodist Protestant Church in the USA, which had rejected episcopacy, and they repeatedly commend Whitehead's biography of Wesley, including Whitehead's critical comments on Wesley's ordina-tions of 1784. McCaine's earlier *History and Mystery of Methodist Episcopacy, Or, A Glance at "The Institutions of the Church, As We Received Them From Our Fathers"* (Baltimore: Richard J. Matchett, 1827) was an early call for democratic reform that led to the forming of the Methodist Protestant Church, but it did not refer to Whitehead as the later works would do.

24 Schmidt, "'Strangely Warmed': The Place of Aldersgate in the Methodist Canon," 110–11.

Celebrating the Wesleyan Centennial

A little less than fifty years after these works were published, British Methodists celebrated the centenary (centennial) of John Wesley's organization of the "United Societies" (1739), which the main body of British Methodists, the Wesleyan Methodists, understood to be the origin of their distinct ecclesial community. For this occasion, the president of the British Conference, Thomas Jackson (1783–1873), prepared a historical narrative entitled, *The Centenary of Wesleyan Methodism* (1839).[25] Jackson served twice as president of the British Methodist Conference, served as the editor of John Wesley's works in what became the standard (Jackson, fourteen-volume) edition, and served in the chair of divinity at Richmond College between 1842 and 1861. He thus held remarkable stature within British Methodism, and his narrative bears the gravity of an authorized voice for the British Conference.

Jackson's centenary volume begins with a chapter titled the "State of Religion in England Before the Rise of Methodism," where Jackson referred to the eighteenth century as "unquestionably the most unevangelical period that had ever occurred in this country, since the Reformation."[26] He pointed to the corruption of clergy, lax morality in general, and the rise of Deism as evidences of the corruption of the English churches, Reformed as well as Anglican, in this age. In this way, Jackson offered his own version of what I have called code module **AnglicanDeclension**, extended to include the dysfunctional state of other churches as well as the Church of England.[27]

Jackson's account of John and Charles Wesley's early lives (chapter 2) includes the following modules: **EpworthUpbringing**, **JWInfluences** (specifically naming Jeremy Taylor, Thomas à Kempis, and

---

25 Thomas Jackson, *The Centenary of Wesleyan Methodism: A Brief Sketch of the Rise, Progress, and Present State of the Wesleyan-Methodist Societies Throughout the World* (London: John Mason, 1839). A comment on p. 213 makes it clear that it was the centennial of the founding of the first of the United Societies that was commemorated by this volume in 1839; cf. also p. 2 although this location does not reveal the precise meaning of the centenary.

26 Ibid., 2; chaps. 1–18.

27 Ibid., 1–6.

William Law), **OxfordSociety**, **SpiritualDysfunction**, and **Georgia-Pietists** (mentioning only Moravians). The chapter concludes with Jackson's account of **AldersgateExperience**.[28] The fact that Jackson's account can be so readily summarized under these headings shows that his work reflects what had already become a standardized telling of the Wesleyan narrative. The next chapter (3) continues this with labeled headings answering to modules **FieldPreaching** and **Classes-Bands**. The chapter also includes a description of the authorization of lay preachers (**MethodistPreachers**), perhaps sensitive to the accusation that this practice stood in tension with Church of England Article 23,[29] then describes the building of separate worship spaces and the Wesleyans' work in book publication.[30] The next chapters detail the spread of Methodism prior to the Wesleys' deaths (chapter 4; module **GrowthOfMethodism**), their deaths (chapter 5; module **JWDeath**), and the spread of Methodism beyond their deaths (chapter 6; continuing **GrowthOfMethodism**).[31] Jackson's narrative can be shown as combining the following sequence of narrative modules:

JACKSON, *CENTENARY OF WESLEYAN METHODISM* (1839)
EpworthUpbringing
JWInfluences (especially Jeremy Taylor, Thomas à Kempis, and William Law)
OxfordSociety
SpiritualDysfunction
GeorgiaPietists (mentioning only Moravians)

---

28 These topics appear in this order in the second chapter, 19–49.

29 The Twenty-Third Article of Religion begins by stating that, "It is not lawful for any man to take upon him the office of public preaching or ministering the sacraments in the congregation, before he be lawfully called and sent to execute the same" in Valerie R. Hotchkiss and Jaroslav Pelikan, eds., *Creeds and Confessions of Faith in the Christian Tradition*, 2:534; cf. E. J. Bicknell, *A Theological Introduction to the Thirty-Nine Articles of Religion of the Church of England* (London: Longmans, Green, and Co., third edition, 1955), 321.

30 Thomas Jackson, *The Centenary of Wesleyan Methodism: A Brief Sketch of the Rise, Progress, and Present State of the Wesleyan-Methodist Societies Throughout the World* (London: John Mason, 1839), 50–91.

31 Ibid., 92–122, 123–58, and 159–94, respectively.

JACKSON, *CENTENARY OF WESLEYAN METHODISM* (1839) (continued)
AldersgateExperience[32]
FieldPreaching
ClassesBands
MethodistPreachers
GrowthOfMethodism
JWDeath
GrowthOfMethodism (continued beyond John Wesley's death)

The conclusion of Jackson's *Centenary of Wesleyan Methodism* claimed that Methodism is a simple, pure form of Christian faith consistent with the Scriptures and proven by its fruits in conversions and in the reform of "manners," denoting morals and broader culture. Jackson also saw Methodism as compatible with the faith and worship of the Church of England and allowed that there had been a great improvement in the Church of England since Wesley's time. He spent considerable space lauding the national church:

> The incomparable Liturgy of the Established Church is used in many of the Wesleyan chapels in England, and in all the Mission chapels of the West Indies, . . . [and] the sanctified learning which is displayed in the profound and orthodox writings of the Divines of the Church of England has ever been of the greatest benefit to the Wesleyan body, as it has to the more serious and religious part of the community in general.[33]

Jackson's centenary volume, then, generally followed the pattern laid out by Coke and Moore, though acknowledging the wider spread of Methodism in his time and continuing to acknowledge a symbiotic

---

32　These first six topics appear in this order in the second chapter, 19–49.
33　Ibid., 195–229; quotations are on 202 and 203, respectively.

relationship of the Wesleyan Conference to the Church of England, at least on the part of learned leaders of the Wesleyan Conference.

In association with the same British Methodist centenary of 1839, a British Methodist missionary to the West Indies, **George Beard (1793–1877)**, wrote a poetic account of the history of Methodism that was published around 1840 under the title, *The History of Methodism, or the Wesleyan Centenary: A Poem in Twelve Books*.[34] Dedicated to Thomas Jackson, Beard's poem was written in heroic couplets, a genre that had flourished in the eighteenth century, for example, in Alexander Pope's translations of Homer, but had come to be regarded as passé in literary circles by Beard's time.[35] It began by invoking the "Genius of holy love," an invocation of the Holy Spirit modeled after the invocation of the muse in classical verse.[36] The poem is divided into twelve short books, also evocative of classical poetic structure. By utilizing this genre, Beard sought to elevate his narrative of Methodist history to the status of a classical epic.

The poem does not cover quite the same material as Jackson's centenary volume. It does devote an entire "book" to a depiction of the corruptions of society and the paucity of clergy in the age before Wesley. This is not quite what I have called module **Anglican-Declension** because in Beard's poem, the fault is ascribed not to the Church of England as such but rather to English society at large (thus **SocialDysfunction**).[37] The poem waxes eloquent about the beauty of England ("Albion, dearest Isle of the blue sea"), though the author admitted in a note that his couplets about England were written while he was in the West Indies.[38] The poem places special emphasis on

---

34 George Beard, *The History of Methodism, or the Wesleyan Centenary: A Poem in Twelve Books* (London: Simpkin, Marshall, and Co., and Southwark: J. C. Beard, n.d., [ca. 1840]).

35 On the diminished reputation of Alexander Pope's verse in the Romantic period, cf. Margaret Drabble, ed., *The Oxford Companion to English Literature*, 6th ed. (Oxford: Oxford University Press, 2000), 804, s.v. "Pope, Alexander"; and in Michael Stapleton, consultant editor, *The Cambridge Guide to English Literature* (Cambridge: Cambridge University Press, 1983), 710–11, s.v. "Pope, Alexander."

36 Beard, *History of Methodism*, 3. *Genius* is a Latin term for "Spirit."

37 Ibid., Book 2.

38 Ibid., 6–7; note and quotation are on p. 6. Cf. also the conclusion of the work, 175–76, which has the Methodists crying, "Live Victoria!" and unfurling the Union Jack on their missionary voyages.

the Wesleys' engagement in the Oxford Methodist society (**Oxford-Society**),[39] but does not mention either the Georgia venture or the Aldersgate experience of 1738. It jumps from the Oxford societies to an account of early Methodist itinerant preaching (**FieldPreaching**)[40] and skips over the organization of Methodist societies to dwell at length on the expansion of Methodism beyond Britain (**GrowthOfMethodism**).[41] The poem celebrates Methodist opposition to slavery, the author noting in his introduction that he was in the West Indies in 1833 when Parliament abolished slavery in British possessions (thus module **OppositionToSlavery**).[42] The narrative of Beard's poem thus utilizes the following sequence of encoded modules:

BEARD, *HISTORY OF METHODISM* (CA. 1840)
SocialDysfunction
OxfordSociety
FieldPreaching
GrowthOfMethodism
OppositionToSlavery
JWDeath

Both the Jackson and Beard narratives express a consistent confidence in the divine guidance of the Methodist movement through its earlier history and in their own time, and their confident sense that Methodism had meant nothing but good but for the world. Jackson made this very clear in his conclusion:

> The Wesleys, and their noble companion in evangelical labour,
> Mr. Whitefield, were indeed extraordinary men; but they were

---

39   Ibid., 18–20.
40   Ibid., Book 4, 21–20, and extending into Book 5.
41   Ibid., most of the book from Book 5 forward deals with the missionary expansion of Wesleyan Methodism.
42   Ibid., the author's introduction (vii) and Book 10 (123–42).

not men casually brought into existence, and whose powers were casually called forth by the circumstances of the times, as a profane and godless philosophy would insinuate. They were raised up by God, as the instruments of his mercy to the world. The peculiar talents with which they were endued were his gift. Their piety, their zeal for the divine glory, their yearning pity for ignorant and wicked men, their meek endurance of opposition, and their patience in toil and suffering, were all the effects of his holy inspiration. The whole of their success in turning men to Christ depended upon the exertion of the divine power; for no man can come to Christ unless he be drawn by the Father.[43]

Beard also saw the practical effects of Methodism as the result of divine providence. Commenting on the name *Methodist*, for example, Beard wrote:

Well chosen name! A CENTURY it has stood,
And Methodistic zeal has stem'd the flood,
Of sin, and folly, in a thousand forms;
And liv'd, and flourish'd, mid surrounding storms.
Long may it live, and ever may it stand,
To bless, renew, and sanctify the land.[44]

The impression one gains from Jackson's and Beard's accounts is of Methodism as a benevolent, simplified, and thus universalized form of Christian faith, well adapted to expansion throughout the world and not only proven effective but also proven to be of divine grace by its practical effects.

EARLY AMERICAN METHODIST USES OF THE WESLEYAN NARRATIVE

American Methodists had made a cleaner break with Anglican structures than their British counterparts by the organization in 1784 of the

---

43 Jackson, *Centenary of Wesleyan Methodism*, 213–14.
44 Beard, *History of Methodism*, 19.

Methodist Episcopal Church. Nevertheless, the very earliest narratives that American Methodists gave of the origins of Methodism focused only on the rise of the Methodist movement but not of the rise of Methodist churches. The earliest American Methodist *Disciplines* were organized in the form of questions and answers following the pattern of the Wesleyan Minutes. These earliest *Disciplines* began with two questions about the rise of Methodism in "Europe" (that is, Britain) and America. The narrative about the rise of Methodism in Britain in response to the first question in the *Discipline* gave a slightly revised version of the narrative given in the Wesleyan Minutes quoted above as the response to question four in the "Large Minutes." The revised narrative is as follows:

> In 1729, two young Men, reading the Bible, saw they could not be saved without Holiness, followed after it, and incited others so to do. In 1737, they saw likewise, that Men are justified before they are sanctified; but still Holiness was their Object. God then thrust them out, to raise an holy People.[45]

This is followed by a question asking about the rise of Methodism in America. The response is as follows:

> During the Space of thirty Years past, certain Persons, Members of the Society, emigrated from England and Ireland, and settled in various Parts of this Country. About twenty Years ago, Philip Embury, a local Preacher from Ireland, began to preach in the City of New-York, and formed a Society of his Countrymen and the Citizens. About the same Time, Robert Strawbridge, a local Preacher from Ireland, settled in Frederick County, in the State of Maryland, and preaching there formed some Societies. In 1769, Richard Boardman and Joseph Pilmoor, came to New-York; who were the first regular Methodist Preachers on the Continent. In the latter End of the

---

45 This is consistent in early *Disciplines* of the Methodist Episcopal Church; it is here cited from *A Form of Discipline for the Ministers, Preachers, and Members of the Methodist Episcopal Church in America, Considered and Approved at a Conference held at Baltimore, in the State of Maryland, On Monday the 27th of December, 1784* (New York: W. Ross, 1787), 3. Cf. Richey, "History in the Discipline," 191.

Year 1771, Francis Asbury and Richard Wright, of the same Order, came over.[46]

Although the narrative of American Methodism given here was simply a recounting of the earliest societies (module **ClassesBands**) and the earliest preachers formally authorized by the British Conference (module **MethodistPreachers**), the narrative of the first rise of Methodism in "Europe" focuses on the quest for holiness, and this was consistent with the way in which the earliest Methodist *Disciplines* in North America reframed the statement of the basic mission of Methodism: "To reform the Continent, and to spread scripture Holiness over these Lands."[47] That is to say, the distinct mission of the Methodist preachers and of the Methodist societies had to do with the quest for Christian holiness but was now placed in the context of the North American continent rather than Britain and the Church of England. The basic pattern of this historical narrative with the reframed statement of the Methodist mission on the North American continent remained consistent in the *Disciplines* of the Methodist Episcopal Church through the end of the nineteenth century. However, American Methodist *Disciplines* from 1801 began to insert a separate section narrating the origins of the Methodist Episcopal Church as a distinct denomination (thus module **AmericanOrdinations**).[48]

Within twenty-five years of the Christmas Conference (1784) at which the Methodist Episcopal Church was founded, American Methodists began producing more expansive histories of Methodism intended for the readership of Methodist leaders and members of the

---

46 Ibid., 3–4.

47 Ibid., 4.

48 Methodist Episcopal *Disciplines* from 1801 repeated the statement about the rise of the Methodist movement (as given above) in the episcopal address, a letter signed by all the acting bishops that appears at the very beginning of the *Discipline*, then a statement "Of the Origins of the Methodist Episcopal Church" in chap. 1, Section 1 of the *Discipline*. I have checked this in the ME Church *Disciplines* of 1801, 1808, 1844, 1860, 1880, and 1888. This pattern prevailed until 1892, when it was significantly revised (see the text below on this revision); cf. Richey, "History in the Discipline," 191–92. The Methodist Episcopal Church, South, included the same material as the Methodist Episcopal Church in the early versions of its *Discipline*, adding a section 2 on the origins of the ME South Church. From 1870, however, the ME South *Disciplines* remove entirely the historical narratives.

societies. Earlier narratives composed by American Methodists generally followed the path blazed by Coke and Moore. One of the first narratives of Methodism in North America apart from the Minutes and the *Disciplines* was given by the early American Methodist preacher **Jesse Lee** (1758–1816) who offered a *Short History of Methodists* in 1810. Lee wanted to offer a response to a request that John Wesley himself had sent him (long before) for "a connected relation, of what our Lord has been doing in America . . . "[49] Placed in this way, the narrative that Lee offered presupposed that the Methodist movement was a divinely inspired work. The first words of Lee's account indicate his sense of the Wesleyan revival as a divinely guided enterprise: "The Rev. John Wesley, (by the grace of God the Father and Founder of Methodism . . . "[50]

Consistent with the attempt in the Wesleyan Minutes to discern "God's design in raising up the Preachers called Methodists," Lee understood the Wesleyan movement as an act of divine grace, but unlike the earlier Minutes and the *Disciplines* that stressed the work of "two young men" (i.e., John and Charles Wesley), Lee's account of the Wesleyan movement focused consistently on John Wesley. Moreover, Lee focused single-mindedly on the history of "Methodism" as a set of institutions: classes, societies, bands (code module **Classes-Bands**), itinerant preachers (code module **MethodistPreachers**), watch nights, and the like. The significance of 1729 in his account was not simply the Wesleys' recognition of the need for holiness, but their first organization of a society that Lee saw as the predecessor of later Methodist classes and societies. There was no mention of Aldersgate, although the Fetter Lane Society is mentioned, nor was there any extended discussion of John Wesley's theology. For example, the Wesleys' recognition, noted in both the Minutes and the early American *Disciplines*, that justification precedes sanctification is not present

---

49 Jesse Lee, *A Short History of the Methodists in the United States of America: Beginning at 1766, and Continued till 1809, to Which is Prefixed a Brief Account of Their Rise in England in the year 1729, &c.* (Baltimore: Magill and Clime, 1810), iii.

50 Ibid., 9.

in Lee's narrative: he only chronicled the beginnings of distinctively Methodist institutions.[51] Nevertheless, it is clear that in Lee's view, these institutions were all part of the providential "design" or purpose of God in raising up the Methodist movement.

LEE, *SHORT HISTORY OF METHODISTS* (1810)
OxfordSociety
GeorgiaPietists (only Moravians, and only mentioned upon his return to England)
ClassesBands
MethodistPreachers
ArminianVsCalvinist
AmericanOrdinations
GrowthOfMethodism (the remainder of the book deals with the growth of American Methodism).

American narratives of the origins of Methodism written after Lee's time show some significant re-coding of this historical narrative. The influential New York Methodist **Nathan Bangs (1778–1862)** offered *A History of the Methodist Episcopal Church* in the same year as Thomas Jackson and George Beard offered their centenary accounts of British Methodism (1839). But Bangs's history began not with England but with the European "discovery" of America, and it recounts the preaching of Jonathan Edwards and George Whitefield as the historical background to the development of American Methodism[52] before backing up and considering John Wesley and the earlier development of the Methodist movement in Britain. Bangs thus introduced what I will call the distinctly American module **AmericanReligion**. In his narrative of the Wesleyan

---

51   Ibid., chap. 1, 9–23.
52   Nathan Bangs, *A History of the Methodist Episcopal Church* (New York: T. Mason and G. Lane, 1839), 1:11–37.

revival, Bangs gave the date of 1729 as the first Methodist society (in Oxford), consistent with the narrative in the *Discipline*, and he recounted the missionary journey to Georgia (thus connecting the Wesleys with America), the Aldersgate-Street experience (code module **AldersgateExperience**, John Wesley's trip to Germany to visit Herrnhut (code module **GeorgiaPietists**), the development of the first societies and the General Rules (code module **ClassesBands**), and the first annual conference in 1744 (code module **Methodist-Preachers**).[53] Bangs concluded that the rise of the early Methodist movement "was eminently the work of God."

In justifying John Wesley's independence with respect to the Church of England, Bangs wrote that Wesley "was forced either to disobey God by relinquishing his work, or to become the leader of a distinct sect. [Wesley] wisely chose the latter, for which thousands will bless God in time and eternity."[54] Although the term "sect" may not have carried in Bangs's time the negative connotations that it would carry later, Bangs nevertheless associated Wesley with the founding of Methodist churches as a deliberate act: he "wisely chose" to become the leader of a separate Christian denomination or church, and this was true insofar as Wesley justified his own actions that led to the establishment of the Methodist Episcopal Church. Wesley had not depicted himself as a church founder, but Bangs did in describing Wesley as the founder of "a distinct sect" (thus module **ChurchFounder**, including the module **AmericanOrdinations**).

Bangs's sense of Wesley as a church founder went well beyond what earlier interpreters including Wesley himself had envisioned. As we have seen, John Wesley and interpreters from the Wesleyan Conference in Britain such as Thomas Jackson were careful *not* to imply that their ecclesial structure amounted to a formal break with the Church of England, and Jesse Lee's earlier American-based narrative described Wesley only as the institutor of particular structures that

---

53 Ibid., 1:38–45.
54 Ibid., 45.

had been imported to America. But Bangs's work is on a larger scale. Framed by the perspective of North American religious history, it depicts Wesley as the originator of a distinctive church well suited to the North American context.

BANGS, *HISTORY OF THE METHODIST EPISCOPAL CHURCH* (1839)
AmericanReligion
GeorgiaPietists
ClassesBands
MethodistPreachers
ChurchFounder (including and expanding module **AmericanOrdinations**)

Some of the Methodist churches that originated in this period as a result of divisions from the Methodist Episcopal Church did not have explicit recourse to the narrative of the Wesleyan movement but gave only a narrative of their own distinct origins. The older *Disciplines* of the AME and AME Zion churches did not include narratives of the Wesleyan revival as the Methodist Episcopal Church had, and they focused instead on the distinct development of their own churches.[55] Nevertheless, these denominations did maintain the Twenty-Five Articles of Religion that John Wesley had edited and had sent to America with Thomas Coke in 1784, and they maintained such distinctive Wesleyan practices as itinerant preaching, lay preaching, class meetings, societies, watch nights, love feasts, and adaptations of the liturgy of the *Sunday Service*. The AME Church,

---

55   The first *Discipline* of the AME church was *The Doctrines and Discipline of the African Methodist Episcopal Church* (Philadelphia: Richard Allen and Jacob Tapisco for the African Methodist Connection in the United States, John H. Cunningham, Printer, 1817), which begins with an address to church members explaining the origins of the denomination in the mistreatment of black members of the St. George Methodist society in Philadelphia in 1787 (3–9). Similarly, an early *Discipline* of the AME Zion Church recounts the origins of that denomination from the John Street Methodist society in New York: *The Doctrines and Discipline of the African Methodist Episcopal Zion Church, Revised by the General Conference, Indianapolis, Indiana, 1924* (Charlotte, NC: A.M.E. Zion Publication House, 1925), the "Founders' Address," 6–8.

moreover, maintained episcopacy in the form in which it had been adapted by the Methodist Episcopal Church (the Zion Church would not adopt episcopacy until later in the nineteenth century), and the AME Church also included in its *Disciplines* the compilation of Wesleyan Minutes that have been historically called the "Doctrinal Minutes."[56] In this way, the early AME and AME Zion churches had recourse to the distinctive doctrine and practices of the Wesleyan movement, even though they did not have explicit recourse to the narrative of the Wesleyan movement. As we shall see, however, the AME Church would later, under Bishop Henry McNeal Turner, make more explicit its connections to the narrative of the Wesleyan Revival, especially in justifying its ministerial orders.

THE WESLEYAN NARRATIVE IN RADICAL WESLEYAN COMMUNITIES IN THE EARLY NINETEENTH CENTURY

Some Wesleyan and Methodist groups in the early nineteenth century began to encode narratives of the Wesleyan revival in very different ways than the Wesleyan Conference or the Methodist Episcopal Church had done. An example from Britain can be seen in a document that is identified as *A Catechism for Wesleyan Methodists* (1834), and was written by "A Member of the Wesleyan Methodist Association," a group in Leeds that had divided from the Wesleyan Conference as a result of an ongoing series of divisions among Wesleyan Methodists there. Set as a dialogue between a pupil ("P.") and a teacher ("T."), the following question and answer reveals their understanding of the basic meaning of the Wesleyan movement:

> P.—What were the ancient characteristics of Methodism?

---

56 The "Doctrinal Minutes" appear from the very first *Discipline* of the AME Church in 1817, though not under that name. In the 1817 *Discipline* they are included as Section 2 (following the Articles of Religion) with no title: *Doctrines and Discipline of the African Methodist Episcopal Church* (1817), 25–55. Later editions of the AME *Discipline* would refer to this document as the "Catechism on Faith."

> T.—Its simplicity; its indifference to form and ceremony; to everything, indeed, except the agency of the Holy Spirit in awakening, converting, and sanctifying the souls of men; the extraordinary zeal and success of its preachers; and the Christian heroism of its self-denying people; who, after the example of the disciples in the apostolic, and the Puritans in more modern ages of the church, boldly avowed the most rigid principles of the Bible, in opposition to the principles, the practices, and the fashions of the world.[57]

This account of the "ancient" Methodist movement stresses only its rigorous moral discipline and its teaching of the way of salvation, although the Wesleyan Methodist Association had also emphasized democratic reforms in the Methodist movement.

Similar movements for democratic reform within Methodism appeared in the United States in about the same period. The democratic reforming impulse appeared in the early constitution of the African Methodist Episcopal Zion Church, which had rejected lifelong episcopacy (despite the word "episcopal" in its name) and insisted on lay representation from its origins. It also appeared in movements that led to the formation of the Methodist Protestant Church (1830), which similarly rejected the institution of episcopacy and insisted on equal lay and clergy representation in all church conferences.

An early apologia for the Methodist Protestant movement was given by Alexander McCaine (1773–1856) in a tract given the hissing title, *The History and Mystery of Methodist Episcopacy* (1827). This work examined in detail Wesley's provisions for establishing the American Methodist church in 1784. McCaine argued that Wesley intended only a presbyteral ordination, never claimed the title "bishop," and did not intend the American Methodist superintendents to take

---

57 [Anonymous] *A Catechism for Wesleyan Methodists: Particularly for Methodist Class Leaders and Local Preachers, Wherein the Various Points at Issue between the Conference and the People are Taken Up and Discussed in Familiar Dialogue* (Liverpool: E. Smith and Co., 1834), 4. The author's name is not given, except that the title page notes that the tract is "by a member of the Wesleyan Methodist Association."

the title "bishop."[58] In their own ways, then, the leaders of democratic Methodist movements offered a significant alternative module (their version of module **AmericanOrdinations**) to that typically used by other Methodist churches, encoding a Methodist identity that minimized the episcopal polity of more traditional American Methodist denominations. In later works, McCaine and other Methodist Protestant writers would claim the authority of Whitehead's biography of Wesley, especially Whitehead's critical comments on Wesley's ordinations, even though Whitehead himself had presupposed commitment to the ecclesial structures of the Church of England.[59]

Conclusion

As Methodist narrators retold accounts of their origins to encode Methodist identities in the early nineteenth century, a number of consistent themes appeared, as well as some highly controverted points in the ways in which early Methodist churches and their constituents described and handed on the Methodist story.

1. The emphasis on the pursuit of Christian holiness as the primary aim of Methodism remained in the formal Minutes of the Wesleyan Conference and in the *Disciplines* of the Methodist Episcopal Church as the primary aim or goal of Methodism. Whitehead's *The Life of Rev. John Wesley* (1793 and 1796) reinforced this sense of spirituality and holiness as the primary aim of John Wesley in his plea that the Methodist movement should have been only a movement and should not have resulted in the formation of Methodist churches, at least in Britain.

2. The call for conversion, represented in the Aldersgate narrative, emerged as a central theme in some versions of the Methodist retelling of their own narrative in this period, specifically, in Coke and

---

58   McCaine, *History and Mystery of Methodist Episcopacy.*
59   McCaine, *Letters on the Organization and Early History of the Methodist Episcopal Church*; Drinkhouse, *History of Methodist Reform.*

Moore's *Life of Wesley* (1792) and then in Thomas Jackson's *Centenary of Methodism* (1839) and Nathan Bangs's *History of the Methodist Episcopal Church* (1839). As we will see, this developed into a more general sense of evangelistic mission in the next period.

3. The inheritance of Wesleyan doctrine, especially doctrine concerning the "way of salvation," was an important element in the identity of early Methodist church bodies. Wesleyan doctrine regarding justification, assurance, and sanctification was included in the Minutes utilized by British Methodists and by the African Methodist Episcopal Church (the document subsequently identified as the "Catechism on Faith"). The Methodist Episcopal Church and the African Methodist Episcopal Zion Church did not have the doctrinal material from the Minutes in their *Disciplines*, although the Methodist Episcopal Church produced doctrinal tracts explaining some of these critical doctrines in the 1790s. The ME, AME, and AME Zion churches all had Wesley's revision of the Articles of Religion, though these did not include distinctly Methodist doctrine. As we have seen above, the biographies of John Wesley offered by Coke and Moore and by Whitehead included doctrinal material in the Minutes and other explanations of Wesleyan teaching.

4. Most divisive among these early Methodist bodies was the issue of what kind of church and church structures John Wesley had intended. The Wesleyan Conference downplayed the importance of the ordinations of 1784 as seen in Coke and Moore's *Life of Wesley*. The Methodist Episcopal Church from 1801 included reference to the ordinations in their disciplinary account of the origins of the Methodist Episcopal Church as a way of justifying their episcopal polity. Whitehead's *The Life of Rev. John Wesley* had questioned the need for the ordinations and Wesley's motives in performing them. The African Methodist Episcopal Zion Church and the Methodist Protestant Church rejected episcopacy (at least lifelong episcopacy) as being unfaithful to Wesley's plan of "superintendents" (the Zion church would later incorporate a form of episcopacy) and British reforming groups rejected the power of the Conference of preachers.

5. In the Methodist Episcopal Church, the sense of a divine calling of Methodism to the new American nation emerged as a very strong theme in the work of Nathan Bangs. As we shall see, this is a theme that would grow in importance in the next period. The African Methodist Episcopal Church and the African Methodist Episcopal Zion Church were developing a parallel sense of mission among African American people in this period.

Other themes could be mentioned, for example, the emphasis on moral discipline represented in the quotation given above from the *Catechism for Wesleyan Methodists*. All of the Methodist bodies that emerged in this period as churches practiced discipline in classes organized into societies, with the keeping of the General Rules as the common discipline they shared. All had inherited other common early Methodist practices such as itinerant ministry, love feasts, and watch nights. Despite similarities in accounts of the origins of Methodism in this period, then, interpreters exercised considerable originality in choosing specific modules of narrative code in their accounts, in developing a new module of narrative code adapted to the American environment (**AmericanReligion**), and in particular ways in which they described such crucial inherited modules as **AmericanOrdinations**.

WESLEYAN NARRATIVES IN AN AGE OF METHODIST ASCENDANCY

LATE NINETEENTH CENTURY

T he nineteenth century, especially the second half of the nineteenth century, was a period of remarkable growth for Methodist churches. In the United States, the membership of the Methodist Episcopal Church (MEC) is estimated to have been around 65,000 in 1800 and then 341,000 in 1825. After the division of the Methodist Episcopal Church, South (MECS), the combined membership of the MEC and MECS was 1.42 million in 1850, 2.2 million in 1875, and 4.1 million when the century ended in 1900.[1] Methodist groups in Britain counted 96,000 members in 1800 and ended the nineteenth century with 770,000 members, though Methodist growth in Britain had slowed considerably after 1830 in the wake of divisions and infighting within Methodist groups there.[2] The same period saw remarkable Methodist expansion throughout the world. By 1900, Methodist

---

1   Membership statistics as given in Nolan B. Harmon, ed., *Encyclopedia of World Methodism* (Nashville: United Methodist Publishing House, 1976), 2712.

2   David Hempton, *Methodism: Empire of the Spirit* (New Haven: Yale University Press, 2005), statistical tables in an appendix on p. 214.

missionary work had planted Methodist churches in Africa, Asia, Australia, the Pacific islands, and Central and South America.

Growth in membership, planting new congregations, and foreign missions were signs of Methodism's ascendancy in this period. Another visible sign was the building of imposing new urban churches, often in the Gothic style that had become fashionable through the middle of the nineteenth century. Earlier Methodist Episcopal *Disciplines* had specified that Methodist structures must be "plain and decent," and in the interpretation of Bishop Asbury that meant the unadorned whitewashed wood-frame church buildings that American Methodists typically built in the early nineteenth century.[3] In the second half of the nineteenth century, Methodists adopted more sophisticated architectural styles. An example of the Gothic style is the Asbury Methodist Episcopal Church (now Asbury Crestwood United Methodist Church) in Crestwood, New York, opened in 1867 in commemoration of the hundredth anniversary of the coming of the first Methodist missionaries to North America. An example from Britain is the Wesley Memorial Church in Oxford, opened in October of 1878. The appearance of Gothic church structures indicates that Methodists in this period were rising in social class as well as in numbers, they had developed stronger educational institutions, they had begun to see themselves as cultured people in contrast to their Methodist forebears of the early nineteenth century, and they wanted to see their churches like other, more historic churches. The Gothic style represented this sense of cultural and social advancement for Methodists.

In this period, we will see not only recreations and recombinations of the typical modules of Wesleyan origins but also an extended controversy in the Victorian era in Britain over John Wesley's Anglican identity that I have called module **AnglicanWesley**. This will serve as a precedent for extended discussions over particular ways of telling narratives of Wesleyan origins in the early twentieth century (over

---

3   Karen B. Westerfield Tucker, *American Methodist Worship* (New York: Oxford University Press, 2001), 241.

module **JWInfluences**) and in the later twentieth century (over module **EcumenicalWesley**).

METHODIST OPTIMISM IN THE VICTORIAN AGE

This period coincides with the Gilded Age in the history of the United States and with the Victorian era in Britain. The ethos of both Britain and the United States in this period was imbued with a strong optimism tied to notions of technological and cultural progress, a vision of "manifest destiny" in the United States, which was in this period being expanded from a national vision into a sense of international expansion on the part of the United States. It was a period that witnessed the flourishing of the British Empire with its own sense of cultural supremacy and a mission to "civilize" the broader world. Methodists in this period of ascendancy—both American and British Methodists—expressed their own version of optimism in this period, an utter confidence that their religious movement had been favored by God as an instrument of revival in the churches and as an instrument for the civilization of the world.

Luke Tyerman (1820–89), to begin with a very prominent example, was a British Wesleyan minister and historian whose 1870 biography, *The Life and Times of the Rev. John Wesley, M.A.*, began with the question, "Is it not a truth that Methodism is the greatest fact in the history of the church of Christ?"[4] With this sense of Methodism's immense importance, and thus John Wesley's importance for the world at large, Tyerman proceeded to produce the lengthiest biography of John Wesley ever written, extending to three fat volumes with a total of 1,842 pages of text.[5]

Tyerman's exhaustive text covered almost all the narrative modules listed above, although the length of his text allowed him to spread many of these into several chapters or (from about the middle of the

---

4   Luke Tyerman, *The Life and Times of the Reverend John Wesley, M.A., Founder of the Methodists* (New York: Harper and Brothers, 1872), 1:1.

5   In the American edition of 1872, excluding front and end matter.

first volume) into chronicles by each calendar year that he narrated. His was a comfortable, leisurely narrative that occasionally admitted Wesley's minor faults but always went on to account for them. Was Wesley religiously indifferent in his early years in Oxford? Perhaps, Tyerman admits, but he soon turned to more serious religious pursuits.[6] Was Wesley's marriage to Mary Vazeille a disaster? Yes, but he lays the fault entirely on her. Describing Mary's use of John's correspondence to defame him to Calvinistic preachers, Tyerman wrote:

> A more infamous episode does not occur in Wesley's history. The charges were cruel insinuations founded upon interpolated letters, stolen by a faithless woman, who, in order to defame a husband of whom she was utterly unworthy, not only committed theft but forgery, and then put herself into the hands of a sect of holy Calvinists, who employed her perfidy and meanness in injuring the man whom, at the altar of the Most High God, she had sworn to love, honour, and obey.[7]

Tyerman's style was that of old-fashioned antiquarian scholarship, chronicling each year of John Wesley's life in succession, extolling the one Tyerman celebrated as the principal human agent in "the greatest fact in the history of the church of Christ."

TYERMAN, *LIFE AND TIMES OF JOHN WESLEY* (1870)

Volume I

Introduction on the Greatness of Methodism

EpworthUpbringing (chap. 1)

Wesley's ordination and **JWInfluences** (Kempis, Taylor, Law; chap. 2)

AnglicanDeclension and **OxfordSociety** (chap. 3)

GeorgiaPietists (chap. 4)

---

6   Ibid., 1:30–31.
7   Ibid., 3:233.

TYERMAN, *LIFE AND TIMES OF JOHN WESLEY* (1870) (continued)

AldersgateExperience interpreted as a conversion experience and **Wesley-Doubts** (explained as his doubts as to whether he was a completely sanctified Christian) followed by Wesley's trip to Germany (chap. 5)

Part II[8]

SocialDysfunction and **FieldPreaching** and **MethodistPreachers** (lay preachers; section 1739)

StillnessMeans, ClassesBands (separation from Moravian societies), and **ArminianVsCalvinist** (section 1740)

ClassesBands (origin of class meetings distinct from or as divisions of earlier societies; section 1742)

ClassesBands (origin of General Rules, section 1743)

MethodistPreachers (origin of the annual conference, section 1744)

ClassesBands ("Rules of Band Societies") and **CWPoetry** (there are notices of publications of poetry involving John and Charles throughout; section 1745)

GrowthOfMethodism (Ireland), and **MethodistBenevolence** (*Primitive Physick*, section 1747)

Volume II (continuing Part II)

JohnAndMary (actually, Charles Wesley's marriage and John's proposed marriage to Grace Murray; although the latter occurred in 1748, they are both narrated in the section on 1749).

JohnAndMary (their marriage), **GrowthOfMethodism** (Scotland, 1751).

Most of Tyerman's narrative from this point does not introduce new versions of the modules I have identified, but chronicles year-by-year the developments in Wesley's life and the growth of Methodist societies.

Part III

WayOfSalvation (debates over entire sanctification, sections 1761, 1762, and 1763)

---

8   Tyerman moves from the earlier chapters to "Part 2" (no "Part 1" was designated), with subsections, really shorter chapters, for each year from this point.

TYERMAN, *LIFE AND TIMES OF JOHN WESLEY* (1870) (continued)
Volume III (the text is also internally designated Volume III)
GrowthOfMethodism (preachers appointed to America, section 1769)
ArminianVsCalvinist (controversy over 1771 Minutes, in sections 1771 and 1772) and **MethodistPreachers** (women preachers; section 1771)
OppositionToSlavery (section 1772)
JohnAndMary (their bitter division, section 1776)
AmericanOrdinations (section 1784)
JWDeath (section 1791)

To Tyerman's insight we may compare the perspective of the American clergyman George Lansing Taylor (1835–1903), writing nineteen years later in *The Gospel River: Or, The Evolution of Christianity* (1889). An elder of the Methodist Episcopal Church also known as a gospel hymn author, Taylor narrated the "evolution" of Christianity in seven stages:

- "The Pentecostal Church at Jerusalem,"
- "The Judeo-Gentile Church at Antioch,"
- "The Pauline, Missionary, and Universal Form of the Church,"
- "The Church of Constantine and the World-Ruling Roman Empire,"
- "The Medieval Church of the 'Dark Ages' of Europe,"
- "The Protestant Church of the Great Reformation," and
- "The Great Modern Evangelical Church."

Taylor saw the latter as the culmination of the evolution of Christianity, especially in the rise of Methodism:

> And how amazingly has the course of the gospel river been fulfilled in the history of Methodism! In a century and a half from its birth, only half as long as from Christ to Constantine,

> Methodism has swelled from the ankle-deep rill of its be-
> ginning in Oxford University in 1739 until it is now a mighty
> river, an ocean in itself, rolling its beneficent billows around
> the world![9]

In this account Taylor took 1739, John Wesley's first itinerant preaching, as the date of the true beginnings of Methodism. From this period, Methodists placed more and more emphasis on John Wesley's Aldersgate-Street experience, and this emphasis led them to refor-mulate their account of the origins of Methodism, focusing not only on the cultivation of holiness but also on the need for the heartfelt religious experience and locating the true origins of Methodism after the Aldersgate-Street experience. For both Tyerman and Taylor, Meth-odism was the culmination of the development of Christianity, favored by God as the instrument of revival in the churches, and its distinctive mission was much broader than simply the cultivation of Christian holiness. Its mission was Christian evangelization, indeed, the evange-lization of the whole world.

The Wesleyan Narrative and Methodism's Destiny in the New World

Many American Methodist leaders in this period reread the narrative of the Wesleyan revival as a narrative intimately linked to a distinctive mission of bringing Christian civilization to the North American con-tinent. This was preceded by the addition of a very short narrative of the rise of Methodism in America in the earliest Methodist Episco-pal *Disciplines*, then in the work of Nathan Bangs (see above). But in this period we may consider the work of **Abel Stevens** (1815–97), an influential leader of the Methodist Episcopal Church associated with the New England Annual Conference throughout his career. Like

---

9   George Lansing Taylor, *The Gospel River: Or, The Evolution of Christianity* (New York: Hunt & Ea-
     ton; and Cincinnati: Cranston and Stowe, 1889), 19. George Beard, whose epic poem celebrating
     the centenary of British Methodism has been noted above, also utilized the image of the "rill"
     (precisely that word) of Oxford Methodism that grew to encompass the world; Beard, *History of
     Methodism*, 31–32.

Bangs, Stevens was never elected to the episcopacy but exerted enormous influence as an editor of denominational publications and as a writer. He served successively as the editor of the Methodist periodicals *Zion's Herald* (1848–52), the *National Magazine* (1852–60), and *The Methodist* (1860–74). His position as editor allowed him to write extensively, and he produced a number of books on Methodist history, including an extensive *History of the Methodist Episcopal Church* (1864) and then a much briefer *Compendious History of American Methodism* (1867–68).[10] The subtitle of this latter work indicates that it was designed as an abridgment of his *History of the Methodist Episcopal Church*, although the title itself shows that Stevens's concern was with all of American Methodism—the Methodist Episcopal Church, South, as well as the Methodist Episcopal Church. Stevens was known as a moderate on the issues that had separated the ME and ME South churches in 1844–45. Strongly opposed to slavery and to any Methodist involvement in slavery, Stevens nevertheless took the view that the Plan of Separation adopted by the 1844 General Conference, which had authorized the foundation of the Methodist Episcopal Church, South, was constitutionally legitimate, and he opposed those in his own church who claimed that the ME South denomination was illegitimate. Writing his *Compendious History*, a significantly abbreviated work despite its title, in the period after the Civil War, Stevens reflected the views of a Northern moderate, anxious to heal the wounds of division left by the war and earlier American Methodist controversies and especially concerned with Methodism's unique and providential role in the evangelization of the United States.

Stevens's *Compendious History* began with an account of John Wesley's visit to Glasgow University in 1757. Although there was no record of Wesley ever having met James Watt (who had come to Glasgow in the same year), Stevens creatively envisioned a meeting

---

10   Abel Stevens, *A Compendious History of American Methodism. Abridged from the Author's "History of the Methodist Episcopal Church"* (New York: Phillips and Hunt, and Cincinnati: Walden and Stowe, 1867, although a preface printed in the book carries the date 1868).

of these two men as making cardinal contributions to the civilization of North America: Watt's invention of the steam engine enabled the opening of the western frontier, and Wesley's revival and its itinerant preaching system "could alone afford the ministrations of religion to the overflowing population" of the American West. Thus Watts and Wesley "were co-workers for the destiny of the new world."[11] We should note the term "destiny of the new world," for it evoked the term *manifest destiny* that had been utilized by Democrats in the United States from 1845 to denote their belief in the providential destiny of the United States to expand into the western territories. Stevens was quite explicitly an apologist for this point of view. He wrote that

> The fervent spirit of [Jonathan] Edwards, seeing, with Bossuet, in all history only the "history of redemption", dreamed in his New England retirement, of a millennium which was to dawn in the western hemisphere, and thence burst upon the nations and irradiate the globe.[12]

Although he mentioned that Methodists had supported "negro emancipation" among other charitable ventures (module **OppositionToSlavery**),[13] Stevens did not describe the vehemence of Wesley in opposition to human slavery or the fact that participation in the slave trade had been forbidden in the General Rules as revised by the early Methodist Episcopal Church.[14] In fact, Stevens stated that the earliest Methodists' "mission being purely spiritual, their practical or disciplinary system was founded purely in their spiritual designs," thus appealing to the notion of the "spirituality of the church," popular in southern Methodist, Baptist, and Presbyterian circles in the period after the Civil War.[15] Stevens's great concern, then, was to offer a

---

11   Ibid., 18–19.
12   Ibid., 19.
13   Ibid., 31.
14   To be fair, Stevens does state explicitly later in the book that the original position of the Methodist Episcopal Church was to forbid slaveholding absolutely, and he notes that after the "Great Secession" of 1844, the Methodist Episcopal Church became the leading antislavery church in North America (525–26).
15   Ibid., 30.

postmillennial vision of America, though stripped of postmillennialism's typical emphasis on social reform. By doing this, Stevens pointed to the spiritual role that Methodism was to play in America's providential destiny.

Stevens's brief narrative of the Wesleyan revival (only half of a chapter) emphasized two points. First, he emphasized the role of vital religious experience, taking John Wesley's Aldersgate experience as a paradigm for Methodist experiential religion (module **AldersgateExperience**) and contrasting the vitality of that experience with Stevens's caricature of Anglicanism: "Both the Wesleys, turning away from St. Paul's, Westminster Abbey, the dead Churches, seek light from heaven in these humble assemblies." Stevens presupposed **AnglicanDeclension** and stated explicitly that Aldersgate was Wesley's experience of the new birth.[16] He characterized Wesley's full understanding of the "way of salvation" as flowing from the inspiration of this experience (thus module **WayOfSalvation**).

Second, Stevens emphasized the distinctive "methods" of Methodism, especially its use of lay preaching and itinerancy (module **MethodistPreachers**) as the means that would enable Methodism to expand both in Britain and in the New World.[17] Thus Stevens placed far greater emphasis on the work of evangelism than on the work of cultivating holiness, and we will see this as a consistent theme among the larger Methodist churches—in contrast to churches representing the Holiness movement—in this era. Summarizing his account of the Wesleyan revival and again lifting up these two emphases, Stevens wrote, "Such, then, was Methodism—such its spirit and its methods. It was a revival Church in its spirit, a missionary Church in its organization."[18] Thus, although Stevens's account of the rise of Methodism in England acknowledged that Methodism had functioned early on within the Church of England, by the end of his account of the Wesleyan revival

---

16 Ibid., 26–27; quotation on p. 26.
17 These two emphases are stated on p. 25 and discussed through pp. 25–30.
18 Ibid., 30.

he had come to represent Methodism as a "Church," and thus to see John Wesley as founder of a distinctive "Church" (module **Church-Founder**). In this way, Stevens's account of the Wesleyan revival as the first stage in his account of American Methodism bolstered his vision of the distinctive mission of Methodism as a church in ascendancy that was playing a central role in the formation of American civilization.

STEVENS, *COMPENDIOUS HISTORY OF AMERICAN METHODISM* (1867)
AmericanReligion
OxfordSociety and **JWInfluences** (Law, Taylor, and Kempis)
GeorgiaPietists
AldersgateExperience contrasted with "dead" Anglican churches (**AnglicanDeclension**)
WayOfSalvation
ClassesBands
FieldPreaching and **MethodistPreachers**
ChurchFounder (including and expanding module **AmericanOrdinations**) with an emphasis on the church as a purely spiritual institution
OppositionToSlavery (very muted and attributed only to Wesley, i.e., not described in relation to American Methodist Churches)

Bishop **Matthew Simpson**'s *A Hundred Years of Methodism* was written specifically for the centennial of US independence in 1876 and reflected a very similar notion of Methodism's destiny in the New World. Simpson (1811–84), in addition to serving as a Methodist Episcopal bishop and president of Garrett Biblical Institute, had been a confidant of President Abraham Lincoln and offered the eulogy at Lincoln's burial in Springfield. The first chapter of *A Hundred Years of Methodism* spoke only of American history and accomplishments, though it has no sustained account of earlier American religious life (**AmericanReligion**).

The next chapter took up the narrative of the Wesleyan revival.

Following brief accounts of Wesley's family background (**EpworthUp-bringing**), the Oxford "Methodist" societies (**OxfordSociety**), and the Georgia venture, including encounters with Moravians (**Georgia-Pietists**), Simpson narrated the story of Aldersgate (**AldersgateExpe-rience**) as the chief and critical event in John Wesley's development: "Then [i.e., after Aldersgate] properly commenced that wonderful career which closed only with his death."[19] Like Stevens, Simpson was concerned with the development of distinct Methodist institutions: outdoor preaching (**FieldPreaching** and **MethodistPreachers**) and Methodist societies and classes (**ClassesBands**), though by this time the bands had disappeared from American Methodist culture.[20] Like Stevens, Simpson emphasized that the Wesleyan message (**WayOfSalvation**) and the Wesleyan methods were "the common platform" of all Methodists (i.e., Northern and Southern, British and American): "But in all the points which touch the masses of people directly, Methodism is one everywhere, for it is simply, in the language of Chalmers, 'Christianity in earnest.'"[21] Like Stevens, Simpson described Methodism as a "Church" by the end of his comments on the beginning of the Wesleyan revival movement in Britain, giving the impression that his narrative of Wesley was a narrative of a church founder whose church had a very distinctive and providentially given mission for the Christianization of the North American continent (modules **WesleyEvangelist** and **ChurchFounder**).[22]

SIMPSON, *A HUNDRED YEARS OF METHODISM* (1876)

AmericanReligion

EpworthUpbringing

---

19 Matthew Simpson, *A Hundred Years of Methodism* (New York: Nelson and Phillips; Cincinnati: Hitchcock and Walden, 1876), 18.

20 All of these narrative modules appear in the introduction and in chap. 2.

21 Ibid., 28. Simpson's reference is to the Scots Presbyterian theologian Thomas Chalmers, whose sermon on "The Importance of Civil Government to Society" referred to "methodism" [sic] as "Christianity in earnest": cf. Chalmers, *Sermons and Discourses,* (New York: Robert Carter, 1844), 1:345.

22 Ibid., 28: "In ten years [from the beginning of the Wesleyan revival] the outlines of the coming Church were already prepared."

SIMPSON, *A HUNDRED YEARS OF METHODISM* (1876) (continued)
OxfordSociety
GeorgiaPietists
AldersgateExperience
FieldPreaching and MethodistPreachers (including lay preachers)
ClassesBands
WayOfSalvation
GrowthOfMethodism
ChurchFounder

Both Stevens and Simpson concluded their narratives by celebrating in florid rhetoric the utter triumph of Methodism in the New World, focusing on the success of its evangelistic mission (**Wesley-Evangelist**). Thus Abel Stevens:

> This lowly Methodistic story is but the reproduction, in substance, of the apostolic history; and presents, in full vitality, that original, that only, example of evangelistic propagandism, which, when all dogmatic conflicts and hierarchical pretensions, with their wasted passions and pomps, are recorded as historical failures, will bear forward to universal triumph the ensign of the Cross by a catholic, living, working Church of the common people.[23]

And thus Matthew Simpson:

> Methodism is sure of the past century. Its fathers are crowned in bliss, and its sons marshaled in the field. If they valiantly fight the great battles of humanity, if they tread fearlessly the path of duty, if they preserve uncorrupted the doctrines of the Gospel, if they seek to bear the image of the blessed Saviour, and if they preserve the cardinal principles of their Church polity, the coming century will be full of glorious achievements. Every

---

23   Stevens, *Compendious History of American Methodism*, 584.

land shall be beautified with its temples, and in every language
shall its prayers and songs ascend before the throne of God.[24]

Stevens and Simpson portray a church in the ascendancy in North America, with a vital piety well suited to the character of American people, and with evangelistic methods (lay preaching, itinerancy, the use of classes and bands) well suited to expansion on the American frontier. Above all, they portray a church confident that it is carrying out the distinctive mission of God in the New World.

In 1892 the episcopal address and the historical statement in *The Doctrines and Discipline of the Methodist Episcopal Church* were revised in ways that show the developing American Methodist self-understanding as a church alongside other (and older) churches. In this period in which American Methodists were evolving from the revivalism that had characterized their development in the early 1800s and recovering more sophisticated forms of liturgy, the episcopal address at the beginning of the *Doctrines and Discipline* of that year states that "The Order of Worship herein set forth we commend to your scrupulous observance. In substance it has been received from our Fathers,"[25] thus taking account of the Wesleyan origin of traditional liturgical forms.

The historical statement in the *Doctrines and Discipline* was significantly revised in that year in ways that also reflect American Methodism's new sense of its identity as a church alongside older existing Christian denominations. The new statement begins as follows:

> The doctrine and spirit of Primitive Christianity have existed at
> different times and in different degrees in all branches of the
> kingdom of Christ among men. They were embodied in a new
> form on this wise.[26]

The statement goes on to quote earlier versions of the historical statement, though some of its revised language indicates the ecclesiastical

---

24 Simpson, *Hundred Years of Methodism*, 352.
25 Methodist Episcopal Church, *The Doctrines and Discipline of the Methodist Episcopal Church* (New York: Eaton and Mains, 1892), 5.
26 Ibid, 13.

leanings of North American Methodism in this period. For example, it referred to "John and Charles Wesley, of Oxford University, and Presbyters of the Church of England."[27] This introduces a module that would be restated many times following, namely, the claim that Wesley was truly Anglican (module **AnglicanWesley**).

The statement also followed the lead of Simpson and Stevens in asserting the unique role of American Methodism within the United States: "Coeval with the Republic, [the Methodist Episcopal Church] has expanded with it, and ministered to its moral and religious life."[28] Perhaps responding to the declaration of papal infallibility that had come twenty-two years earlier at the First Vatican Council, the Methodist Episcopal *Doctrines and Discipline* concluded with a rhetorical flourish, asserting that

> [The Methodist Episcopal Church] has always believed that the only infallible proof of the legitimacy of any branch of the Christian Church is in its ability to seek and save the lost and to disseminate the Pentecostal spirit and life.[29]

This reflects a very consistent note of Methodism in this period: the claim that Methodism's principal role was in evangelism (thus module **WesleyEvangelist**). This stood in tension with the earlier claim stated explicitly by Wesley himself that the principal aim of the early Methodist movement was the cultivation of Christian holiness. At its conclusion, the 1892 historical statement again asserted the evangelistic mission of the Methodist Episcopal Church and alongside this, its vocation to collaboration in this enterprise with other churches:

> The sole object of the rules, regulations, and usages of the Methodist Episcopal Church is that it may fulfill to the end of time its original divine vocation as a leader in evangelization, in all true reforms, and in the promotion of fraternal relations among all the branches of the one Church of Jesus Christ, and

---

27 Ibid.
28 Ibid., 15.
29 Ibid., 16.

as a coworker with them in the spiritual conquest of the world for the Son of God.[30]

Although the cultivation of holiness remained as a part of the ethos of Methodism in this period, the emphasis on evangelism grew consistently more pronounced, especially as American Methodists clashed with advocates of the Holiness movement (see below on their conceptions of Wesleyan and Methodist identity).

The ethos of Methodist ascendancy also affected other North American Methodist groups. **Henry McNeal Turner** (1834–1915) was a bishop of the African Methodist Episcopal Church whose study of *The Genius and Theory of Methodist Polity* (1885) was approved in its entirety by the General Conference of that denomination and has remained a standard for the AME Church. Although the earlier versions of the *Doctrines and Disciplines* of the AME Church had not included a narrative of the Wesleyan revival (see above), Turner's study of *Methodist Polity* included many references by which he connected the tradition of the AME Church to the Wesleys.[31]

Turner was particularly concerned with the issue of the historic episcopate, which had been an issue in the early history of the AME Church due to the relationship between AME founder Richard Allen and Allen's friend and fellow worker, Absalom Jones, who became the first African American ordained to the priesthood in the Episcopal Church in the United States (in 1804). The issue of historic episcopate and the apostolic succession had been increasingly important to Anglicans as a result of the Oxford Movement, and the restoration of historic episcopate would be framed as one of four conditions for future church unions on the part of the Episcopal Church in the year after Turner's work appeared (the "Chicago Quadrilateral" of 1886, approved two years subsequently by Lambeth Conference of bishops of the Anglican communion).

---

30   Ibid.

31   Henry McNeal Turner, *The Genius and Theory of Methodist Polity, or the Machinery of Methodism: Practically Illustrated through a Series of Questions and Answers* (Philadelphia: Publication Department, A.M.E. Church, 1885), chap. 1, "Whence the Church?" 1–9.

Although Turner rejected the notion that validity of sacraments or ministries depended on maintaining an unbroken succession of bishops, he nevertheless gave a distinctive version of the module **AmericanOrdinations** that laid great importance on the fact that a presbyteral (his term) succession of ministry had been maintained through John Wesley's ordinations of 1784, by the Methodist Episcopal Church, and through them by the African Methodist Episcopal Church. He even made the point that Anglican priest Absalom Jones had participated in some of the early ordinations in the AME Church.[32] Turner's recollections of the Wesleyan origins of the Methodist movement and his careful analysis of patristic, Reformation, and Wesleyan attitudes toward historic episcopate and ministerial succession show the concerns of a church that, like the Methodist Episcopal Church and the Wesleyan Conference in its time, was becoming more ecclesially and theologically sophisticated and wanted to be seen as a church on par with other historic Christian denominations.

THE WESLEYAN NARRATIVE AND BRITISH METHODIST ACCOUNTS OF JOHN WESLEY'S "CHURCHMANSHIP"

Relationships with Anglicans also played an important role in the culture of British Methodists in the age of ascendancy. A particular issue faced by British Methodists in this age was that Anglican scholars in the late nineteenth century began to make the claim, over against conventional Methodist views of John Wesley, that Wesley himself was never a member of a Methodist church and that, moreover, he displayed many traits of "High Church" Anglicanism. This led to an extended controversy over a very specific element of the Wesleyan narrative, what I have called module **AnglicanWesley**. Methodists in this age were compelled to recode in some ways the Wesleyan narrative in response to these Anglican claims.

---

32 The entirety of chap. 2 of Turner's *Methodist Polity*, comprising questions 36 through 90, is devoted to the issue of "Ministerial Succession," 9–35.

This controversy was initiated by an Anglican barrister and legal scholar, **Richard Denny Urlin** (1830–1907), in his 1870 study of *John Wesley's Place in Church History: Determined with the Aid of Facts and Documents Unknown to, Or Unnoticed by, His Biographers.*[33] In the preface, Urlin stated that his work should "be regarded as supplementary to the existing biographies, the latest of which was written forty years ago."[34] Thus he was not aware of Tyerman's biography, which came out in the same year as his book (1870). Urlin was particularly critical of (British) Wesleyan interpretations of Wesley:

> The Wesleyan writers, from whom a minute analysis of their founder's system might have been expected, have omitted to point out that Methodism was originally a revival of the traditions and usages, within the enclosure, of the "one Catholic and Apostolic Church;" and, while minutely describing his reception in the year 1738, of one great truth, they completely fail to recognise Wesley's power of selecting from many sources whatever appeared to be valuable, and his studious regard for the teachings of Catholic antiquity, not less remarkable in the latter than in the earlier stages of his remarkable career.[35]

Urlin was also critical of the Oxford Movement, holding that Wesley's "innovations" were grounded in the practices of antiquity, whereas the "innovations" of the Oxford Movement were "derived rather from medieval and Roman than from ancient and Eastern sources."[36] He pointed to Wesley's use of the medieval Catholic spiritual writer Johann Tauler, Wesley's identification with Caroline (though he does not use the term) Anglican sources, and Wesley's use of sources from the ancient Eastern Christian traditions, which included the use of lay preaching, stationary fasts and other "usages" associated with the Manchester group of Non-Jurors, and liturgical practices derived

---

33   Richard Denny Urlin, *John Wesley's Place in Church History: Determined with the Aid of Facts and Documents Unknown to, Or Unnoticed by, His Biographers* (London, Oxford, and Cambridge: Rivingtons, 1870).
34   Ibid., v.
35   Ibid., 9–10.
36   Ibid., 11.

from ancient Eastern Christian traditions.[37] Urlin argued that the Wesleyan movement, though "unauthorized" by the Church of England, was originally intended to "supplement" the ministries of the Church of England, and Wesleyan Methodists had never formally declared themselves in schism with the national church despite the fact that they had set up separate church structures.[38] Urlin, then, called into question the ways in which the Wesleyan narrative was transmitted by leading British Methodists in his age, offering a way to understand Wesley as consonant with commitment to Anglicanism.

Urlin's characterization of John Wesley was challenged by Wesleyan scholar James Harrison Rigg (1821–1909) in a pamphlet entitled *Was John Wesley a High Churchman? A Dialogue for the Times* (1882).[39] Rigg's title was suggestive of the "Tracts for the Times," the Anglican publications from the 1830s—some of them elaborate scholarly treatises—that had inaugurated the Oxford Movement (also known as Tractarianism). Rigg had entered Wesleyan ministry in 1845. In 1853, he founded the *London Quarterly Review* and shortly after wrote a textbook titled *Modern Anglican Theology* (1857). In 1874 he published a biographical study of *The Living Wesley*, which emphasized those aspects of John Wesley's life and work that favored the "low-church" or Reformed Anglican traditions.[40] In 1878 he became president of Wesleyan Conference, in which position he had supported admission of laymen into the conference, first allowed in that year. According to a biographer, "Rigg was a life-long exponent of the side of the Wesleyan tradition which looked for inspiration to the Established Church rather than to Non-Conformity."[41]

The tract or pamphlet by Riggs entitled *Was John Wesley a High*

---

37 Wesley's use of Tauler (chap. 3, 34–45); his identification with Caroline Anglican sources (chap. 4, 46-58); Wesley's use of Eastern Christian sources (chap. 5, 59–86).

38 Urlin wrote a subsequent study, *The Churchman's Life of Wesley* (London: Society for Promoting Christian Knowledge, 1880) advocating his views of Wesley.

39 James Harrison Rigg, *Was John Wesley a High Churchman? A Dialogue for the Times* (London: The Wesleyan Methodist Book Room, 1882).

40 James Harrison Rigg, *The Living Wesley* (London: Charles H. Kelley, 3rd edition, 1905; the 1st ed. was 1874; cf. 115–21 on Wesley's "churchmanship."

41 John Kent, article on Rigg in the *Encyclopedia of World Methodism* (s.v. "Rigg," p. 2021).

Churchman? was written as a dialogue between an Anglican rector and the Wesleyan minister in his parish. Rigg's "rector" (and one must remember that this is Rigg putting words in the mouth of the "rector") refers to the recent "Œcumenical Methodist Conference" (1881) in London and the report that Methodists numbered as their adherents between 20 and 23 million constituents.[42] The tract responds directly to the issue of Wesley's identification as a "High Churchman" by stating that it is not an easy question because,

> a clergyman might have steadily held the opinions and profession of a High Churchman all his life in the last century and yet not hold one of the characteristic opinions of a Ritualising High Churchman of to-day.[43]

Rigg admitted that Wesley had been a "ritualising High Churchman" earlier in his career, in Oxford and in America "before his conversion."[44] But he then went into some detail of historical documents illustrating the change in Wesley's views after 1738, dealing specifically with Wesley's denial (after 1746) of the doctrine of "apostolical succession," Wesley's views of baptism, Wesley's view of the presence of Christ in the sacrament of the Lord's Supper, and Wesley's authorization of lay preachers, all of which Rigg saw as being very significantly different than the views of "ritualising" High Anglicans of his day.[45] Rigg thus offered a historically nuanced version of the module **AnglicanWesley** in response to Urlin's claims.

The dialogue in historical scholarship between Urlin and Rigg illustrates how urgently Methodists needed to uphold their own traditioning of John Wesley in the age of Methodist ascendancy. It was a

---

42 Ibid., 4.

43 Ibid., 7; Rigg's pamphlet refers to Abbey and Overton's *History of the Church of England in the Eighteenth Century* on this point about the meaning of "High Church" in the eighteenth century.

44 Ibid., 8–9.

45 Ibid., 8–30 in general. On specific points: Wesley's denial (after 1746) of the doctrine of "apostolical succession" (17–19), Wesley's views of baptism (19–21), Wesley's view of the presence of Christ in the sacrament of Holy Communion (21–24), and Wesley's authorization of lay preachers (24–27). Rigg followed this pamphlet with a subsequent study of *The Churchmanship of John Wesley: And the Relations of Wesleyan Methodism to the Church of England*, rev. ed. (London: Wesleyan-Methodist Book-Room, 1886).

nuanced study, and the fact that Methodists could produce a scholar such as Rigg shows how Methodism had evolved through the nineteenth century. At the heart of their disagreement, however, was the vital question of the identity and the distinctive mission of Methodism. We might paraphrase it as the question of "Who owns John Wesley?"

RETELLING THE WESLEYAN NARRATIVE ON THE PART OF THE HOLINESS MOVEMENT

We have seen how an appeal to the narrative and teachings of the Wesleyan revival was made on the part of Wesleyan groups seeking democratic reforms, such as the Wesleyan Methodist Association in Britain or the Methodist Protestant Church in the early nineteenth century. It was during the period of Methodist ascendancy that the Holiness movement began to develop in American Methodist churches, and this movement would claim the precedent of the Wesleyan revival in defending its understanding of Christian holiness. Holiness leaders, at first within the context of existing Methodist churches, taught believers to expect entire sanctification as a conscious, momentary experience that might happen soon after a believer's conversion. We might say, then, that the leaders of the Holiness movement had a distinctive take on the module **WayOfSalvation**, one that they believed to be faithful to John Wesley himself. As the Holiness movement developed, Holiness leaders began to hand on and interpret the Wesleyan tradition in a distinctive way.

The American Methodist evangelist **Phoebe Palmer** (1807–74), whose work was a fountainhead of the Holiness movement, referred repeatedly to John Wesley's teaching on sanctification in her 1849 study of *The Way of Holiness*.[46] Another early Holiness advocate, **Jesse Truesdale Peck** (1811–83), wrote around 1856 an influential

---

46 Phoebe Palmer, *The Way of Holiness* (New York: Lane and Scott, 1849); The version I have consulted is that available via the Wesley Center for Applied Theology at Northwestern Nazarene University (wesley.nnu.edu), consulted on 11 June 2008. This version is identified as a product of the Holiness Data Ministry. A search of this machine-readable text shows at least six explicit references to John Wesley's teaching on sanctification.

work on the doctrine of sanctification, a doctrine he advocated as *The Central Idea of Christianity*. In this work, Peck wrote,

> The Wesleyan reformation was eminently a movement in favor of holiness. The true doctrine of Christian Perfection was perhaps more clearly taught and powerfully enforced than at any former time since the days of primitive purity.[47]

In fact, testimonies to experiences of entire sanctification among nineteenth-century Holiness advocates often contained specific reference to John Wesley's teaching on sanctification as the ground of their experience.[48] In general, Methodist churches remained committed through the nineteenth century to the teaching that believers should expect entire sanctification in this life. The bishops of the Methodist Episcopal Church, South, declared in 1894, responding to Holiness advocates,

> The privilege of believers to attain unto the state of entire sanctification or perfect love, and to abide therein, is a well-known teaching of Methodism. . . . Let this doctrine still be proclaimed, and the experience still be testified.[49]

Two years later, in 1896, the bishops of the Methodist Episcopal Church declared,

> We have insisted on the glorious privilege and duty of all men becoming saints, of immediately being made perfect in love,

---

47 Jesse T. Peck, *The Central Idea of Christianity* (Louisville, Kentucky: Pentecostal Publishing Co., n.d., although the work is thought to have been written around 1856), in a section or chapter on "The Historical Argument." The version I have consulted is that available via the Wesley Center for Applied Theology at Northwestern Nazarene University (wesley.nnu.edu), consulted on June 11, 2008. This version is identified as a product of the Holiness Data Ministry.

48 This can be seen in a work of Holiness preacher and Organizer John S. Inskip, who published a collection of writings on Holiness, including testimonies to experiences of entire sanctification. Among the testimonies he included, those of John Allen Wood and Daniel Steele included explicit reference to Wesleyan teaching on sanctification: Inskip, ed., *Holiness Miscellany* (Philadelphia: National Publishing Association for the Promotion of Holiness, 1882) in the sections giving the testimony of Woo and Steele; the version I have consulted is that available via the Wesley Center for Applied Theology at Northwestern Nazarene University (wesley.nnu.edu), consulted on June 11, 2008. This version is identified as a product of the Holiness Data Ministry.

49 The Bishops' Address, in the *Journal of the General Conference of the Methodist Episcopal Church, South* (Nashville: Publishing House of the Methodist Episcopal Church, South, 1894), 25.

and of gradually ripening into Christian maturity in all facul-
ties. This doctrine was never more definitively stated, clearly
perceived, nor consistently lived by greater numbers than
now. But how lamentably the Church falls short of the divine
possibility![50]

By the time these declarations were made, the Holiness movement was growing increasingly independent of the formal structures
of American Methodism. Holiness leaders worked through a network
of already existing camp-meeting associations and other organiza-
tions that were closely related to Methodist churches but legally independent. In the late nineteenth century, in the very age when the
constituency of older Methodist churches was becoming more middle class, and when Methodist people were thinking of themselves
as more culturally sophisticated, Holiness groups often appealed to
the rural and urban poor. Methodist objections to Holiness teachings,
then, were sometimes a veiled means of decrying the social status of
Holiness people and the "enthusiastic" religion of Holiness people
that had been the characteristic of almost all Methodists only a few
decades before.

The bishops of the Methodist Episcopal Church, South, in 1894
went on after the statement quoted above to decry the presence of
a "holiness party" that, in their opinion, often valued "excited moods
and loud professions" more than the life of holiness, and the 1894
General Conference of the denomination went on to adopt a reso-
lution critical of the emotional excesses of the Holiness movement.
By the end of the nineteenth century, Holiness groups had begun to
organize themselves into separate denominations.

Even after the separation of Holiness churches, leaders of Holiness
churches continued to insist that they were carrying on the teaching about holiness and the ministry to the poor that had been the
hallmarks of the Wesleyan movement and of the earlier work of the

---

50   Address of the Bishops, in the *Journal of the Methodist Episcopal Church* (New York: Eaton and
     Mains, and Cincinnati: Cuts and Jennings, 1896), 38.

Methodist churches. **Phineas F. Bresee** (1838–1915), a former Methodist Episcopal presiding elder who became a key figure in the organization of the Church of the Nazarene, wrote,

> I examined with a good deal of interest Charles Wesley's hymns on consecration and sanctification as often in the Methodist Hymnal—about sixty of them. Their teaching is very clear in reference to the doctrine of entire sanctification. Over and over is repeated the deep, impassioned cry, the promise of God and the way to enter in. That men are to enter now, by faith, is plainly taught. They give rare, little glimpses of experience which comes after one has entered, but viewed more as a hope.[51]

The earliest *Manual* of the Church of the Nazarene stated the mission of the denomination as follows:

> We seek holy Christian fellowship, the conversion of sinners, the entire sanctification of believers and their upbuilding in holiness, together with the preaching of the Gospel to every creature. We also seek the simplicity and Pentecostal power manifest in the Primitive New Testament Church.[52]

The *Manual* followed the pattern of Methodist *Disciplines*, with a historical statement (only about the origins of the Church of the Nazarene), a statement of doctrine based on the Methodist Articles of Religion, and a set of General Rules based on those of the Methodist churches.[53]

Conclusion

In the period of ascendancy in the late nineteenth century, Methodist churches continued to encode their identity by retelling the narrative

---

51 Phineas F. Bresee, a sermon titled "The Lifting of the Veil" in *Twenty-Nine Sermons* (Los Angeles: Nazarene Publishing, 1903); the version I have consulted is that available via the Wesley Center for Applied Theology at Northwestern Nazarene University (wesley.nnu.edu), accessed on June 11, 2008. This version is identified as a product of the Holiness Data Ministry. Although this was written in 1903 before the formal organization of the national [Pentecostal] Church of the Nazarene (1908; the word *Pentecostal* was subsequently eliminated from the name), Bresee was already working with a group in Los Angeles that had taken the name "Church of the Nazarene," as the name of the publisher of this work suggests.

52 *Manual of the Pentecostal Church of the Nazarene* (Los Angeles: Nazarene Publishing, 1908), 27.

53 Ibid., 11–21 (historical statement), 22–31 (doctrinal statement), 31–34 (General Rules).

of the Wesleyan revival and by reference to the distinct teachings and practices that came from the Wesleyan revival. Although references to holiness as the distinct vocation of Methodists remained in place, they were overshadowed in this period by the broader emphasis on evangelism in mainstream (as contrasted with Holiness-oriented) Methodist churches. In North America, this emphasis on evangelism was tied to the growing sense of "manifest destiny" on the part of Americans and the triumphal Methodist sense of a divine mission to evangelize the continent. When the Methodist Episcopal *Doctrines and Discipline* was revised in 1892, its basic statement of mission was altered to state that:

> We believe that God's design in raising up the Methodist Episcopal Church in America was to evangelize the continent and spread scriptural holiness over these lands.[54]

The words *evangelize the continent* replaced the earlier formulation, *reform the continent*. By this time, the quest for holiness had become muted in the experience of many, if not most, Methodists, and that lay in the background of the rise of the Holiness movement and its claim to faithfully carry on the original distinctive vocation of Methodism based on its understanding of the Wesleyan revival.

Another issue faced by Methodist churches in this period also forced them to reconsider their Wesleyan roots, and that was the continuing question of Methodism's relationship to Anglicanism. This can be seen in the case of the Wesleyan Conference in Rigg's responses to Urlin and in the case of the African Methodist Episcopal Church in Turner's lengthy vindication of Methodist episcopacy and the legitimacy of Methodist ministerial succession. But within the Methodist Episcopal Church and the Methodist Episcopal Church, South, the late nineteenth century could be described as a period of "Gothic" Methodism, a period when imposing Methodist church structures, like the

---

54 *Doctrines and Discipline of the Methodist Episcopal Church* (New York: Hunt and Eaton, and Cincinnati: Cranston and Curts, 1892), 3. The same appears in the 1896 *Discipline* (New York: Eaton and Mains, and Cincinnati: Curts and Jennings, 3).

Italian Renaissance structure of the Lovely Lane Methodist Church in Baltimore, rose as a sign of Methodism's claim to be church in the same way as Presbyterians and Anglicans and Lutherans were recognized to be church. Thus, although Urlin and other Anglicans may have found the Wesleys' "high church" tendencies to be an argument against Methodist churches and in favor of Anglican churches, Methodist interpreters in this period found the "high church" image of Wesley to suit their own evolving conception of the role of Methodism among the larger family of Christian communities in the world. Even the notion of John Wesley as a kind of generic evangelist, increasingly described apart from Wesley's emphasis on the cultivation of holiness, served to reinforce the sophistication to which Methodists aspired in this age.

This chapter has considered how the Wesleyan narratives evolved in the late nineteenth century as Methodist communities looked to the Wesleyan past to find clues for the contemporary mission of their churches. In the next chapters we will trace the development of this tradition into the twentieth century as we consider the traditioning of the Wesleyan past in the contexts of modernist culture and in a period beyond Modernism.

WESLEYAN NARRATIVES IN AN AGE OF METHODIST MODERNISM

EARLY TWENTIETH CENTURY

The previous chapters have shown how Wesleyan communities had retold narratives of Wesleyan origins and utilized these narratives to encode their senses of distinctive mission and identity. Chapter 1 showed how this narrative tradition developed even in the time of John Wesley. Chapters 2 and 3 continued the narrative through the nineteenth century, considering how early Methodist churches looked back to the Wesleyan revival for the source of their identity, and how Methodist and Holiness communities in the late nineteenth century, in the period of Methodist ascendancy, continued to reinterpret the Wesleyan revival as a source of their own senses of distinct Christian missions in their time by recasting John Wesley in the principal role of evangelist and deemphasizing his role as an advocate of Christian holiness (in mainstream Methodist churches) or by emphasizing the crisis moment of entire sanctification (in Holiness churches).

By the end of the nineteenth century, Methodist and other Wesleyan churches were passing into a new phase in their development in which they began to deal much more directly with broader issues that had been raised in Western culture since the time of the Enlightenment. Methodism had always been, in some senses, a modern movement. It arose in the social context of the Industrial Revolution in Britain, and John Wesley was himself aware of developments in modern epistemology, for example, the thought of John Locke. Wesley sometimes utilized language derived from Locke and Malebranche and other contemporary philosophers associated with early modernity.[1] But in the very late nineteenth century and the early twentieth century, Methodist churches engaged the modern world in a new way as their congregations and constituencies grew more culturally sophisticated and as their leading clergy tended more and more to reflect education in colleges, universities, and theological institutions. In this cultural context, Wesleyan communities began to encode Wesleyan identities in new ways, in some cases by rediscovering truths about Wesleyan origins that had gone unnoticed in the past.

A particular form that modernity took in this age has been described as *Modernism*. Not to be equated with *modernity* in its vast sweep from the seventeenth century to the present, Modernism represented a very specific European and North American cultural movement from the late nineteenth century through at least the 1960s that rejected traditional forms of culture and encouraged innovation in a number of areas including art, architecture, and music.[2] The period of Modernism saw new forms of large-scale social unities, such as the Union of Soviet Socialist Republics, the United Nations, and the World Council of Churches, that were believed to be possible only by overcoming older forms of regionalism, nationalism, and denominationalism that were seen as inhibiting the formation of modern unities.

In Christian cultures, more specifically, Catholics spoke directly of Catholic "Modernism" whereas Protestants preferred to speak of

---

1   Cf. Dreyer, "Faith and Experience in the Thought of John Wesley" *American Historical Review* 88 (1983): 12–30; Brantley, *Locke, Wesley, and the Method of English Romanticism*; and Matthews, "'Religion and Reason Joined': A Study in the Theology of John Wesley."

2   Art Berman, *Preface to Modernism* (Urbana and Chicago: University of Illinois Press, 1994), 3–9.

"liberal" theologies and outlooks that flourished in this age. Modernism also denoted, in Christian culture, a concern for the betterment of societies based in concrete engagement with the concerns of the working poor, especially in growing cities, represented by American Methodist engagement with the "Social Gospel" movement. A particular Christian form of the modernist vision of unity can be seen in the ecumenical movement that was growing in prominence throughout this period, culminating in the organization of the World Council of Churches in 1948. As Methodist churches emerged at the end of the nineteenth century from the cultural isolation associated with their earlier sectarian attitudes toward the broader society, reinforced by self-administered forms of clergy education (i.e., the "course of study school"), they came into direct contact both with modernity and with its more specific subculture of Modernism. Modernity and Modernism were both to impact Methodist culture very deeply in the early twentieth century.

One expression of Modernism in Methodist life was the accomplishment of large-scale Methodist unions in the early twentieth century. In Britain, the three largest Methodist groups—the Wesleyan Conference, the Primitive Methodist Connexion, and the United Methodist Free Churches—came together in the period between 1929 and 1932 to form the Methodist Church in Great Britain and Northern Ireland. In the United States, the Methodist Episcopal Church, the Methodist Episcopal Church, South, and the Methodist Protestants came together in 1939 to form the Methodist Church. In America and Britain these unions overcame more than a century of Methodist divisions, some of them over crucial issues like the democratic reforms that had been demanded by the Methodist Protestant Church in the United States and by the Primitive Methodist Connexion and the predecessors of the United Methodist Free Churches in the United Kingdom. The union in the United States overcame regional differences lingering from the Civil War, although it ended up reinforcing racial division with the creation of a segregated Central Jurisdiction whose structures lasted beyond 1970.

An early instance of Modernism appeared in American Methodist theological circles at the end of the nineteenth century in the Personalist philosophy and theology that flourished at Boston University associated with Borden Parker Bowne, Edgar Sheffield Brightman, and others. The Personalist philosophy of this age developed from German idealist philosophy, and many of its advocates found little relevance in the older Wesleyan theology.[3] It prompted Harvard philosopher William James to comment in a footnote to his famous Gifford Lectures, *The Varieties of Religious Experience*, "See how the ancient spirit of Methodism evaporates under those wonderfully able rationalistic booklets (which every one should read) of a philosopher like Professor Bowne."[4]

But although Methodism was changing in this age, signs of its late nineteenth-century ascendancy continued. The Gothic style continued to be favored by urban Methodists in this period and was renewed in the early twentieth century, seen in the gray collegiate Gothic buildings of Garrett Biblical Institute in Evanston, Illinois (built in 1924), the Gothic edifice of the Highland Park Methodist Church in Dallas (built in 1926), and the extensive stone Gothic structures of Duke University's West Campus (built between 1927 and 1935). The façade of Duke Chapel has stone images of John and Charles Wesley, Francis Asbury, George Whitefield, and Thomas Coke.[5] As we shall see, the triumphalist telling of Methodist history continued in monuments such as these and in popular Methodist literature in this age, though it was also challenged by more critical historical accounts.

---

3   On Personalism, see Thomas A. Langford, *Practical Divinity: Theology in the Wesleyan Tradition*, rev. ed. (Nashville: Abingdon Press, 1998), 1:105–110, 164–170, 2:114–136, 161–173. Bowne does refer to John Wesley in a lengthy essay titled "The Christian Life" in his *Studies in Christianity* (Boston: Houghton Mifflin Co., 1909), where he was concerned with the traditional Methodist doctrine of assurance and maintained that John Wesley himself did not insist on a certain kind of religious experience as evidence that one was justified (195–297).

4   William James, *The Varieties of Religious Experience: A Study in Human Nature* (New York: The Modern Library, 1902), 492.

5   Though the image of "Thomas Coke" is mistakenly of a seventeenth-century English privy counselor of that name rather than the Methodist Thomas Coke.

THE OLD METHODISM AND THE NEW

An indication of the shifts in Methodist culture occurring around the turn of the twentieth century can be seen in a series of lectures, *The Old Methodism and the New*, delivered by British Wesleyan minister **George Jackson** (1864–1945) at Wesleyan University in Middletown, Connecticut, celebrating the two hundredth anniversary in 1903 of John Wesley's birth.[6] Jackson offered the perspective of a British Methodist speaking to American Methodists and elaborating a series of comparisons between Methodism as it existed at the end of the eighteenth century (roughly in 1800) and Methodism as it existed at the time of his lecture in 1900.

In his first lecture on the "ecclesiastical position" of Methodism, Jackson argued that whereas a hundred years before his time British Methodists still in some ways considered themselves tied to the Church of England and refused to acknowledge themselves as Dissenters, in the last hundred years Wesleyan Methodists had grown further from Anglicanism and closer to the church cultures of Dissenters. In his second lecture on Methodist doctrines, Jackson argued that Methodists continued to hold a strong doctrine of biblical authority but were open to new discoveries in biblical archeology and the literary criticism of the biblical texts. He maintained that Methodists continued to hold a strong doctrine of conversion but were open to different (i.e., more gradual) ways in which conversions might occur. He asserted that Methodists continue to hold a strong and consistent teaching that one can know that one's sins are forgiven, though Methodists may not insist that such an assurance is necessary. He insisted, moreover, that Methodists continued to teach a strong doctrine of eternal judgment even though Methodists might not insist on a doctrine of conscious eternal punishment.

In his third lecture on the characteristic "spirit of Methodism,"

---

6   George Jackson, *The Old Methodism and the New* (London: Hodder and Stoughton, 1903), "An address delivered at Wesleyan University, Middletown, Conn., U.S.A., on June 28, 1903, on the two hundredth anniversary of John Wesley's birth" (opposite title page).

Jackson stated that the early Methodist spirit that focused on offering Christ and salvation to all lived on, even though Methodists in his day had developed broader ethical concerns and needed further depth in studies of theology and Christian ethics. He concluded by appeal to the example of Welsh Methodist leader Hugh Price Hughes who had died in the previous year and to whom the volume is dedicated (see below on Hughes), holding up Hughes's life and work as an example of the revival of the early Methodist spirit in a new time and especially Hughes's concern for the urban poor, which Jackson saw as consistent with Wesley's identification with the poor (thus modules **SocialDysfunction** and **MinistryWithPoor**). His narrative also seems to presuppose the image of John Wesley as a generic evangelist with little reference to or interest in Wesley's role in the cultivation of Christian holiness. Jackson, then, is a good example of how Methodists were struggling with modernity and Modernism at the beginning of the twentieth century, not denying central and consistent Methodist themes, but consistently seeking to broaden their scope.

THE WESLEYAN NARRATIVE IN MODERN CHURCH HISTORY

As Methodists told their own story by way of published histories in this period, they very often continued the triumphalist narrative from the earlier age, especially in more popular works intended for lay readers. An example of this species of Methodist historiography is *The Story of Methodism* (1926) by **Halford Edward Luccock** (1885–1961) and **Paul Hutchinson** (1890–1956), subsequently revised and updated (after the US Methodist union of 1939) with added chapters by **Robert Wesley Goodloe** (1888–1966) in 1949.[7] Concluding their first chapter, they wrote that as a result of John Wesley's work,

---

7   Halford E. Luccock and Paul Hutchinson, with two final chapters by Robert W. Goodloe, *The Story of Methodism*, 2nd rev. ed. (New York and Nashville: Abingdon-Cokesbury Press, 1949).

under God's guidance, "there spread in England a movement known to history as the Methodist Revival that still exerts a mighty influence on human affairs."[8] The next chapter compares the villages of Scrooby, Nottinghamshire, from which the "Pilgrim fathers" set out for North America, and Epworth, Lincolnshire, just fourteen miles away, from which the Wesleys came, invoking the narrative module described above as **AmericanReligion**. The chapter, then, follows a parallel track to that offered by Abel Stevens and Matthew Simpson in asserting the destiny of Methodism in bringing civilization to the New World: "Scrooby and Epworth! From the first, in truth if not in actual chronicle, the Mayflower set sail to plant a new world. From the second, John Wesley went out to save an old one."[9] A derivative work designed to train children in the Methodist heritage was written by Luccock with the aid of Webb Garrison and was entitled *Endless Line of Splendor* (1950, with multiple revised editions up to 1992). Again John Wesley appears as the generic evangelist—an evangelist whose principal concern was enlarging the scope of Christian communities rather than deepening the spirituality and sanctity of constituents.

But although the triumphalist strain of Methodist history continued in popular circles in the early twentieth century, new trends were appearing in Methodist historiography that would significantly impact the ways in which Methodists told their own story, that is to say, the ways in which Methodists handed on the Wesleyan tradition to new generations. An important and early example of this was offered by **James M. Buckley** (1836–1920), who entered the ministry of the Methodist Episcopal Church in 1859 and served from 1880 as editor

---

8 Ibid., 27.

9 Ibid., 28–34; quotation is on p. 34. On this volume, cf. Russell Richey, "History as a Bearer of Denominational Identity," 282–84. Richey notes that the Luccock and Hutchinson volume came out well after Buckley's *History* (see below in this text), and Richey writes, "Yet, their very easiness with the providential claims is striking, perhaps worrisome. Do Buckley's critical premises haunt their breezy confidence? Do their assertions betray superficiality or conviction?" While it may be true that Luccock's and Hutchinson's assertions of providence and triumph might somehow betray their own doubt, this is not expressed overtly in their book, and I think it is best to read the work as a continuation of the triumphalist narrative that emerged in the period of ascendancy.

of the *New York Christian Advocate*. Hugely influential at the turn of the twentieth century, Buckley was a delegate to every Methodist Episcopal General Conference between 1872 and 1912.

Buckley showed some signs of old-fashioned Methodist conservatism. Early in his career as a writer he offered a volume published by the Methodist Book Concern, *Christians and the Theater* (1875), which carefully studied sixty plays currently in production in New York and concluded that although some might be unobjectionable, the theater remained "a symptom and fruit of that moral and spiritual enervation which thus far in the history of Christianity has been the concomitant, and, perhaps, the inevitable effect, of luxury."[10] Buckley had been a member of the committee that had revised the Methodist Episcopal *Discipline* of 1892, including its historical statement (see the previous section). In 1905 he offered the Quillian Lectures at Emory College in Georgia, *The Fundamentals and Their Contrasts*, offering a defense of "the principles fundamental to all religion" in response to contemporary doubters.[11] Along with the eminent Methodist layman and ecumenical pioneer Dr. John R. Mott, Buckley offered an eloquent eulogy at the funeral of Chicago evangelist D. L. Moody in 1900.

As a historian of Methodism and one who handed on the Wesleyan tradition, however, Buckley showed himself to be of a very different generation than Tyerman and other Methodist historians before him. His *A History of Methodists in the United States* (1896) was offered in the American Church History series published under the auspices of the American Society of Church History, of which Buckley was an early member.[12] An illustrated edition of the book (1899) was

---

10   J. M. Buckley, *Christians and the Theater* (New York: Phillips and Hunt; and Cincinnati: Cranston and Stowe, 1886 (but copyrighted 1875), 156.

11   James M. Buckley, *The Fundamentals and Their Contrasts* (New York: Eaton and Mains; and Cincinnati: Jennings and Graham, 1906); quotation is on p. 7. Buckley does show a trend toward liberality in his assumption, held along with many Evangelical Christians of his age, that certain fundamental teachings were actually held by all major religious systems.

12   James M. Buckley, *A History of Methodists in the United States* (New York: Christian Literature Co., 1896).

reviewed positively by Episcopal Church historian Henry C. Vedder of Crozer Theological Seminary.[13] Vedder's comment on Buckley's history is revealing:

> The most admirable quality, perhaps, that one finds in the book is its candor. Denominational histories, for the most part, do not belong to historical literature, but should be classed as apologetics, or possibly polemics. The temptation to indulge in this style of writing must be strong when an enthusiastic Methodist undertakes to tell the story of his own denomination.[14]

Vedder went on to compliment, in particular, Buckley's honesty in dealing with Wesley's attitude toward the American colonies, Wesley's attitude toward ordination (especially the ordinations of 1784, with Buckley's own retelling of module **AmericanOrdinations**), the controversy over slavery among Methodist churches (invoking module **OppositionToSlavery**), and the more recent controversy over the Methodist Book Concern.[15]

Buckley did in some passages reflect the earlier Methodist tendency to ascribe the work of providence to the Methodist movement, but Russell E. Richey points out that Buckley seldom did this in his own voice, more typically allowing the voices of others by way of quotations to carry the theme of the providential direction of Methodism.[16] Like traditional Methodist accounts of Wesley, Buckley emphasized the Aldersgate-Street conversion experience (module **AldersgateExperience**), but Buckley acknowledged Wesley's later doubts about his earlier claims that he had not been a Christian prior to Aldersgate, citing Wesley's own addition of notes to the published *Journal* account that "I had even then the faith of a *servant* though

---

13   Henry C. Vedder, *History of Methodists in the United States*. 1899 ed. by J. M. Buckley, *American Journal of Theology* (1900), 200–203.
14   Ibid., 201.
15   Ibid., 202–3.
16   Richey, "History as a Bearer of Denominational Identity," 279–82.

not the faith of a *son*."[17] Buckley narrated the Aldersgate experience factually, giving Wesley's own words but without the triumphal comments that Methodists had in the past added to it, and Buckley went on to recount how the Moravians refused communion (fellowship as much as participation in the Lord's Supper) to Wesley in the summer after Aldersgate, suggesting that they themselves were still not convinced of the validity of his conversion experience,[18] and thus invoking module **WesleyDoubts**. Similarly, Buckley later referred to the "conversion, in the technical term" of John and Charles Wesley,[19] raising the possibility that their experiences in 1738 may not have been "conversion" in other senses of the term. As George Jackson had indicated that "the new Methodism" had begun to value more gradual religious experiences (see above), Buckley suggested that Wesley's own experience at Aldersgate, the old paradigm of the Methodist conversion experience, may not have been as dramatic or its effects as instantaneous as Methodists had earlier represented it as being.

Buckley's narrative recounted the development of distinctive Methodist institutions, such as itinerant preaching (module **MethodistPreachers**) and the use of societies (module **ClassesBands**), though at some points Buckley was concerned to show ways in which some of these institutions had parallels in the experience of other Christian communities (for example, the Moravian origins of Methodist "bands"). In describing the characteristic teachings of John Wesley, Buckley again stressed the common Christian elements in Wesley's proclamation:

> The *doctrines* taught by Wesley and his itinerant and lay preachers included the fundamental principles of Christianity as held by the Reformed churches generally, but excluded ritualism and sacramentarianism, and divided from Calvinism on

---

17   Buckley, *History of the Methodists in the United States*, 72.
18   Ibid., 73–77.
19   Ibid., 93.

unconditional election, predestination, final perseverance of the saints, and kindred doctrines.[20]

Buckley acknowledged that Wesley and the early Methodist preachers placed an emphasis on "the possibility of instantaneous conversion, and on the witness of the Spirit, which was explicitly defined and inculcated as the privilege of every believer," but Buckley's statement on this subject is carefully worded to show instantaneous conversion as a "possibility" and the witness of the Spirit as a common "privilege," but neither as being strictly necessary (his version of module **WayOf-Salvation**). Similarly, perhaps responding to concerns raised by the Holiness movement, Buckley described the doctrine of Christian perfection as the fulfillment of the great commandment, and Buckley made it clear that this "perfection" was, according to Wesley himself, "not a perfection which does not admit of continual increase."[21] In these cases, then, the sharp contours of the older Wesleyan message, insisting on the necessity of an instantaneous and conscious experience of conversion and on a parallel experience of entire sanctification, were rounded out and interpreted as being more like the experiences of Christians of other traditions.

BUCKLEY, *HISTORY OF THE METHODISTS IN THE UNITED STATES* (1896)
AldersgateExperience
WesleyDoubts
MethodistPreachers
ClassesBands
WayOfSalvation
AmericanOrdinations
OppositionToSlavery

20   Ibid., 90–91.
21   Ibid., 91.

The more scientific and critical approach to American Method-ist history pioneered by Buckley was carried on in the early twenti-eth century by **William Warren Sweet** (1881–1959), who served on the faculty of the University of Chicago for twenty years (1927–46), then briefly at Garrett Biblical Institute (1946–48) before finishing his career at the School of Theology of Southern Methodist University (1948–52). Sweet's consistent focus was on the religion of the Amer-ican frontier, and he advocated the view that the Methodist itinerant system (module **MethodistPreachers**) had been uniquely fitted for the evangelism of the frontier because of the flexibility that it allowed Methodist preachers in opening new areas for the formation of new Methodist societies (congregations). Sweet would eventually pioneer an extensive project sponsored by the University of Chicago that col-lected and published documents illustrating the frontier expansion of US churches, and in this project Sweet himself edited the volumes of Baptist as well as Methodist materials.

In 1933 Sweet published a volume, *Methodism in American His-tory*, to which he subsequently added a new chapter, bringing the volume up to 1953 including the US Methodist union of 1939.[22] Sweet's narrative began with the condition of religion in North America in the eighteenth century, emphasizing the effects of the first Great Awakening (module **AmericanReligion**), then he pro-ceeded to a brief chapter on the emergence of Methodism in En-gland under John Wesley's influence. His account of Wesley covered some of the typical topics about Wesley's upbringing in Epworth, his time at Oxford University and his development of the Holy Club there, and his sojourn in Georgia including his encounters with the Moravian community (see the table following).[23] Sweet described Wesley as "a rigid High-Churchman and a strict sacramentarian," perhaps writing his impression of Tractarian Anglicanism back into

---

22 William Warren Sweet, *Methodism in American History,* 2nd ed. (Nashville: Abingdon Press, 1954).

23 Ibid., 9–33.

Wesley's time. Sweet emphasized Wesley's frustration with the Georgia mission and in Wesley's relationship with Sophia Hopkey, stating that Wesley's *Journal* revealed his "depression of spirit" upon his return to England. Sweet's narrative has a brief paragraph on Wesley's Aldersgate-Street conversion experience (module **Aldersgate-Experience**),[24] noting the newly found "certainty and victory" that John and Charles Wesley had found in their conversion experiences. In this way, Sweet reflected a trend in the early twentieth century toward psychological interpretations of religious experiences, a trend that would be seen just a few years later (1938) in the work of G. Elsie Harrison.[25]

Sweet's description of the condition of the Church of England in the eighteenth century is perhaps the most exaggerated example of what I have called narrative module **AnglicanDeclension**:

> The depth and apathy and shame to which organized religion in eighteenth-century England had sunk beggars description. In 1731, Montesquieu reported, after a visit to England, that the people had no religion, and that not more than four or five of the members of the House of Commons attended church. The whole Church of England, from the Archbishop of Canterbury down, was honeycombed with indifference and complacency. Many of the clergy spent their time in gambling, fox-hunting, and drinking, and made little pretense of caring for the spiritual well-being of the perishing people about them.[26]

As we shall see, contemporary scholarship has severely challenged this view of the eighteenth-century Church of England, but Sweet's description can stand as a classic expression of the module **AnglicanDeclension** that shaped Methodist consciousness about the Anglican background of Methodism until the last few decades. Sweet also paid attention to the Industrial Revolution as a critical context for the

---

24 Ibid., 33–36.
25 G. Elsie Harrison, *Son to Susanna: The Private Life of John Wesley* (Nashville: Cokesbury Press, 1938).
26 Sweet, *Methodism in American History*, 37.

Wesleyan movement (module **SocialDysfunction**).[27] He emphasized John Wesley's doctrinal liberality[28] and the development of Methodist classes (module **ClassesBands**) and itinerant preaching (modules **FieldPreaching** and **MethodistPreachers**) as a prelude to Methodist expansion on the American frontier. Sweet emphasized the doctrinal liberality of the early Methodist movement, for example, the fact that the movement did not set doctrinal requirements for participation in Methodist societies (module **DoctrinalLiberality**). Sweet's narrative of John Wesley had only the briefest mention of such characteristic Methodist teachings as the new birth, assurance of pardon, or entire sanctification (module **WayOfSalvation**).

SWEET, NARRATIVE OF WESLEYAN ORIGINS IN *METHODISM IN AMERICAN HISTORY* (1933 AND FF.)

AmericanReligion

EpworthUpbringing

OxfordSociety

GeorgiaPietists (Wesley's "depression of spirit" in this period)

AldersgateExperience (as giving confidence)

SocialDysfunction and **AnglicanDeclension** (strong emphasis)

ClassesBands

FieldPreaching and **MethodistPreachers** (including lay preachers; emphasized as laying the foundation for Sweet's thesis on the importance of itinerant preaching on the American frontier)

WayOfSalvation (very brief)

DoctrinalLiberality (emphasized)

Sweet's narrative of Methodist origins, though written for a lay readership, came not from a Methodist church leader but from a

---

27   Ibid., 36–37.
28   Ibid., 41–42.

historian located solidly in the academy. But Sweet's work was famous, especially for his elaboration of the "frontier hypothesis," and
his history came to influence generations of well-read Methodist
leaders, especially as education in theological schools came to be the
norm in American Methodist church circles from the middle of the
twentieth century. His influential history reflects many of the trends of
the Modernist period, including his psychologizing of Wesley's Oxford
and then Aldersgate experiences and his claims about John Wesley's
doctrinal liberality. Sweet's narrative has little reference to the Wesleyan teaching about holiness. In fact, his frontier thesis presupposed
that John Wesley's principal work, and the principal work of American
Methodists, was in expanding Christian communities rather than en-
riching their depth and their sanctity. In many other respects, despite
his academic location, Sweet's narrative of Wesley reflected conventional versions of this narrative, most notably in his exaggerated account of Anglican declension in the eighteenth century.

MODERNIST INTERPRETATIONS OF THE WESLEYAN MOVEMENT

The turn to modernist culture in Methodist churches can be seen in
this period in new interpretations of John Wesley and of the Methodist movement, both in Britain and in the United States. British (Wesleyan) Methodist scholar **Herbert Brook Workman** (1862–1951),
for example, offered a brief study of *The Place of Methodism in the
Catholic Church,* an essay originally published in 1909 as an introduction to a two-volume work, *A New History of Methodism*, and subsequently expanded and republished in 1921.[29] Workman argued, "Few
would deny that the primary *Idea* of Methodism lies in its emphasis of
[sic] experience."[30] He saw the Reformation as a protest against the
idea of "solidarity" (i.e., communal identity) in the medieval church,

---

29 Herbert Brook Workman, *The Place of Methodism in the Catholic Church,* rev. ed. (1st ed. 1909,
    London; Epworth Press, 1921).

30 Ibid., 16.

and saw the Methodist emphasis on religious experience as a further out-working of the principle of individual identity and experience that began with the Reformation. Workman drew a strong parallel between the thought of Wesley on religious experience and that of Friedrich Schleiermacher.[31] He understood the distinctive Methodist doctrines of assurance, sanctification, conversion, and Methodist Arminianism as particular expressions of the central idea of religious experience.[32] Thus Workman argued that the idea of religious experience, and the particular Methodist emphasis on religious experience, is its unique gift to the "catholic" Christian community.

Another instance of a modernist interpretation of John Wesley was offered in this period by **Umphrey Lee** (1893–1958), who from 1939 through 1954 served as president of Southern Methodist University. Lee's study of *John Wesley and Modern Religion*, based on his Columbia University dissertation,[33] made the case that John Wesley was a "modern" Christian theologian and prophet, understanding that "the modern movement" involves "a preference for emotion, individualism, diversity, and growth, over reason, uniformity, and regulation."[34] But despite Wesley's emphasis on emotion and religious experience generally, Lee rejected traditional Methodist readings of Wesley that stressed his vivid and instantaneous religious experiences, a view that he parodied as seeing John Wesley as a "stained-glass saint" in an Evangelical mold rather than the "living prophet" that Lee preferred to see in John Wesley.[35] Consistent with this view, Lee stressed Wesley's emphasis on "practical religion," Wesley's reaction against "speculative" teachings, and thus Wesley's broad tolerance in doctrinal matters.[36]

---

31 Ibid., 23–26.
32 Ibid., 33–43 (assurance), 51–53 (sanctification), 53–54 (conversion), and 54–56 (on Methodist Arminianism).
33 Umphrey Lee, *John Wesley and Modern Religion* (Nashville: Cokesbury Press), 1936.
34 Ibid., 16.
35 Ibid., 17.
36 Ibid., 112–13, and again 144–45.

Lee offered a whole chapter on Wesley's Aldersgate-Street experience (module **AldersgateExperience**), arguing, in contrast to traditional Methodist views, that Wesley later reinterpreted the experience not as his "conversion" in the sense of his first real experience of Christian belief, but rather as "a mystical conversion—that is, the conversion of a religious man to a higher state of religious devotion."[37] Lee saw Wesley's doctrine of prevenient grace as a rejection of the Augustinian and Reformation doctrine of original sin and as preserving divine initiative while at the same time allowing a free human response to divine grace.[38] Lee claimed that Wesley held together the doctrines of justification and sanctification that had been separated since the Reformation, that Wesley's mature understanding of Christian perfection was that it involved both an instantaneous moment but also continual increase, and that Wesley reflected a tendency towards Christian asceticism in his understanding of how Christians are to pursue perfection.[39]

Like Workman before him, Lee compared Wesley's emphasis on religious experience (and Lee calls this "mystical experience") with Schleiermacher's similar emphasis.[40] Lee's conclusion was as follows:

> It is this combination of mystical experience with the ethical, the rational, and the institutional elements in religion which gives Wesley his place in the history of Christianity. Phrased in another way, it may be said that he joined the tendencies toward regulation and control, toward uniformity and universality, with the tendencies toward emotion, diversity, and freedom. And he did this without sacrificing either the doctrine of grace or the ethical interests of religion."[41]

---

37 Ibid., chap. 5, 83–109; quotation is on p. 103.
38 Cf. ibid., 125.
39 Ibid., 171–72 (justification and sanctification), 186–87 (progressive sanctification), and 196–207 (asceticism and Christian perfection).
40 Ibid., 302–3.
41 Ibid., 321.

Lee thus offered a distinctively modernist reading of Wesley. His concern with religious experience had more than a little justification in Wesley's claim that "perceptible inspiration" was "the main doctrine of the Methodists."

Other Methodist interpretations of John Wesley in this period emphasized Wesley's concern for the conditions of the poor. The Welsh Wesleyan evangelist **Hugh Price Hughes** (1847–1902), who established the *Methodist Times* in 1884 and then in 1887 founded the West London Mission as a Wesleyan outreach to the poor of London, taught a very traditional Methodist theology. Hughes maintained central tenets of Christian orthodoxy that, he believed, were common to Christians since the time of the Council of Nicaea (module **EcumenicalWesley** and reflecting his version of **DoctrinalLiberality**).[42] His view of Wesley's conversion was consonant with that of traditional Methodist piety, emphasizing the complete change of character brought about by conversion,[43] and Hughes's own preaching, as that of traditional Methodists, held out the terrifying fear of divine judgment as a ground for conversion.[44]

But Hughes's appreciation for Wesley lay in his sense that, contrary to the middle-class identification of Victorian Wesleyans, John Wesley's movement had practically helped the poor of England in the time of the Industrial Revolution (modules **SocialDysfunction** and **MinistryWithPoor**). In a posthumously published introduction to John Wesley's *Journal*, Hughes had written,

42 Hugh Price Hughes, sermon, "'Robert Elsmere' and Mr. Gladstone's Criticism of the Book," in *Social Christianity: Sermons Delivered in St. James Hall, London* (London: Hodder and Stoughton, 1890), 99–100: "It is a remarkable fact, as Mr. Gladstone points out, that ever since the fourth century the Christian conception of Christ has been absolutely unchanged. Amid all our controversies and schisms we have never doubted or disputed the claims of Christ. To-day, if you were to shut up in a room the Archbishop of Canterbury, Mr. Spurgeon, Cardinal Manning, General Booth, the Chairman of the Congregational Union, and the President of the Methodist Conference, and tell them that they must remain there until they were all agreed in a common definition of the claims of Christ, they would not be detained for five minutes."

43 Ibid., 105–6.

44 See his concluding sermon, "A Timely Warning," in *Social Christianity*, 271–81: "The hour of final choice grows nearer, nearer, nearer. You may have entered upon it now. Repent Escape for your life. Flee to Christ, and all will yet be well" (at the conclusion, p. 281).

Then came John Wesley and his "helpers." They were the first preachers since the days of the Franciscan friars in the Middle Ages who ever reached the working classes. In England, as in France, Germany, and everywhere else, the Reformation was essentially a middle-class movement. It never captured either the upper classes or the working classes. That explains its limitations.

As Dr. Rigg has shown, Wesley's itineraries were deliberately planned to bring him into direct contact neither with the aristocracy nor with the dependent or poverty-stricken poor, but with the industrious, self-supporting workmen in town and country. The ultimate result was that "the man in the streets" became Methodist in his conception of Christianity, whatever his personal conduct and character might be.[45]

Thus Hughes wrote around the turn of the twentieth century. But by the early twentieth century Methodist interpreters of their own history and tradition had to respond to vociferous critics who, sometimes writing the morals of Victorian Methodism back into the Methodism of John Wesley's age, argued that Methodism had hindered and not helped the working people of England in the Industrial Revolution. Their attitudes were summed up by **Marjorie Bowen** (pseudonym of Gabrielle Margaret Long née Campbell, 1885–1952), who in 1938 published a study entitled *Wrestling Jacob: A Study in the Life of John Wesley and Some Members of the Family*.[46] Bowen wrote,

It has been estimated that in the period during which John Wesley worked nearly half the population were paupers; it was these unemployed outcasts and criminals to whom the evangelist appealed, giving them religion as a drug and a comfort.[47]

---

45 Hugh Price Hughes, introduction to *The Journal of John Wesley* (New York: Fleming Revell Company of New York, 1903); (repr ed., Chicago: Moody Press, 1974), 11–12.

46 London: Religious Book Club, 1938.

47 Marjorie Bowen, *Wrestling Jacob: A Study in the Life of John Wesley and Some Members of the Family,* quoted in Robert F. Wearmouth, *Methodism and the Common People of the Eighteenth Century* (London; Epworth Press, 1945), 266.

Noting the similarity of this phrase to Marx's thoughts on religion as an "opiate of the people," Primitive Methodist circuit preacher and historian **Robert Featherstone Wearmouth** (1882–1963) responded in a 1945 study of *Methodism and the Common People of the Eighteenth Century* based on his University of London PhD dissertation. Wearmouth argued that Wesley and the eighteenth-century Methodists had consistently sought to empower poor and working-class people by recognizing their gifts and offering education and organization as well as religious formation.[48] Both Hughes and Wearmouth had responded to the modernist critique of traditional religion by highlighting the practical as well as spiritual concerns of John Wesley and early Methodists for the common people of the eighteenth century (again invoking modules **SocialDysfunction** and **MinistryWithPoor**). In this way, they reinterpreted the Wesleyan tradition as it related directly to their contemporary efforts to reclaim the distinct mission of "the people called Methodists" to "the depressed classes."[49] In doing so, they set in motion a thread of interpretation within Wesleyan churches that saw Wesley's identification with the poor as lying at the heart of the Wesleyan tradition itself.

In 1938 Methodists throughout the world celebrated the bicentennial of John Wesley's Aldersgate-Street conversion experience. A collection of essays given at a Georgia conference on this occasion interpreted module **AldersgateExperience** in a variety of ways. The topic of the conference at which the essays were delivered was "The Primacy of Personal Religious Experience in the Life and Work of Methodism."[50] The notion of "personal religious experience" evokes the idea, very common in this period, that Methodists' emphasis on religious experience was a distinctly modern concern, as we have seen

---

48 Wearmouth, *Methodism and the Common People of the Eighteenth Century*, 263–68, the concluding argument of the book as a whole.

49 The term is that of Wearmouth, 267.

50 W. G. Gram, preface to *What Happened at Aldersgate*, ed. Elmer T. Clark (Nashville: Methodist Publishing, 1938), 5.

in reference to the works of Herbert Brook Workman and Umphrey Lee considered above. An introductory essay by Elmer Clark made the case for the complexity inherent in Wesley's Aldersgate-Street experience, including Wesley's subsequent notations about his earlier descriptions of it and the doubts that Wesley continued to have after the experience (module **WesleyDoubts**).[51] Other Methodist leaders in these essays consistently expressed the need for Methodists to return to the heartfelt experience of Wesley at Aldersgate.[52] Jean Miller Schmidt, commenting on these essays, notes that as a whole they express "a quest for identity and a hungering for spiritual power" on the part of modern Methodists.[53]

WESLEYAN NARRATIVES AT MID-TWENTIETH CENTURY

The period from the late 1960s to the present has seen a remarkable growth of interpretations of the Wesleys and of Methodism. It seemed possible that Methodists at the beginning of this period might abandon the narrative approach to identifying the distinctive identity of the Wesleyan movement. A strong current in this period was to emphasize the theological content of the Wesleyan movement over narratives of Wesleyan origins, especially in the wake of ecumenical encounters with leaders of other denominational traditions. This ecumenical perspective would lead to a significant revisioning of Wesleyan origins (see the next section). But a series of three volumes of the *History of American Methodism* that appeared in 1964, coinciding with the bicentennial of the first Wesleyan missionaries to the British North American colonies, had no sustained narrative of Wesleyan origins but only an introductory chapter by David C. Shipley giving an

---

51 Elmer T. Clark, "What Happened at Aldersgate," in *What Happened at Aldersgate*, 11–42.

52 Cf., for example, the conclusion of Methodist Protestant James H. Straughn's essay, "Aldersgate the Basis of Methodist Doctrine," in *What Happened at Aldersgate*, 142–44, and especially the last paragraph on p. 144, where Straughn wondered if modern historical investigations into Aldersgate amount to merely archaeological inquiries or nostalgic longings for a bygone era.

53 Schmidt, "'Strangely Warmed': The Place of Aldersgate in the Methodist Canon," 118.

account of the distinctive Wesleyan culture that American Methodists inherited from their "European" (British) origins.[54]

In the period after the Second World War, British and American Methodist interpreters offered narratives of the development of Methodism that began with John Wesley as a clue to Methodist identity. These extended narratives followed the concerns of the Modernist period. One single-volume account of John Wesley in this period, that of A. Skevington Wood, offered a scholarly reworking of the nineteenth-century Evangelical pattern of describing John Wesley's experience as normative for Methodist identity (see the following).

Between 1965 and 1988 a four-volume series, *A History of the Methodist Church in Great Britain* was published, edited by Rupert E. Davies and E. Gordon Rupp. The volumes were written across the periods I have described as Methodist Modernism and Methodism beyond Modernism. But the first volume including a narrative of Methodist origins in the eighteenth century was published in 1965 and fits within the Modernist period described here. The volume was written by the Methodist historian **Maldwyn Lloyd Edwards** (1903–74), a native of Liverpool with MA degrees from the University of Wales and Cambridge and a PhD degree from the University of London. Edwards was a prominent British Methodist leader of his generation who served as president of the British Methodist Conference.[55] He had written some works dealing with contemporary social issues faced by Christians and had also written a three-part history of British Methodism with the first volume entitled *John Wesley and the Eighteenth Century.*[56]

A History of the Methodist Church in Great Britain commenced

---

54 David C. Shipley, "The European Heritage," in Emory S. Bucke., ed., *History of American Methodism* (Nashville: Abingdon Press, 1964), 1:9–42.

55 Maldwyn Edwards, chapter on "John Wesley," in Rupert E. Davies and E. Gordon Rupp, eds., *A History of the Methodist Church in Great Britain* (London: Epworth Press, 1965–88), 1:37–79.

56 Maldwyn *Edwards, John Wesley and the Eighteenth Century* (London: Epworth Press, 1933). The other two volumes in the series were *After Wesley: A Study of the Social and Political Influence of Methodism in the Middle Period (1791–1849)* (1935) and *Methodism and England: A Study of Methodism in its Social and Political Aspects during the Period 1850—1932* (1943).

in 1965, two years after an initial report, *Conversations between the Church of England and the Methodist Church* (1963), had been published, and the ongoing ecumenical talks between the Church of England and the Methodist Church in Great Britain can be understood as a context of the series. Edwards's chapter in the first volume of this series follows a chapter by Herbert Butterfield on "England in the Eighteenth Century" dealing with the technological, economic, political, and cultural background of the eighteenth century in Britain. Butterfield's chapter dealt very little with the state of the Church of England in that century.[57] Edwards's narrative following this dealt with the following aspects of John Wesley's life as a foundation for the remainder of Methodist history.

MALDWYN EDWARDS, CHAPTER TITLED "JOHN WESLEY" IN *A HISTORY OF THE METHODIST CHURCH IN GREAT BRITAIN* (1965)

EpworthUpbringing including commentary on the ancestry of Samuel and Susanna Wesley and their commitments to Anglicanism including their sacramental theology and their commitment to "orthodox Arminian teaching"

OxfordSociety and **JWInfluences** considered together and with some reflections on the importance of Charterhouse for John Wesley. Edwards emphasized Wesley's readings in the Cambridge Platonists as well as such spiritual literature as Kempis, Jeremy Taylor and William Law.

GeorgiaPietists emphasizing Moravians as influences in Georgia

AldersgateExperience with no reference to Wesley's later doubts; Edwards pauses to refute Piette's catholicizing reading of Wesley's Aldersgate-Street experience.

FieldPreaching and the early development of lay preachers and conferences

Extraordinary emotional effects of the revival and **MethodistPersecution** including riots associated with this

ArminianVsCalvinist and other conflicts in the middle part of Wesley's career

---

57   Edwards, in *History of the Methodist Church in Great Britain*, 1–33.

MALDWYN EDWARDS, CHAPTER TITLED "JOHN WESLEY" IN
A HISTORY OF THE METHODIST CHURCH IN GREAT BRITAIN
(1965) (continued)

GrowthOfMethodism emphasizing specific regions of the country where Wesley focused his efforts (London, Bristol, Newcastle, Cornwall, and areas contiguous with them), the general absence of work among "the fashionable rich" and agricultural workers, and the eventual attraction of middle-class people to Methodism later in Wesley's career

An explanation of the appeal of Wesley's message, thus **WayOfSalvation** emphasizing his emphasis on divine love (rather than divine power) and the optimism of his doctrine of sanctification

An explanation of the success of Wesley's forms of organization especially focused on **MethodistPreachers**

A description of Methodist involvement in various social issues facing Britain at the time including discussions of **MethodistBenevolence** and **Opposition-ToSlavery**

Discussion of Wesley's provisions for the continuation of Methodism beyond his own life, focusing entirely on the structures he put in place in Britain

A discussion of the later years of John Wesley including his strained relationship with his wife, thus **JohnAndMary**

A discussion of the final days of John Wesley and his death (**JWDeath**), and then a concluding discussion of Wesley's character emphasizing his self-control, learning, charity, and tolerance for those who differed with him

Edwards's history was a very modest one: a narrative brief in scope that emphasized some of John Wesley's continuities with Anglican Christianity and placed a particular emphasis on the good that Methodists had accomplished with respect to the social issues prominent in the eighteenth century. He encoded a narrative of Methodism that fit the aspirations of British Methodism moving in the direction of unity with the Church of England.

A very different interpretation of John Wesley's life in relation to Methodism was offered by **Arthur Skevington Wood** (1916–93), an English Methodist minister and scholar who consistently identified himself with the Evangelical side of British Methodism. Wood had served as a circuit minister, as a frequent speaker at the Keswick Convention, as a British leader in the Billy Graham evangelistic crusades, and as principal of Cliff College from 1977 through 1983. His study of *The Burning Heart, John Wesley: Evangelist* (1967) offered a scholarly interpretation of Wesley's life emphasizing Wesley's work as an evangelist. Wood's book was deeply grounded in primary texts but also reflected the most recent Wesleyan scholarship of his day including works by Robert Monk, Albert C. Outler, John Walsh, and the German Lutheran scholar Martin Schmidt whose two-volume study of *John Wesley: A Theological Biography* had appeared in German in 1953 and 1966.[58]

Wood's narrative placed a great deal of emphasis on John Wesley's Puritan heritage and then on the crucial role of the Aldersgate-Street experience. Wood was aware that the Puritan tradition had continued within the Church of England as well as in Dissenting churches, and he saw Samuel and Susanna and John Wesley continuing to reflect Puritan emphases on discipline and on the initiative of divine grace in salvation. He saw John Wesley in particular as reverting to such Puritan practices as itinerant ministry and the exercise of lay preaching authorized outside of episcopal ordination, "where existing church order stood in his way, for he did not hesitate to set it aside."[59] With respect to the Aldersgate-Street experience, Wood respectfully considered modern interpreters who wanted to see John Wesley's 1725 conversion to religious seriousness as Wesley's primary religious "conversion." He rejected this idea, citing what he believed to be a "consensus of recent scholarly opinion" favoring "the traditional view" that Aldersgate was the great watershed moment in Wesley's career, and especially in his career as an evangelist.[60]

58 A. Skevington Wood, *The Burning Heart, John Wesley: Evangelist* (Exeter: Paternoster Press, 1967). Wood had access to the German edition of Martin Schmidt's *John Wesley* (Zürich and Frankfurt am Main: Gotthelf-Verlag, 1953–66) and to Robert C. Monk's *John Wesley: His Puritan Heritage: A Study of the Christian Life* (Nashville: Abingdon Press, 1966).

59 Wood, *Burning Heart*, 28.

60 Ibid., 59–69, quotations on p. 69.

As the subtitle of his work indicates, Wood's focus was on John Wesley's role as an evangelist, and Wood's narrative was structured around Wesley's evangelistic work, devoting considerable attention to the development of outdoor preaching, itinerant preaching, and the utilization of lay preachers and other lay assistants for evangelistic work. Consistent with this emphasis, Wood's book focused on what I have called code module **WesleyEvangelist** and gives the strong impression of Wesley's evangelistic work overshadowing his work in the cultivation of holiness; holiness appears as a crucial outcome of the primary work of evangelization. This can be seen in Wood's chapter on holiness. He acknowledged the importance of holiness as "the grand *depositum*" for early Methodism and acknowledged the Wesleyan teaching of a crisis experience of entire sanctification culminating the process of sanctification, in keeping with Keswick and Holiness understandings of entire sanctification. But Wood understood the message about complete holiness not as Wesley's primary goal but as a natural outgrowth of his evangelistic mission: "This intensive reiteration of the need to make progress was the best possible fellowship message for Wesley's converts."[61]

Wood placed huge emphasis on Wesley's preaching and preaching occasions, with a relatively brief discussion of classes and bands, and these are treated as "follow-up" to the work of evangelism.[62] So Wood did not see evangelism as one aspect among many of Wesley's interests or emphases; he depicted Wesley's evangelistic mission as Wesley's principal work. In this respect, Wood's narrative continued the strain of evangelistic interpretation of Wesley that had come to prominence in the late nineteenth century when Methodists, buoyed by their success in evangelism through the nineteenth century and by then engaging in polemics with Holiness teachers, began to take

---

61   Ibid., 269; Wood's chapter on holiness is on pp. 260–69.
62   Ibid, 186–95. He uses the term *follow-up* on p. 186. The index to Wood's work shows only two single-page references to bands and two single-page references to classes, contrasted with numerous references to preaching. The outline of the structure of Wood's book given in the text below shows several successive chapters on Wesley's preaching and his hearers.

evangelism itself rather than the cultivation of holiness as the principal mission of Methodism.

Also consistent with earlier Methodist historiography, Wood represented the Wesleyan movement as a direct result of divine guidance. His utilization of typical encoded modules can be represented as follows:

A. SKEVINGTON WOOD, *THE BURNING HEART* (1967)

EpworthUpbringing with emphasis on Samuel and Susanna Wesley's Puritan heritage (chapters 1–2)

OxfordSociety (chapters 2–3)

JWInfluences mentioning his reading of early Christian sources, and Catholic spiritual writers, with special emphasis on his study of Jeremy Taylor, William Law, and Thomas à Kempis (chapter 3)

GeorgiaPietists emphasizing the crucial role of Moravians (but not Lutheran Pietists) on Wesley extending beyond his time in Georgia (chapters 4–5)

AldersgateExperience as the crucial watershed in Wesley's life, his true conversion experience, and the ground of his evangelistic work (chapters 5–6)

MethodistPersecution including Wesley's early exclusion from preaching in Anglican parishes (chapter 7)

FieldPreaching and the extension of Wesley's ministries into **Wesley-Evangelist**, occupying several chapters of Wood's narrative (chapters 8–14)

MethodistPersecution focusing on opposition to Wesley's preaching on the part of Anglican leaders (chapter 15)

The testimony of Wesley's converts (chapter 16)

ClassesBands as "follow-up" to Wesley's evangelistic work (chapter 17)

Wesley's later life and his character as "an honourable man" (chapter 18)

An account of John Wesley's teachings including his belief in biblical authority (chapter 19) and several chapters on aspects of the **WayOfSalvation** including justification by grace through faith (chapter 20), original sin (chapter 21), regeneration (chapter 22), growth in holiness (chapter 23), entire sanctification (chapter 24). Wood also has a chapter in this section on Wesley's eschatology (chapter 25).

A. Skevington Wood thus encoded the identity of Methodism as a principally evangelistic society grounded in the heroic and divinely inspired evangelistic work of John Wesley. He offered a powerful and well-documented vision of Wesley and Wesleyanism with this focus on evangelism as reaching persons who were either not Christians or only nominally Christians, a vision that has so deeply influenced strands of modern Methodism that it seems almost a *datum*, a fact beyond dispute.

In 1974, American Methodists had a new textbook on their history authored by Garrett-Evangelical Professor **Frederick Abbott Norwood** (1914–95), *The Story of American Methodism* (1974).[63] Trained at Yale University, Norwood began serving as professor of church history at Garrett Theological Seminary in 1952. Norwood's text expresses the desire for a more inclusive narrative than Methodists had offered in the past, even if his book did not consistently succeed in offering such a narrative. It is the case that when he was writing in the late 1960s and the early 1970s, there were fewer editions of primary historical resources for American Methodism on the basis of which a more inclusive narrative might have been developed.[64] His book was designed to coincide with the 1976 bicentennial celebration of US independence. Although it appeared at the beginning of the period after Modernism, Norwood himself consistently reflected a modernist approach to historical study. The book was published by Abingdon Press, the primary publishing imprint of The United Methodist Church, and it stood through the end of the twentieth century as the standard textbook utilized in studies of the history of The United Methodist Church for ministerial candidates.

Norwood opened his book by observing the importance of United Brethren in Christ founder Phillip William Otterbein and Evangelical

---

63 Frederick A. Norwood, *The Story of American Methodism: A History of the United Methodists and Their Relations* (Nashville: Abingdon Press, 1974), 23–60.

64 Cf. the introduction, 19–20, where Norwood acknowledged that the diversity of American Methodism required that the subject must not be reduced to the history of The United Methodist Church. But Norwood's text overwhelmingly did so.

Association founder Jacob Albright in the history of The United Methodist Church in addition to the Wesleys, but his work then proceeded to four chapters giving a narrative focused almost exclusively on John Wesley, following conventional lines of Wesleyan narratives.[65] His general structure is as follows:

NORWOOD, CHAPTERS ON METHODIST ORIGINS IN *THE STORY OF AMERICAN METHODISM* (1974)
Chapter 1:
EpworthUpbringing
OxfordSociety
JWInfluences (specific early influences: Taylor, Kempis, Law)
GeorgiaPietists
AldersgateExperience and **WesleyDoubts** together
FieldPreaching
MethodistPersecution
Chapter 2:
ClassesBands
MethodistPreachers including the conferences of preachers, the building of preaching houses, the elaboration of circuits, and the allowance for women preachers in the 1760s and 70s
StillnessMeans
ArminianVsCalvinist
Chapter 3:
JWInfluences (more broadly elaborated)
WayOfSalvation including references to Charles Wesley's hymns as illustrating specific points in the "way of salvation"

---

65 Although it could be argued that Albright (b. 1759) should have come later in a chronological narrative, Otterbein (b. 1726) was closer to a contemporary of John and Charles Wesley and came from a significantly different cultural and ecclesiastical background as to warrant considering him as a parallel figure to John Wesley.

Chapter 4:

Distinctly Wesleyan understandings of ecclesiology, communal practices that developed in the Wesleyan movement, and progressive social efforts (including **MethodistBenevolence** and **OppositionToSlavery**) that grew out of the movement

In some respects, Norwood's narrative was more inclusive than previous ones. He did, for example, recognize the formal roles played by women as exhorters and preachers in the Wesleyan societies. His account of Wesley's theology (generally following Colin Williams's *John Wesley's Theology Today*, 1960) acknowledged multiple strands of influence of Christian traditions in Wesley's work. Norwood's narrative also acknowledged the social context of early Methodism with reference to the Industrial Revolution. His narrative of Wesley principally served his goal of describing the evolution of American Methodism, setting up a number of points in Wesley's experience (e.g., **OppositionToSlavery**) that would come to prominence in later American Methodism. Norwood's account of Wesley is in some ways more complex than earlier accounts, and in this respect it sets up his attempt to describe American Methodism—and especially The United Methodist Church—as a complex, modern entity growing from multiple and complexly interwoven sources.

ECUMENICAL INTERPRETATIONS OF THE WESLEYAN MOVEMENT

In roughly the same period, a trio of three scholars all working in the United States led a renaissance in Wesleyan studies, and each of these was influenced by involvement in the ecumenical movement: Australian Methodist Colin W. Williams, British Methodist Frank Baker, and American Methodist Albert C. Outler. Of these, only Baker produced a strictly narrative history, but the works of Williams and Outler as well as Baker developed the code module I have described as **Ecumenical-Wesley** that became so prominent in this period.

The vanguard of the ecumenical interpretation of the Wesleyan tradition in relation to the ecumenical movement was **Colin W. Williams** (1921–2000), an Australian Methodist theologian and ecumenist who spent most of his career in the United States, eventually serving as dean of Yale Divinity School (1969–79). Williams had been a delegate to the Second Assembly of the World Council of Churches in Evanston, Illinois in 1954 (he was serving as an assistant professor of theology at Garrett Biblical Institute in Evanston when the Assembly was held there) and then served as an adviser to the third Assembly of the World Council in New Delhi in 1961.

It was during this period of ecumenical involvement that Williams wrote what was to become a standard textbook for decades to come, *John Wesley's Theology Today* (1960). In the preface to this work, Williams noted that it was specifically in response to ecumenical dialogue that he developed this text.[66] His work displayed a multifaceted knowledge of Christian traditions in dialogue with which he placed John Wesley's theology—especially the Protestant traditions that had dominated the ecumenical movement prior to the Second Vatican Council. He saw Wesley's theology as a mediating theological outlook that reconciled many of the antinomies of the Reformation period (**EcumenicalWesley**), but he also understood Wesley's theology as offering a distinctive ecumenical gift in four specific emphases, namely, emphases on (1) salvation by faith as expressed in the "order of salvation" (the category from continental Lutheran and Reformed theology that Williams consistently utilized to describe Wesley's understanding of the "way of salvation"; code module **WayOfSalvation**), (2) the assurance of pardon as a distinctly Wesleyan note, (3) the quest of Christian holiness as an antidote to the typically Protestant focus on "justification by faith alone," and (4) Christian fellowship as

---

66 Colin W. Williams, *John Wesley's Theology Today* (Nashville: Abingdon Press, 1960), [5–10] (unnumbered in the 1993 reprint that I consulted).

a means of grace, especially as this was expressed in the Wesleyan use of voluntary societies. Williams utilized the term *ecclesiolae* as an ecumenical perspective on the Wesleyan classes, bands, and societies (his version of module **ClassesBands**). Williams's vision of John Wesley, then, was inspired by the ecumenical movement, which allowed Williams to see points of conjunction in Wesley's thought that others may have found problematic but which he saw as uniquely appropriate to contemporary ecumenical dialogue.

Williams's study included an appendix on John Wesley's ecclesiology in relation to that of the Church of England. The issue of John Wesley's relationship to the Church of England was taken up in a narrative form by British Methodist historian **Frank Baker** (1910–99), who had grown up in the Primitive Methodist Church, which had gone into union with other British Methodist groups in 1932 to form the Methodist Church of Great Britain. From 1960 until his retirement in 1980, Baker served as a professor of Wesleyan studies at Duke Divinity School, and in his early years at Duke he wrote an extensive (422 pages) and meticulously researched study of *John Wesley and the Church of England* (1970), which he offered directly in response to then-ongoing negotiations for unity between the Methodist Church of Great Britain and the Church of England. Baker, unlike Williams, was much more a historian than a theologian, and his Wesley research was grounded in years of study in Wesleyan texts and documents, many of which he had personally collected. His study of *John Wesley and the Church of England* detailed the many incremental steps by which the Wesleyan movement, though never formally separated from the Church of England in John Wesley's lifetime, found itself separate *de facto* (this was Baker's own expression) by the time of John Wesley's death in 1791.[67] Baker's ecumenical contribution in this work, then, was to show how a movement could become a separate church even when separation had not been the intent of the leaders (John and Charles Wesley) of that movement—indeed, had been explicitly forbidden by them.

---

67   Baker, *John Wesley and the Church of England.*

A third leader in the renaissance of Wesleyan studies in the second half of the twentieth century was **Albert C. Outler** (1908–89), who from 1951 served as a professor of systematic theology at Perkins School of Theology at Southern Methodist University in Dallas, Texas. Like Williams and Baker, Outler had also been formed by the ecumenical movement, and his ecumenical formation would strongly shape his vision of John Wesley's relevance for contemporary churches. Having written his Yale dissertation on Origen's use of the "rule of faith" (1938) under Robert Lowry Calhoun, Outler became involved in the work of the Faith and Order Commission of the World Council of Churches. He served as a Methodist representative to the third World Conference on Faith and Order held at Lund, Sweden in 1952, where he proposed an ecumenical study of "our common history as Christians." This would lead to the landmark ecumenical consensus document, "Scripture, Tradition, and traditions" that was adopted at the Montreal Plenary meeting of Faith and Order in 1963. At the same time as the Montreal meeting, Outler was serving as a Protestant observer at the Second Vatican Council.

In the 1960s Outler turned his attention to studies of John Wesley's theology, offering a volume of John Wesley's theological writings in the Library of Protestant Thought series in 1964.[68] In the early 1970s, he offered a series of lectures later published as a book titled *Theology in the Wesleyan Spirit*.[69] Outler's concern in this work was to understand John Wesley as a pivotal figure who held an eclectic vision of Christian faith, a unique vision drawn from Protestant, Catholic, and ancient Eastern Christian sources, a vision that Outler believed had become increasingly relevant as churches began to learn of the gifts of each other's traditions.[70] Whereas Williams had focused on

---

68 Albert C. Outler, ed., *John Wesley: A Representative Collection of His Writings* (New York: Oxford University Press, 1964).

69 The lectures were given as the Fondren Lectures at SMU in 1973. The book was *Theology in the Wesleyan Spirit* (Nashville: Tidings, 1975).

70 See Outler's essay on "A New Future for Wesley Studies: An Agenda for 'Phase III,'" in Meeks, ed., *Future of the Methodist Theological Traditions*, 38–40.

Wesley's Continental Protestant sources, Outler's involvement in dialogue with Orthodox and Catholic as well as Anglican leaders led him to recognize some significant sources of Wesley's thought in Catholic and early Eastern Christian traditions as well as the Anglican background of Wesley's thought.

Williams, Baker, and Outler were not the only ones of their generation to make critical contributions to Wesleyan studies in the later twentieth century: Lawrence Meredith, E. Dale Dunlap, William Cannon, John Deschner, Robert E. Chiles, Lycurgus M. Starkey, and others contributed to the growing literature on the Wesleys, especially on the Wesleys' theology.[71] I would call attention to one characteristic note of these interpreters of the Wesleys in the latter half of the twentieth century, especially of Williams and Outler: they took the Wesleys to be normative for Methodist life and thought in a way that deprecated to varying degrees the experience of Methodism in the nineteenth century.[72] Their nominal reasons for doing this were that the Wesleys were the fountainhead of the Methodist church traditions and that a corpus of John Wesley's works, in particular, served as established doctrine for historic Methodist communities. This may have been a matter of academic or even aesthetic taste, using the analogy of a preference for Baroque music over that of the Romantic period, but their rediscovery of the Wesleys' theological roots gave the Wesleys a kind of "classical" status within the Methodist church traditions from which later Methodist developments such as camp-meeting revivalism

---

71 Lawrence Meredith, "Essential Doctrine in the Theology of John Wesley with Special Attention to the Methodist Standards of Doctrine" (PhD dissertation, Harvard University, 1962); E. Dale Dunlap, "Methodist Theology in Great Britain in the Nineteenth Century: With Special Reference to the Theology of Adam Clarke, Richard Watson, and William Burt Pope" (PhD dissertation, Yale University, 1956; repr. ed., Ann Arbor, MI: University Microfilms International); William R. Cannon, *The Theology of John Wesley, with Special reference to the Doctrine of Justification* (Nashville and New York: Abingdon-Cokesbury Press, 1946); John Deschner, *Wesley's Christology: An Interpretation*, rev. ed. (Dallas: Southern Methodist University Press, 1985); Robert E. Chiles, *Theological Transition in American Methodism, 1790–1935* (New York and Nashville: Abingdon Press, 1965); Lycurgus M. Starkey, *The Work of the Holy Spirit: A Study in Wesleyan Theology* (New York: Abingdon Press, 1962).

72 I say "to varying degrees," because although I sensed this deprecation of the nineteenth-century Methodist experience very strongly in Outler, I never sensed it so strongly in Baker, though Baker did take John and Charles Wesley as being normative for Methodist life and thought.

or the elaboration of Methodist institutional structures in the nineteenth century were seen as signs of declension from the original Wesleyan pattern.

CONCLUSION

Looking back over the period of Methodist Modernism surveyed in this chapter, we can see four consistent concerns that informed the ways in which Methodist re-traditioned and encoded the Wesleyan heritage in the very late nineteenth and early twentieth centuries. The first is the sense of religious experience, or *personal* religious experience, as a critical contribution of Methodism and a central idea in Methodist identity. On the positive side, this was the ground of Umphrey Lee's claims about Methodism as an expression of modern Christian trends and of Herbert Brook Workman's idea that religious experience was the general ground on which all other distinctively Methodist ideas were based. It came to be tied up with understandings of Aldersgate. George Jackson had claimed that one of the signs of the "new Methodism" in his age was that it allowed that a person might know their sins forgiven through a particular religious experience, though the Methodists no longer insisted on such an experience. Buckley, reflecting his own ambiguity towards the Aldersgate experience, would refer to it as Wesley's "conversion, in the technical term."[73]

On the negative side, a similar concern appears in the 1938 celebration of the bicentennial of Aldersgate, with its repeated calls for Methodists to "rekindle" the spirit of Aldersgate, but with an underlying sense that this was a nostalgic look to a bygone era of Methodist experience. This same attitude toward religious experience might be seen as underlying James Buckley's depiction of Methodist history, a depiction far less confident in the immediacy of divine activity than portrayals of Methodist history in the past. Methodists continued to recognize religious experience as a distinct contribution of their

---

73   Buckley, *History of the Methodists in the United States* (1896), 93.

church tradition, but it had become a much more generalized sense of "religious experience," and not at all the very specific sense of specific experiences ("awakening" to an awareness of one's need for God, "assurance" of the pardon of one's sins) that Methodists had confidently proclaimed as needed by all people in the past. Aldersgate, then, was being reinterpreted as a sign of the general human experience of the divine rather than the distinctive experience it had represented in earlier Methodists' telling of their own story.

A second theme that emerged strongly in the period of Methodist Modernism was the openness of Methodists to new ways of interpreting the Scriptures, especially in the light of modern biblical criticism. Methodist doctrinal statements had not historically adopted the language of "inerrancy" or "infallibility" that were popular in the Fundamentalist movement, and the historic Methodist tendency toward an optimistic, postmillennial interpretation of the future of humanity stood in tension with the premillennialism that had become popular in US Evangelicalism in the early twentieth century. Thus George Jackson described the "new Methodism" as open to new ways of reading the Scripture, and the liberal American Methodist theologian Harris Franklin Rall could cite Wesley against premillennialism.[74]

A third theme that emerged in this period was the Methodist concern to ground modern ministries to the poor in their understanding of John Wesley's work, what I have described as module **SocialDysfunction**. Thus Jackson concluded his lectures on the "new Methodism" by appealing to the work of Hugh Price Hughes, who himself had developed inner-city missions based on his understanding of Wesley's ministries with the poor. In the same way, Wearmouth responded to criticisms of Methodism by external historians by pointing

---

74 Harris Franklin Rall, *Modern Premillennialism and the Christian Hope* (New York and Cincinnati: Abingdon Press, 1920), 101–2 (on Bengel) and 249–50 (on Wesley's following Bengel's bimillennial interpretation of Revelation 20), and more generally 245–53, which is an appendix addressing the question, "Was John Wesley a Premillennialist?" where Rall laid out the general Methodist resistance to premillennialism and Wesley's and later Methodists' progressive stance towards societal improvement, grounded in Methodist postmillennialism, although Rall did not utilize that term. The essay *Was John Wesley a Premillennialist?* was subsequently published separately (Toronto: Methodist Book & Publishing House, 1921; The Ryerson Essays, no. 1).

to Wesley's engagement with the poor and the early Methodist societies' engagement with the poor in the Industrial Revolution (module **MinistryWithPoor**). Robert Wearmouth's work was directed against social-scientific critics of the Wesleyan movement, and William Warren Sweet also called attention to the Industrial Revolution as the social context of early Methodist work.

A fourth theme that emerged in the Modernist period was that of Wesley's relevance for Methodist church unions and for engagement with Christians of other traditions (module **EcumenicalWesley**). In a sense this carried on the discussion of Methodist churches in relation to Anglicanism that had become prominent in the period of Methodist ascendancy, but in the work of Herbert Brook Workman it had become a broader quest to understand *The Place of Methodism in the Catholic Church*. Large-scale Methodist unions in Britain (1929–32) and in the United States (1939) appealed to Wesley as the ground of the original unity of the Methodist movement, and it was hoped that by reuniting the divided streams of the Methodist family, they could recover the vitality of the early Methodist movement. As we have seen in the previous section, the work of Williams, Baker, and Outler all contributed to the understanding of Wesley's relevance to ecumenical issues that were contemporary in their age.

WESLEYAN NARRATIVES BEYOND MODERNISM

LATE TWENTIETH AND EARLY TWENTY-FIRST CENTURIES

This chapter deals with the evolution of the Wesleyan narratives beyond Modernism in the late twentieth and early twenty-first centuries. The expression *beyond Modernism* signals my reluctance to use terms such as *Postmodernism* and *postmodernist* to refer to the evolution of Wesleyan narratives, not only because these terms have proven very difficult to define, but especially because they involve defining our own contemporary cultural predicament, always dangerous for historians. More important, *Postmodernism* or *postmodernist* may not relate as well to Methodist cultures in this period as they do to broader cultural trends. However, Methodist cultures also reflected a move beyond Modernism from the 1970s forward, even if it's difficult to identify their cultural shifts straightforwardly with Postmodernism.[1]

---

1 I want to be clear here that in speaking of a period "beyond Modernism," I mean to denote an age of cultural reactions against the Modernism that flourished in the early twentieth century, answering to what some (but not all, by far) interpreters have called "postmodernist" interpretations of cultures. I do not mean to suggest that the cultures of the late twentieth century have been "postmodern" in the sense of a rejection of modernity, the whole complex of cultural, technological, and scientific developments that have occurred since the seventeenth century in Western culture. I am not convinced that we are past the period of "modernity" in this broader sense.

What I want to describe in this chapter is a range of Wesleyan narratives that emphasize the distinctive nature of this tradition, perhaps parallel to "postmodernist" interpretations of cultures that have prevailed since the late 1960s or the early 1970s, or at least, interpretations that have emphasized the particularities of cultures and traditions in contrast to both traditional and modernist claims about broader cultural unities.[2] And yet, what I will describe as interpretations of the Wesleyan tradition "beyond Modernism" originally grew out of the engagement of Methodists in the ecumenical movement and its own quest to find a core of Christian tradition shared between denominational traditions. Wesleyan narratives in this period tend to paint complex pictures of the early Wesleyan movement, commensurate with the complex communities that Wesleyan churches had become by the late twentieth century.

The period from the late 1960s to the present has seen some consistent trends in Methodist church life. After the American Methodist union in 1968 that resulted in The United Methodist Church, the ensuing period witnessed spectacular ecumenical failures in which Methodist bodies were engaged. A proposed Methodist-Anglican union that had been discussed in the United Kingdom from 1955 was approved by the British Methodist Church but failed by a very close vote to gain the required level of support in one of the houses of the Church of England's General Synod of 1972. The roughly coeval American Methodist engagement with the Consultations on Church Union led to approval by the larger Methodist bodies in the United States but failed in the late 1990s to gain the necessary support from other church bodies that would have led to the formation of a "Church of Christ Uniting" in the United States. The failure of these large-scale ecumenical ventures left Methodist church communities contemplating their own futures independent of other denominational groups.

The period from the mid-1960s and forward has also seen the

---

2   Cf. Steven Connor's account of Postmodernism in his study of *Postmodernist Culture: An Introduction to Theories of the Contemporary* (Oxford: Basil Blackwell, 1989), esp. 3–23.

devolution of many of the global branches of British and American Methodist churches into independent Methodist denominations, which often maintain ties with their parent churches but function as independent and indigenous church structures. Perhaps most important for the Methodist psyche in this period, the older Methodist churches of Britain and the United States began to see significant losses of membership, professions of faith, and attendance at church services. These can be explained as resulting from an increasingly secular cultural outlook in both places and perhaps as a result of the passing of an older culture in both places that valued church membership even on the part of nominal church members.[3] But the declines were especially troubling for Methodists internally, since through their history Methodists had kept meticulous accounts of membership and attendance and had pointed to increasing membership in the nineteenth century and the early twentieth century as a sign of the divine approval of their movement.

By the 1970s and 1980s a new generation of scholars had arisen, especially in the United States, from both Methodist and Wesleyan-Holiness church traditions, offering a wide range of DPhil or PhD dissertations, books, and articles exploring Wesleyan theology.[4] The activities of these scholars led to the ongoing existence of the Wesleyan Studies Unit of the American Academy of Religion (since 1983) and a renewed focus on Wesleyan studies in the Oxford Institute of Methodist Theological Studies and in the Wesleyan Theological Society since the 1970s. Parallel to previous chapters, this chapter does not attempt to give a broad or comprehensive survey of Wesleyan scholarship in this period, but it focuses on narratives of Wesleyan origin written during the period that describe the identity of existing

---

3   I have documented some of these phenomena in *The Sky Is Falling, the Church Is Dying, and Other False Alarms* (Nashville: Abingdon Press, 2015), especially chap. 2, "Facts," 17–35.

4   Some of this literature is summarized in my article, "Is It Just Nostalgia? The Renewal of Wesleyan Studies," *Christian Century* 107:13 (18 April 1990): 396–98. The work of David Lowes Watson and Richard P. Heitzenrater served as a bridge between the generation of Williams, Outler, and Baker (with whom Heitzenrater and Watson studied at Duke) and the latter generation (including myself) described in this paragraph.

Wesleyan and Methodist church communities. As with previous chapters, the narratives considered here may be either scholarly or more popular narratives.

CONNECTING HOLINESS AND PENTECOSTAL COMMUNITIES TO THE WESLEYAN NARRATIVE

Williams, Baker, and Outler, discussed in the previous chapter, were Methodist leaders who wrote from the perspective of Methodists deeply involved in the ecumenical movement. As influential as they were for rekindling interest in the Wesleyan theological tradition, the works of Williams and Outler were primarily theological and not primarily narrative, though their interests in Wesley's reflection of highly varied strains of Christian traditions contributed to reshaping the Wesleyan narrative as a way of coding the identities of Wesleyan communities. But other writers and other church communities began to offer narratives that reflected a concern for broader inclusion than earlier Wesleyan narratives had offered. These late twentieth-century narratives have paid attention to roles of women, ethnic-minority persons and communities, the role of popular religion and religious experience, and the communities that have grown from older Wesleyan communities, including Christian communities of Holiness and Pentecostal traditions. They have often broken the direct linkage between the narrative of the early Wesleyan revival and the later development of Wesleyan churches that earlier narratives had maintained. The ecumenical movement and the work of such writers as Colin Williams, Frank Baker, and Albert C. Outler brought John Wesley to the attention of Christians outside of Methodist churches, and some Holiness and Pentecostal leaders began to understand their own traditions in broader contexts as growing from multiple earlier streams of Christian tradition, including the traditions of the Wesleys and of Methodist churches.

Holiness churches had grown from Wesleyan churches and continued to claim Wesleyan origins, as the chapter on Wesleyan narratives in an age of Methodist ascendancy has shown. Some Pentecostal leaders in the period beyond Modernism tried to link Pentecostalism to its deeper roots in Christian heritage and tradition, including their roots in the Wesleyan movement, parallel to the ways in which Wesleyan interpreters at the same time were attempting to root the culture of Wesleyan communities in older Christian traditions. In contrast to earlier streams of Pentecostal exceptionalism that maintained that earlier Christian leaders (including John Wesley) had not really experienced the baptism of the Holy Spirit,[5] a number of Pentecostal leaders including David du Plessis (d. 1987), Jerry L. Sandidge (d. 1992), and Cecil M. Robeck Jr., were, and in the case of Robeck continue to be, directly involved in ecumenical dialogues.[6] At the same time, the expansion of the Pentecostal movement into older churches during the charismatic movement brought local Pentecostal leaders into direct contact with leaders of other Christian communities. A very important development in scholarship came in 1998 when the Society for Pentecostal Studies began to meet regularly with the Wesleyan Theological Society sponsored by the Christian Holiness Association. These meetings have afforded Pentecostal and Holiness scholars occasions to meet with each other to pursue their common histories, and the ecumenical connections and deeper roots of these movements—including their roots in the Wesleyan movement—have often been explored.

But it is not only scholars who have sought to connect Pentecostal and Holiness movements to the broader Christian heritage via their Wesleyan roots. In the context of the charismatic movement, to take a specific example, the Pentecostal and charismatic leader **James**

---

5   Charles F. Parham, for example, once wrote, "Do you mean to say that John Wesley and others since, did not have this Baptism? Exactly; he and many since have enjoyed a mighty anointing that abideth, and spoke like the holy men of old as they were moved by the Holy Ghost but the power of this Pentecostal Baptism of the Holy Spirit is a different thing entirely." In Charles F. Parham, *A Voice Crying in the Wilderness*, 4th ed. 1984 (1901, Charleston, SC: privately published), 32.

6   Cecil M. Robeck Jr., gives an account of some of their work in dialogue with Catholicism in his article, "When Being a 'Martyr' Is Not Enough: Catholics and Pentecostals," in *Pneuma: Journal of the Society for Pentecostal Studies* 21:1 (Spring 1999), 3–10.

Gordon Lindsay (1906–73) produced around 1972 a series of popular profiles of historic Christian leaders whom he understood to be precursors of the Pentecostal movement under the title *Men Who Changed the World*. One of these pamphlets gives a narrative of the life of John Wesley.[7] Lindsay seems to have read a number of older accounts of John Wesley's life and had visited Wesley's house and Chapel on City Road in London.[8] Lindsay's work seems formulaic for the most part and repeats a good deal of the code modules covered by earlier histories. It does not begin with a description of the background or contexts of John Wesley's ministries but includes at least brief versions of these modules:

LINDSAY, *JOHN WESLEY* (CA. 1972)
EpworthUpbringing (including an account of John Wesley's miraculous deliverance in the Epworth Rectory fire)
GeorgiaPietists
AldersgateExperience including an account of the Wesleys' subsequent (January 1, 1739) ecstatic religious experience
FieldPreaching
ClassesBands following a version of **SocialDysfunction** emphasizing the corruptions of English society as setting the need for such societies
JohnAndMary
MethodistPersecution including an account of the Wednesbury mob
ArminianVsCalvinist
JWDeath

Two things stand out in Lindsay's account of Wesley. In the first

---

7   Gordon Lindsay, "John Wesley and William Carey," vol. 4 of *Men Who Changed the World* (Dallas: Christ for the Nations, ca. 1972). I am indebted to the research of an SMU graduate student, David Luckey, whose work on Gordon Lindsay provided valuable background for this section.
8   Lindsay describes his visit to the City Road house on p. 27.

place, *he reflected the earlier sense of divine providence guiding Wesley's life* that had been such a feature of earlier biographies but which had been seriously weakened in more academic Methodist accounts of Wesley from the late 1800s, roughly from the time of James M. Buckley's history of 1896. "Protestantism," just to give one typical example of Lindsay's perspective, "owes an enormous debt to Wesley, as an instrument in the hands of God."[9]

Consistent with this, the second matter that stands out in Lindsay's account is *his emphasis on Wesley's belief in the supernatural, especially miracles including miraculous healing.* He added an entire section on this topic and vividly recounted Wesley's spiritual experiences.[10] For example, Lindsay called attention to the Wesleys' ecstatic experience of January 1, 1739, at a joint Moravian/Anglican love feast at Fetter Lane.[11] John Wesley described this experience in his *Journal*, "About three in the morning, as we were continuing instant in prayer, the power of God came mightily upon us, insomuch that many cried out for exceeding joy, and many fell to the ground."[12]

Gordon Lindsay understood Wesley, along with Francis of Assisi and Martin Luther and a host of other men, as precursors of the Pentecostal and charismatic movements. He had probably read earlier Methodist accounts of the narrative of Wesleyan origins with their strong sense of divine guidance leading the Wesleys and the early Methodist movement, and he emphasized vivid religious experiences and miracles, especially healing, in the Wesleyan narrative. Lindsay himself was associated with healing ministries: his earlier publication had been *The Voice of Healing.* He thus reshaped the Wesleyan

---

9   Ibid., 3.

10   Ibid., section 11, 23–25.

11   This was 1738/39, and January 1 was not the civil or ecclesiastical New Year in the United Kingdom prior to 1752; but Moravians at this point, following Continental customs, probably did reckon January 1 to be the New Year.

12   Wesley, *The Works of John Wesley: Journals and Diaries*, vol. 19, ed. Heitzenrater and Ward, 29; cf. Lindsay, 9. The company went on to pray the medieval *Te Deum Laudamus* from the Prayer Book ritual for daily Morning Prayer, though Lindsay did not note this detail and perhaps did not recognize the *Te Deum* and its place in the liturgical tradition.

narrative in such a way that it offered an encoded clue to Pentecostal and charismatic identity, parallel to the ways in which the narrative had been utilized as a way of encoding Methodist identities. His pamphlets on Wesley and other earlier Christian leaders reflected—they may have inaugurated—a particular strand of Pentecostal culture that sees Pentecostalism as continuous with earlier charismatic expressions of Christian faith.[13]

A very different and creative approach to connecting a particular Holiness tradition to its Wesley roots and its deeper roots in Christian traditions is offered by **Stan Ingersol** in *Nazarene Roots: Pastors, Prophets, Revivalists, and Reformers* (2009).[14] Rather than beginning with a single Church of the Nazarene founder, such as Phineas F. Bresee, or with John Wesley, the book begins with a series of biographical sketches of pre-Methodist Christian saints and leaders including Ignatius of Antioch, Augustine, Luther, and Spener, whom Ingersol understands as precursors of Holiness teachings.[15] He then offers a chapter on "A Methodist Heritage" where he discusses Charles Wesley, John Wesley, and the evolution of the Wesleyan tradition after the Wesleys; then he writes about Francis Asbury and the development of American Methodism and follows these with a sequence of American Methodist and Holiness teachers.[16]

Ingersol's account of the Methodist heritage of the Church of the Nazarene begins with a quotation from Nazarene founder Phineas F. Bresee:

> We feel ourselves a part of that body of believers raised up to
> spread sanctified holiness over these lands, and thus that we

---

13 Cf. Eddie Hyatt, *2000 Years of Charismatic Christianity: A 21st Century Look at Church History from a Pentecostal, Charismatic Perspective* (Dallas: Hyatt International Ministries, 1998). See the contrasting quotation from Parham's *A Voice Crying in the Wilderness* cited in note 5 in this chapter above. The material cited from Aimee Semple McPherson in the first chapter, however, might trend more in the direction that Lindsay took.

14 Stan Ingersol, *Nazarene Roots: Pastors, Prophets, Revivalists, and Reformers* (Kansas City: Stan Ingersol and the Beacon Hill Press, 2009).

15 Ibid., 17–44.

16 Ibid., 45–80.

are a part of that company who are the real successors of John Wesley and the early Methodists.[17]

Ingersol begins his narrative of Methodist roots with Charles rather than John Wesley. He describes the Wesley family in relation, first, to Charles (code module **EpworthUpbringing**), and credits Charles Wesley as the originator of the Oxford "Holy Club" (thus code module **OxfordSociety**). Ingersol also discusses the Georgia venture including the Wesleys' encounter with Moravians in his narrative of Charles Wesley (code module **GeorgiaPietists**), and narrates Charles's conversion experience of May 21, 1738, following this (anticipating code module **AldersgateExperience**). The remainder of his narrative of Charles Wesley focuses on Charles's poetic contributions (**CWPoetry**).[18]

Ingersol's section on John Wesley connects John Wesley as well as Charles to the narrative of **EpworthUpbringing**, discusses some of the devotional and theological literature that John Wesley had studied (code module **JWInfluences**), and then describes John Wesley's role in leading the Oxford society (**OxfordSociety**). Having mentioned John's sojourn in Georgia in the previous section on Charles, Ingersol gives only a brief account of John Wesley's Aldersgate-Street experience, emphasizing the assurance of pardon that John experienced there (code module **AldersgateExperience**). He mentions John's itinerant preaching (code module **FieldPreaching**) and organization of small groups (code module **ClassesBands**), then focuses on John Wesley's consistent priority for ministries with the poor (code module **MinistryWithPoor**). He described John Wesley's understanding of the "way of salvation," focusing on Wesley's teaching on entire sanctification as a precedent for Holiness (including Nazarene) teachings (code module **WayOfSalvation**).[19]

Ingersol's account of the origins of the Church of the Nazarene

---

17 Bresee, in the *Nazarene Messenger* (July 15, 1909), 7; in Ingersol, *Pastors, Prophets, Revivalists, and Reformers*, 45.

18 Ibid., 47–49.

19 Ibid., 50–54.

itself does not focus on a single founder such as Phineas F. Bresee, as many traditional accounts had done. Instead, Ingersol offers profiles of Bresee along with other early Nazarene leaders.[20] He thus paints a complex picture of Nazarene origins and the continuing history of the Church of the Nazarene that allows him to show a great degree of inclusion including German Pietist forerunners, narratives of women preachers, African American Methodist and Holiness leaders, German-speaking Wesleyan groups, and Spanish-speaking Nazarene work. And even if more cautious than earlier narratives, Ingersol speaks directly of God's work in the history and continuing heritage of the Wesleyan and Holiness movements, as many Wesleyan narratives before the period of Modernism had done.[21]

RETELLING WESLEYAN NARRATIVES IN THE LATE TWENTIETH CENTURY

Near the end of the twentieth century, scholars of the Wesleyan movement began to produce single-volume biographies of John Wesley disconnected from a longer narrative of Methodist history. At the same time, some accounts of American Methodist history appeared with little reference to John Wesley.[22] The shift in genre is important in both respects. It suggests that Methodist scholars, at least, have begun to move away from the notion of a connected narrative that begins with Wesley as the foundational narrative for Wesleyan communities.

The tercentennial (tercentenary) of the birth of John Wesley in 2003 spurred the production of books on his life. For example, in

---

20 Ibid., 81–114.

21 For example, "By God's grace, great things can flow from small origins" (ibid., 47).

22 I have noted in the previous chapter that the three-volume series on *The History of American Methodism* began with only a cursory glance at the Methodist culture inherited from Britain and Ireland by Methodists in the United States. Similarly, Charles W. Ferguson's *Organizing to Beat the Devil: Methodists and the Making of America* (Garden City, NY: Doubleday, 1971). As discussed below, *The Methodist Experience in America*, vol. 1: *A History* by Russell E. Richey, Kenneth E. Rowe, and Jean Miller Schmidt (Nashville: Abingdon Press, 2010) also presupposed but did not explicitly deal with the Wesley narrative, acknowledging the previously published biography by Richard P. Heitzenrater, *Wesley and the People Called Methodists*.

the twenty-six years between 1989 and 2015,[23] the following nine single-volume biographies of John Wesley appeared from different publishers (in chronological order here):

Henry D. Rack, *Reasonable Enthusiast: John Wesley and the Rise of Methodism* (1989, with revised editions in 1993 and 2002)[24]

Barrie Tabraham, *The Making of Methodism* (1995, revised editions in 2009 and 2010)[25]

Richard P. Heitzenrater, *Wesley and the People Called Methodists* (1995, second edition in 2013)

Kenneth J. Collins, *A Real Christian: The Life of John Wesley* (1999)[26]

Ronald H. Stone, *John Wesley's Life and Ethics* (2001)[27]

John Munsey Turner, *John Wesley: The Evangelical Revival and the Rise of Methodism in England* (2002)[28]

Roy Hattersley, *The Life of John Wesley: A Brand from the Burning* (2003)[29]

Stephen Tomkins, *John Wesley: A Biography* (2003)[30]

Timothy J. Crutcher, *John Wesley: His Life and Thought* (2015)[31]

These texts did not all attempt to tell a narrative of Wesley's life as a way of coding Methodist identity, but the four that have either "Methodism" or "Methodists" in their subtitles (works by Rack, Tabraham, Heitzenrater, and Turner) do connect their narratives with

---

23 I might mention here works in 1978–79 by Robert G. Tuttle Jr., and Stanley Edward Ayling as precursors to this sequence of studies leading up to the tercentennial of the birth of the Wesleys. Tuttle's *John Wesley: His Life and Theology* (1978) offered a narrative of John Wesley's spiritual development and is mentioned in the conclusion to this book. Ayling's *John Wesley* (Cleveland and New York: William Collins, 1979) was principally a biography, not connected directly to a narrative construal of Methodist identity as others had been.

24 Rack, *Reasonable Enthusiast.*

25 Barrie Tabraham, *The Making of Methodism*, Exploring Methodism series (Peterborough: Epworth Press, 1995, revised in 2009 and 2010).

26 Kenneth J. Collins, *A Real Christian: The Life of John Wesley* (Nashville: Abingdon Press, 1999).

27 Ronald H. Stone, *John Wesley's Life and Ethics* (Nashville: Abingdon Press, 2001).

28 John Munsey Turner, *John Wesley: The Evangelical Revival and the Rise of Methodism in England* (Peterborough: Epworth Press, 2002).

29 Roy Hattersley, *The Life of John Wesley: A Brand from the Burning* (New York: Doubleday, 2003).

30 Stephen Tomkins, *John Wesley: A Biography* (Grand Rapids: Eerdmans, 2003).

31 Timothy J. Crutcher, *John Wesley: His Life and Thought* (Kansas City: Beacon Hill Press, 2015).

the development of Methodism, and I will focus on them. These four works were written by historians connected to Methodist churches. They depict early Methodism as a complex phenomenon, hinting at the complex communities that Methodist churches had become by their time.

The first in this group is **Henry D. Rack**'s *Reasonable Enthusiast: John Wesley and the Rise of Methodism.*[32] Rack has served as lecturer in ecclesiastical history at the University of Manchester and also as a minister in the British Methodist Church. His biography of John Wesley in many respects seeks to rescue Wesley from many of the impressions of Wesley traditionally favored by Methodists. The subtitle of his book reveals that he does in fact mean to narrate Wesley's life in relationship to the evolution of the eighteenth-century Methodist movement.

Rack's biography resists the temptation to identify Wesley with any one of the many intersecting cultural and ecclesiastical outlooks of Wesley's age. In fact, the title of the book indicates the cultural paradox in which he placed Wesley, at the intersection of the Enlightenment ("reasonable") and flourishing movements for a "religion of the heart" ("enthusiast"). Rack expressed concern about

> laying too much stress on the books Wesley read and their original religious pedigree and meaning. Too many analyses of Wesley's experience and theology have proceeded in this bookish way. It is true that the books mentioned did influence him, some of them (even the mystics) long after his conversion. But he read and abridged them very selectively and built them into patterns of his own.[33]

Rack's narrative, then, emphasizes the complex cultural and social worlds in which Wesley lived and in which early Methodism arose, and Wesley's complex interactions with these worlds.

Rack's assessment of the state of the Church of England in

---

32   Rack, *Reasonable Enthusiast.*
33   Ibid., 97.

Wesley's time avoids the pitfalls of traditional Methodist versions of **AnglicanDeclension**, though it is not quite what I have called **AnglicanVitality**.[34] Rack's biography cites J. C. D. Clark's *English Society, 1688–1832*, the work that set in motion more recent assessments of the vitality of the eighteenth-century Church of England, but other works that elaborated this theme were not yet available.[35] Rack's sense of the eighteenth-century Church of England anticipated some of these subsequent works by recognizing the ways in which Anglican clergy and bishops were responding to the crises of their times, including the Industrial Revolution.

Rack paints a nuanced picture of Wesley's responses to the social situation of his time. Responding to the critique that Wesley's sermon, "The Use of Money" could have encouraged *laissez-faire* economic attitudes, Rack notes Wesley's strictures on how money was to be properly earned:

> In all this it seems clear that Wesley is not really encouraging the ruthless, competitive entrepreneur but the small manufacturer and tradesman with limited horizons and rather old-fashioned ways. Moreover, he is to aim primarily at providing for his family and dependents.[36]

Rack's biography is full of nuanced historical judgments like this that stand in contrast to the exaggerations of much conventional Wesley literature, both of Wesley's religious advocates and of his social-scientific critics.

Rack's resistance to conventional Methodist historiography led him to write a history that did not follow a sequence of the typical code modules I have described above, and he gave different nuances to those elements that he did utilize. The following table, then, shows

---

34 Ibid., 10–33.

35 The work of Walsh, Haydon, and Taylor, *The Church of England, c. 1689–c. 1833* was published in 1993 and William Gibson's *The Church of England, 1688–1832* in 2001.

36 Rack, *Reasonable Enthusiast,* 367.

some of the segments answering to typical modules of the narrative of Wesleyan origins, with some notes on Rack's distinctive contributions.

RACK, *REASONABLE ENTHUSIAST* (1989, 1993, 2002)
AnglicanVitality (leaning more in that direction than **AnglicanDeclension**)
SocialDysfunction[37] and cultural trends in Wesley's age
EpworthUpbringing[38]
OxfordSociety[39] with **JWInfluences**[40]
GeorgiaPietists (both Moravians and Salzburgers)[41]
AldersgateExperience and **WesleyDoubts** together with a nuanced account of what "conversion" could have meant in Wesley's context.[42]
[Rack places a significant break in the narrative at 1738]
FieldPreaching with an accounting of convulsions and other supernatural phenomena accompanying the Revival[43]
ArminianVsCalvinist at particular points in the narrative[44]
StillnessMeans[45]
MethodistPreachers[46]
ClassesBands[47]

---

37 Ibid., 1–10.
38 Ibid., 45–60.
39 Ibid., 61–81.
40 Ibid., 81–106.
41 Ibid., 107–36 on the Georgia mission in general and 120–24 on the influences of Moravians and Salzburger Pietists in particular.
42 Ibid., 137–57, with Rack's extended discussion of the possible meanings of "conversion" in regard to the Aldersgate-Street experience specifically, 145–57.
43 Ibid., 191–94 on Wesley's first outdoor preaching and 194–197 on the convulsions and other supernatural phenomena in the revival.
44 Ibid., 197–202 (early relations with Whitefield and other Calvinists); 282–91 (relationships with Calvinists in the period up to 1760); 450–61 (controversies following the Minutes of 1770).
45 Ibid., 202–7.
46 Ibid., 207–12 on Wesley's use of lay preachers; 227–50 on the organization of the conference and other structures of the movement under John Wesleys leadership.
47 Ibid., 212–13.

RACK, *REASONABLE ENTHUSIAST* (1989, 1993, 2002) (continued)

CWPoetry[48]

JohnAndMary[49]

MethodistPersecution emphasizing the "xenophobia" that accompanied early Methodism as a new and little understood religious movement[50]

A distinctive segment or module indicating Wesley's tensions with Anglicanism in the years prior to 1760[51]

DoctrinalLiberality though Rack emphasizes evidence of Wesley's anti-Catholicism and his failure to acknowledge "that one man's 'opinion' was another man's 'essential.'"[52]

[Rack places a significant break in the narrative at 1760.]

Tensions1760s[53]

WesleyCommunicator: Rack introduces a module on Wesley as "propagandist and cultural mediator."[54]

MethodistBenevolence[55]

A discussion of Wesley's political views[56]

WayOfSalvation[57]

A segment or module on the importance of religious experiences and the supernatural in Wesley's work and thought[58]

---

48 Ibid., 251–57.

49 Ibid., 257–69.

50 Ibid., 270–81; Rack acknowledges his indebtedness to John Walsh's article, "Methodism and the Mob" in *Studies in Church History* 8 (1977), 213–27.

51 Ibid., 291–305; here Rack acknowledges his indebtedness to Baker's *John Wesley and the Church of England* in showing early instances of Wesley's growing distance from structures and leaders of the national Church.

52 Ibid., 305–13; the quotation is on 312.

53 Ibid., 333–42.

54 Ibid., 343–60.

55 Ibid., 360–70.

56 Ibid., 370–80.

57 Ibid., 381–409.

58 Ibid., 420–36.

RACK, *REASONABLE ENTHUSIAST* (1989, 1993, 2002) (continued)
AmericanOrdinations emphasizing Wesley's practical motivations rather than theological or ecclesiastic precedents[59]
JWDeath[60]

Of the distinctive segments of Rack's biography, I would especially note his emphasis on Wesley's roles as communicator and educator.[61] There has been a growing recognition that Wesley and Whitefield and other Evangelical leaders had employed very current media for communications such as broadsheets and letters published in newspapers and magazines to disseminate their views.[62] In this way Rack's biography has anticipated what I describe as John Wesley's role as a culture coder, and because Heitzenrater has similar material (see below), I identify this as a distinctive code module, **WesleyCommunicator**.

Although it was designed for a different readership than Rack's biography, **Barrie Tabraham**'s *The Making of Methodism* is as concerned as Rack and other contemporary authors to make sense of the narrative of early Methodism within the historical context of eighteenth-century Britain and within the context of complex contemporary Wesleyan/Methodist churches. Tabraham has served as a teacher in secondary schools and as a Methodist circuit minister who has also been active in Wesleyan and Methodist historical scholarship in the UK. His work is published by the Epworth Press, the publishing house of the Methodist Church in Great Britain, and is intended for lay readership. It functions as an initial historical introduction to British Methodist history within a series of works entitled "Exploring Methodism." The book utilizes sophisticated typography and graphic

---

59   Ibid., 506–26.
60   Ibid., 526–34
61   Ibid., 343–60.
62   On Whitefield's use of performance styles and media, cf. Harry S. Stout, *The Divine Dramatist: George Whitefield and the Rise of Modern Evangelicalism* (Grand Rapids: Eerdmans, 1991), xvii–xxiv passim.

layout, and it offers a distinctive element of blocks of primary historical sources interspersed within its text.

Although briefer than Rack's work, Tabraham's narrative also offers a complex picture of Methodist origins against their eighteenth-century context. It does not seek to identify Wesley or the early Methodist movement as particularly evangelical or "high-church" or socially activist as some interpreters had done. It offers readers a sense that the complex phenomenon that British Methodism had become by the early twenty-first century reflects its own complex roots. It offers an honest narrative that depicts Methodism against its own British background as part of the history and experience of British people from the eighteenth century to the present time.

TABRAHAM, *THE MAKING OF METHODISM* (1995, 2009, AND 2010)

An introduction to the British context of the rise of Methodism that combines elements of **SocialDysfunction** with a hint of **AnglicanDeclension** (chapter 1)

The background to the Wesleys' careers including **EpworthUpbringing** and **OxfordSociety** (chapter 2)

A chapter on the Wesleys' theological sources (Scripture, reason, tradition, and experience, chapter 3)

GeorgiaPietists and **AldersgateExperience**, noting the broader context of the Aldersgate experience including John Wesley's earlier (1725) conversion to religious seriousness (chapter 4)

WayOfSalvation (chapter 5)

FieldPreaching, MethodistPersecution (at least opposition), **Classes-Bands, MethodistPreachers** including the origins of the Conference, **AmericanOrdinations** with an elaboration on their implications for the evolution of British Methodism, and **JWDeath** (chapter 6)

StillnessMeans and a more general description of the ecclesial structures that developed in early Methodism (chapter 7)

Rack's and Tabraham's narratives focused principally on the story of British Methodist churches. After Frederick Norwood's *Story of American Methodism*, a comprehensive narrative of American Methodist history did not come until 2010. By that time, **Richard P. Heitzenrater**'s *Wesley and the People Called Methodists* had appeared. With Heitzenrater's work in place as a widely utilized textbook, the authors of *The Methodist Experience in America: A History* (Russell E. Richey, Kenneth Rowe, and Jean Miller Schmidt) chose not to include a Wesleyan narrative and focused their work on the narrative of American Methodism. So, although Heitzenrater's biography could not be closely tied to *The Methodist Experience in America*, the authors of the latter took it as a complementary text giving the British prehistory of the Wesleyan movement as well as John Wesley's involvement in the founding of the Methodist Episcopal Church in North America.

Moreover, as the title indicates, Heitzenrater's work is not simply a biography of John Wesley but also an account of the evolution of "the people called Methodists" in John Wesley's time and under Wesley's leadership. This emphasis on the development of the Methodist people also serves to connect Heitzenrater's narrative to the history of Wesleyan communities beyond John Wesley's time. The epilogue to the book makes this very clear with discussions of "Methodism after Wesley" and "The Wesleyan Heritage."[63]

In one respect, Heitzenrater's work bears a similarity to Rack's, and that is in Heitzenrater's insistence that a historical account of Wesley and early Methodism must scrupulously avoid the Methodist hagiography of the past. "Every account of origins," Heitzenrater writes in the first sentence of his work, "is laden with myths and legends," and so his work seeks to "distinguish fact from fantasy" in telling such a narrative.[64] In other respects, Heitzenrater's work differs significantly from that of Rack. Rack's biography is written in direct dialogue with secondary historical literature on Wesley and on eighteenth-century British social and cultural contexts of the Wesleyan movement. Heitzenrater's account generally avoids discussion of secondary literature, focusing on

---

63 Heitzenrater, *Wesley and the People Called Methodists*, 347–61.
64 Ibid., xi.

a narrative grounded in primary historical texts, though it does offer suggestions for reading in secondary sources at the conclusion of each chapter. Heitzenrater's work is structured more as a textbook, with illustrations, charts, and highlighted key terms and names to aid students.

The following chart summarizes Heitzenrater's organization of the work, but while names of the conventional code modules are used here, Heitzenrater typically gives very different content to each. In fact, Heitzenrater does not use the conventional code modules as discrete units but, for example, introduces outdoor preaching, conflicts with Moravians and Calvinists, and the initial development of John Wesley's societies, bands, and classes within the scope of a single narrative, then returns to these themes repeatedly. The chart shows beyond initial segments of the narrative (up to 1738) a set of themes to which Heitzenrater returns consistently through his narrative.

HEITZENRATER, *WESLEY AND THE PEOPLE CALLED METHODISTS* (1995, 2013)

An account of the background of the Church of England from the time of the Reformation, and then Pietism and English Religious societies as a more immediate background to the Wesleyan movement[65]

EpworthUpbringing noting the engagement of Samuel and Susanna Wesley with Anglican benevolent and religious societies[66]

OxfordSociety ("The First Rise of Methodism") with some discussion of **JWInfluences**[67]

GeorgiaPietists (both Moravians and Salzburgers; "The Second Rise of Methodism")[68]

AldersgateExperience and **WesleyDoubts** together (within "The Third Rise of Methodism" in London) and growing nuances in Wesley's understanding of what had happened at Aldersgate Street[69]

---

65   Ibid., 1–27.
66   Ibid., 27–35.
67   Ibid., 37–64.
68   Ibid., 64–80.
69   Ibid., 81–103.

HEITZENRATER, *WESLEY AND THE PEOPLE CALLED METHODISTS* (1995, 2013) (continued)

[From this point, Heitzenrater deals with most of the conventionally labeled code modules as themes to which he returns repeatedly rather than discrete blocks of narrative code.]

FieldPreaching and **MethodistPreachers** including several distinct steps in the development of Methodist preaching as well as the early acquisition of preaching houses and chapels, the development of the conference, and early tensions towards independence, e.g., celebration of the Lord's Supper apart from Anglican churches; this theme includes the module **Tensions1760s**.[70]

StillnessMeans[71]

ArminianVsCalvinist including controversies over perfection as well as predestination[72]

ClassesBands including societies and larger lay-led Methodist structures[73]

MethodistBenevolence Heitzenrater introduces Methodist benevolent works (visiting prisoners, charity sermons) early in the narrative commensurate with the work of the London society.[74]

WesleyCommunicator: a segment ("Defense and Apology") parallel to Rack's observations on Wesley's enterprises in communication and education[75]

GrowthOfMethodism initially describing the extension of John Wesley's itineraries northward from London and Bristol, but (as in other cases) a theme to which Heitzenrater returns at various points in his narrative[76]

Sections on attempts at unity within the Evangelical movement[77]

A section of general narrative weaving together many of the themes listed above as they affected Wesley and Methodist people in the period 1775–81[78]

---

70   Ibid., 107–13, 124–29, 155–61, 165–71, 203–22, 230–33, 236–39, 261–90, 313–17.
71   Ibid., 117.
72   Ibid., 117–20, 234–36.
73   Ibid., 113–16, 120–24.
74   Ibid., 137–41, 184–90.
75   Ibid., 141–47, 171–84, 196–201, 223–28.
76   Ibid., 148–55.
77   Ibid., 191–96, 228–29.
78   Ibid., 291–312.

HEITZENRATER, *WESLEY AND THE PEOPLE CALLED METHODISTS* (1995, 2013) (continued)

AmericanOrdinations[79]

JWDeath[80]

The fourth narrative on which I focus in this period is that of John Munsey Turner, *John Wesley: The Evangelical Revival and the Rise of Methodism in England*. Based on Turner's earlier essays, his narrative deliberately rejects the idea that a description of the rise of Methodism could be reduced to a narrative of the career of John Wesley. His reference to "those . . . who may be tempted still to imagine [John Wesley] as an eighteenth-century Billy Graham" might be directed specifically at A. Skevington Wood (above).[81] Turner's book can be laid out schematically as follows.

TURNER, *JOHN WESLEY: THE EVANGELICAL REVIVAL AND THE RISE OF METHODISM IN ENGLAND* (2002)

Chapter 1: A discussion of the Evangelical Revival as the general context of early Methodism, emphasizing **EuropeanPietism** and in a sense **AmericanReligion** insofar as Turner saw the Evangelical movement as a transatlantic phenomenon.

Chapter 2: **EpworthUpbringing**, **OxfordSociety**, **GeorgiaPietists** as an extension of **EuropeanPietism**; **AldersgateExperience** emphasizing that the experience was not as dramatic as earlier interpreters made it out to be; **SocialDysfunction** with an emphasis on social dislocation as a prelude to **FieldPreaching**, followed by a narrative of the development of Methodism including versions of **MethodistPersecution**, **JohnAndMary**, **GrowthOfMethodism**, and **JWDeath**.

---

79   Ibid., 317–25.
80   Ibid., 325–44.
81   Turner, *John Wesley*, vii.

Perhaps more than any other work in this period, Turner's narrative points to the complexity of early Methodism, refusing to see John Wesley as the distinctive focus of the movement, and refusing to see Wesleyan Methodism as the most legitimate fruit of early Methodism, hence his concluding chapter on the importance of Primitive Methodism in Britain.

THE QUEST FOR A "WESLEYAN TRADITION" BEYOND MODERNISM

Many of the trends identified in this and the previous chapter have continued as distinct lines of inquiry, mostly apart from narrative frameworks, in the later twentieth century and the early twenty-first century. The theological interpretation of John Wesley has produced a voluminous literature in this period, much of which has been associated with the Oxford Institute of Methodist Theological Studies, the Wesleyan Studies Unit of the American Academy of Religion, and the Wesleyan Theological Society.[82] A series of studies related to Methodism and the poor have been inspired, in part, by liberation theologies and have explored the eighteenth-century social and economic background of early Methodism as well as the Wesleys' own views of poverty and Christian responses to the poor.[83] In addition to these venues of research, there has been a new flourishing of studies of nineteenth-century Methodism led by scholars associated with the American Society of Church History, such as Nathan Hatch, John Wigger, and David Hempton.[84] Moreover, scholars associated with Evangelical and Holiness movements, some of these who present regularly at the Wesleyan Theological Society and in the Wesleyan Studies Unit of the American Academy of Religion, have produced a rich field of scholarship on the Wesleys and early Methodism.

One of the most significant signs of the interpretation of the Wesleyan tradition beyond the Modernist period is the very idea of a "Wesleyan tradition." This may reflect one of the distinctive traits of cultures beyond Modernism, namely, the attempt to revive or renew traditional cultures.[85] The same period, from the 1970s to the present, that has seen the flourishing of studies of the "Wesleyan tradition" has also seen the flourishing of a wide range of studies of Christian denominational cultures and subcultures, including studies of Baptist tradition and Pentecostal traditions and even the Stone-Campbell Restoration tradition, an "anti-tradition" if ever there was such. The term *tradition* has been applied in these contexts to understand the cultures—we might say the ways of being Christian—historically

---

82 The literature on this is far too voluminous to summarize; cf. my summary observations in "The Origins and Early Growth of Methodism, 1730–1791," in William Gibson, Peter Forsaith, and Martin Wellings, eds., *The Ashgate Research Companion to World Methodism* (Farnham, Surrey: Ashgate, 2013), 21–24.

83 I have offered a brief survey of literature on these approaches similar to that mentioned in the previous note, in "The Origins and Early Growth of Methodism, 1730–1791," 26–30.

84 Cf. Hempton, *Methodism: Empire of the Spirit*, and John Wigger, *Taking Heaven by Storm: Methodism and the Rise of Popular Religion in America* (Urbana and Chicago: University of Illinois Press, 1998).

85 Connor, *Postmodernist Culture*, 74–75, describes the "openness to the past" on the part of postmodern architectures in contrast to Modernist architecture.

transmitted by these denominational groups, so for example, a more general sense of Baptist cultures as contrasted with the history of specific Baptist denominations.[86] Similarly, the notion of a "Wesleyan tradition" or "Methodist tradition" has become a popular concept in recent decades as a way of describing the distinct culture of Wesleyan and Methodist churches.

Beyond Modernism, understandings of a "Wesleyan tradition" underwent significant reconsideration and reinterpretation. But although the generation of Colin Williams, Frank Baker, and Albert C. Outler may have presupposed the strength of Methodism, subsequent generations of interpreters of the Wesleyan tradition advocated in this period a renewal of the tradition in response to indications of the decline of Methodist churches. Methodist churches in both the United States and in the United Kingdom had seen declining church membership and participation throughout the twentieth century. From the 1970s this trend had come to widespread recognition,[87] and it was a very significant factor in the culture of Methodist churches, who in the past had consistently claimed their increasing numbers of adherents as a sign of divine favor. Methodist churches had come to see themselves in many respects as reflecting the issues that faced Anglicanism in John Wesley's day, and in this situation the past of the Wesleyan movement appealed to Methodists as it offered hope for renewal of Wesleyan churches.

Sometimes the concern for tradition in cultures beyond Modernism

---

86   Just as an example, consider the following titles with direct or indirect reference to Baptist tradition: William Powell Tuck, *Our Baptist Tradition* (Macon, GA: Smith and Helwys, 2005); Timothy George and David S. Dockery, *Theologians of the Baptist Tradition* (Nashville: Broadman and Holman, 2001); Steven R. Harmon, *Towards Baptist Catholicity: Essays on Tradition and the Baptist Vision,* Studies in Baptist History and Thought series, (Waynesboro, GA: Paternoster Press, 2006); W. Glenn Jonas Jr., *The Baptist River: Essays on Many Tributaries of a Diverse Tradition* (Macon, GA: Mercer University Press, 2006).

87   For example, the publication in 1972 of *Why Conservative Churches are Growing* by United Methodist Dean M. Kelley made readers in the United States aware of declining church membership among "old-line" or "mainline" American denominations and the growth of Evangelical churches: Dean M. Kelley, *Why Conservative Churches are Growing: A Study in Sociology of Religion* (New York: Harper and Row, 1972); cf. Campbell, *The Sky Is Falling, the Church Is Dying, And Other False Alarms,* 2–6, and also the cautions I have given against the notion that old-line or mainline denominations in the United States are dying, 17–35.

has involved not only the attempt to connect with one's own immediate roots or cultural traditions but also the attempt to connect to deeper roots or more distant traditions by way of one's own tradition. It is in this way that we can understand the flourishing of literature in the 1980s and beyond that attempts to connect Methodists with older Christian traditions by way of John Wesley's own formation and his uses of such traditions. In the 1980s the quest for ancient sources in John Wesley's works became something of a passion among Wesleyan scholars in the United States and elsewhere. K. Steve McCormick, an elder of the Church of the Nazarene, offered a 1983 Drew dissertation titled "John Wesley's Use of John Chrysostom on the Christian Life."[88] I myself completed a dissertation in 1984 at Southern Methodist University (with Outler as an *amicus curiae* to the dissertation committee) on Wesley's vision of ancient Christianity as a model for religious revitalization.[89] In the next a year, a dissertation was presented at St. Louis University titled "John Wesley and the Church Fathers" by Arthur C. Meyers, a professor of economics at that university whose exposure to Catholic Christianity there prompted him to investigate his own Methodist tradition's Catholic roots. At about the same time, in Sweden, a young scholar named Bengt Haglund began work on a dissertation in this area as early as 1982, but Haglund died tragically in 1987 without finishing his research. Throughout this period, Professor Roberta Bondi of Emory University had taught a course in Wesley's patristic roots and published at least two articles reflecting this interest.[90] A Korean student of Professor Bondi, Dr. Hoo-Jung Lee (now academic dean of the Methodist Theological University in Seoul) offered a dissertation at Emory in 1991 titled "The Doctrine of

---

88 Kelley Steve McCormick, "John Wesley's Use of John Chrysostom on the Christian Life" (PhD dissertation, Drew University, 1983).

89 Campbell, "John Wesley's Conceptions and Uses of Christian Antiquity"; subsequently published as *John Wesley and Christian Antiquity: Religious Vision and Cultural Change*.

90 Roberta Bondi, "The Meeting of Oriental Orthodoxy and United Methodism," in *Christ in East and West*, ed. Paul Fries and Tiran Nersoyan (Macon, GA: Mercer University Press, 1987), 171–84 and "The Role of the Holy Spirit from a United Methodist Perspective," *Greek Orthodox Theological Review* 31:3–4 (1986): 351–60.

New Creation in the Theology of John Wesley," including a chapter on Wesley's appropriation of ancient Eastern Christian literature.[91]

In addition to these individual works, at least two scholarly conferences addressed the issue of the ancient or Eastern roots of John Wesley's theology. The Wesley Studies Working Group of the 1982 Oxford Institute of Methodist Theological Studies, which I was in and included Outler, Bondi, and Haglund, heard a paper from Professor Bondi on this topic and included in its published recommendations the suggestion that this research should be pursued further.[92] Eight years later, the 1990 annual meeting of the Wesleyan Theological Society, meeting at the Nazarene Theological Seminary in Kansas City, Missouri, focused on the theme of "Wesleyanism and Eastern Orthodoxy" and heard a number of papers on these themes. The Wesleyan Theological Society represents the Holiness tradition of North American Wesleyanism, and it is quite significant that this group would have taken up the question of Wesley's roots in ancient Eastern Christianity.

Throughout the decade of the 1980s and beyond, the subject of John Wesley's knowledge and uses of ancient Eastern sources became a consistent thematic enterprise in Wesleyan studies and has continued in the last three decades. Coming from North America, Sweden, and Korea, from men and women, from older and younger scholars, from conservative Evangelicals and scholars from Methodism's liberal traditions, it represents Methodism's recovered self-identity as a Christian tradition with deep roots and reflects a culture beyond Modernism as it appears in the interpretation of the Wesleyan tradition.

The work of Professor **Hoo-Jung Lee** mentioned above serves as a connecting link to another expression of Wesleyan identity in the period beyond Modernism, and that is the attempt on the part of Wesleyan Christians outside of British and North American contexts to reinterpret the Wesleyan tradition in the light of their own cultural and

---

91 Hoo-Jung Lee, "The Doctrine of New Creation in the Theology of John Wesley" (Ph.D. dissertation, Emory University, 1991), especially chap. 5, 154–245.

92 In Meeks, *Future of the Methodist Theological Traditions*, 62.

socioeconomic contexts. Since 1982, the Oxford Institute of Methodist Theological Studies has sponsored pre-Institute conferences of Two-Thirds World participants who have offered reports highlighting aspects of the work of John Wesley and the broader Methodist theological tradition relevant to their own situations.

Throughout the period of Methodism beyond Modernism described here, Wesleyan Christians have continued to celebrate cardinal events that have become fixed elements in a recurring Wesleyan cycle. The year 1984 marked the 200th anniversary of John Wesley's ordinations leading to the Christmas Conference of 1784 and the foundation of the Methodist Episcopal Church in the United States. In 1988, Methodists throughout the world celebrated the 250th anniversary of John Wesley's Aldersgate-Street experience, and this occasion allowed Wesleyan scholars to offer some new interpretations of the Aldersgate experience.[93] The bicentennial of John Wesley's death was remembered in Wesleyan and other communities in 1991, and although this was not as large a celebration as others, some Anglican churches offered celebrations of this occasion in the light of the fact that many Anglican churches had introduced a recognition of "John and Charles Wesley, Priests" in their sanctoral calendars either on the third of March, the day after John Wesley's death date (the second of March was already taken by the commemoration of St. Chad of Lichfield) or on Aldersgate Day (24 May).[94] The years 2003 and 2007 saw the commemorations of the 300th anniversaries of the birth of John and Charles Wesley, respectively, and each of these events was celebrated throughout the world. Methodists in Hong Kong, for example, held a large-scale series of celebrations of the life of John Wesley in 2003.

Beyond simply celebrating these Wesleyan and Methodist anniversaries, other Wesleyan leaders have attempted to state what specific aspects of early Methodist movements might be most relevant to a

---

93 See the essays in Randy Maddox, ed., *Aldersgate Reconsidered.*

94 Anglican prayer books in the United States and Canada had included a recognition of "John and Charles Wesley, Priests" from the time of prayer book revisions in the 1970s, and the Anglican Cathedral of St. James in Toronto held a commemoration of the bicentennial of the death of John Wesley in March, 1991. The calendar of the Church of England celebrates John Wesley on May 24.

newly revitalized Wesleyan movement. A volume of essays edited by Mary Elizabeth Mullino Moore published in 2013 offered reflections on the Wesleyan narrative (by Richard P. Heitzenrater), considered a number of areas of potential revitalization including theological recovery (the introductory and concluding essays by Moore), the role of Susanna Annesley Wesley and other early Methodist women leaders (essays by W. Stephen Gunter and Diane Leclerc), the practice of hospitality as an aspect of early Methodist life (Amy G. Oden), approaches to health and healing (an article begun by Paul Bassett and completed by Randy L. Maddox), a renewed sense of vocation of all of God's people (Rebekah L. Miles on behalf of the bishops of The United Methodist Church), and a renewed commitment to identify with victims of repressive states (Elaine A. Robinson).[95]

One of the essays in this work by William B. McClain suggests a renewed discovery of the Wesleyan tradition on the part of African American Methodists and a renewed discovery of African Methodism on the part of other Methodists.[96] This sense of renewal is developed by **Dennis C. Dickerson** in *African Methodism and Its Wesleyan Heritage* (2009). Dickerson, in his role as historiographer of the African Methodist Episcopal Church, notes that the history of the AME and other historically African American denominations has been largely told with respect to the conditions of enslaved and disenfranchised African Americans. He makes the case for linking these narratives to the narrative of the Wesleyan movement, which bore the seeds of Christian abolitionism and a form of Wesleyan inclusivism.[97]

Conclusion

In the period beyond Methodist Modernism, Wesleyan Christians continued to encode their identities, though with less confidence than in

---

95 Mary Elizabeth Mullino Moore, ed., *A Living Tradition: Critical Recovery and Reconstruction of Wesleyan Heritage* (Nashville: Kingswood Books, 2013).

96 Ibid., 45–63.

97 Dennis C. Dickerson, *African Methodism and Its Wesleyan Heritage: Reflections on AME Church History* (Nashville; AMEC Sunday School Union, 2009).

the past. The age of Victorian Methodist triumphalism was a distant memory. The more recent optimism of the early ecumenical movement was also fading away in this period. Narratives of Wesleyan origins in this period exhibit opposing tendencies.

On the one hand is a kind of dissipation of the Wesleyan narrative into a complex story in which characters like John Wesley and perhaps his brother Charles and his mother, Susanna, become parts of a much more complicated narrative that accounts for social and cultural and even political as well as religious factors; which is to say, these narratives can be much more realistic and correspondingly less romantic than Wesleyan narratives in the past, depicting an early history of Methodism commensurate with the complexity of Wesleyan communities today. This is most pronounced in the works of Rack, Heitzenrater, Tabraham, and Turner considered above. Authors of these complex contemporary narratives may even regret personally the effect this has, though at the same time recognizing that complexity itself reveals a very real condition of the past too often overlooked in premodern and Modernist romanticizations of past ages.

A second and complementary trend we can see in this period is the deep desire on the part of contemporary interpreters to connect themselves to the past, even if it is a complex and less heroic past than represented in conventional narratives. This can be seen in the work of Pentecostal and Holiness authors (Lindsay and Ingersol) who connect themselves to a broader Christian tradition by way of the Wesleyan past, in the work of McClain and Dickerson to connect the heritage of African American Methodists to their Wesleyan past, and in the efforts of Methodist interpreters including myself to understand the deeper roots of the Wesleyan heritage in the Christian past.

A third trend I perceive in this period is simply the broadening of the range of material that contemporary interpreters find relevant in the early Wesleyan movement. In the past, the relevance of the movement had been seen in its quest for holiness, its evangelistic work, and its theology. Authors in this period find more aspects of early Methodist life that they might want to see renewed, including women's leadership, care for physical health and healing, the roles of ethnic and cultural minority traditions, and the empowerment of the poor and working-class people.

CONCLUSION

T his book has considered how Wesleyan and Methodist communities have told and retold narratives of their origins as ways of transmitting their communal identities across generations. John Wesley himself set in motion a powerful cultural current that utilized narrative as a normative way to describe the identity of Methodist people by way of his *Journal* (chapter 1). Given this beginning, it should come as no surprise that Methodist people have continued to tell narratives of their origins to describe the identities of their communities utilizing many of the modules of narrative code that Wesley himself had authored. Not surprising either is the fact that as Wesleyan communities have grown and diversified through the centuries, ways of telling narratives of Wesleyan origins and the identities encoded in them have shifted significantly, as this book has demonstrated. Throughout this historical process, narrators received, modified, and handed on strains of encoded narratives. The extent to which they simply handed on the narratives they received or creatively refashioned their narratives varied with each individual retelling.

I have considered four metaphors for understanding the use of a foundational narrative to describe the identity of a community: (1) a play within a play, (2) the construction of the past on the part of storytellers and interpreters, (3) the inheritance of DNA (memes), and (4) computer coding. The metaphor of a play within a play was my initial way of thinking about the complexities of multilevel interpretation of the past. But this metaphor only goes so far because historical narratives claim to describe the past faithfully in ways that plays do not. Neither *A Midsummer Night's Dream* nor the play about Pyramus and Thisbe enacted within it claimed to describe historical events, and they did not function to describe the identity of communities. Readers and audiences understand that a play is mainly about the skills and creativity of a dramatist and a company of actors.

The metaphor of social construction faces a similar problem because, although it allows for change, it tends to look for change through an evolutionary process on the part of communities, minimizing the creative work of narrators. The truth in this is that Wesleyan narratives so often have been simply told and retold, like stories told around the campfire, with gradual modifications. But it does not acknowledge the roles that creative storytellers may play in altering inherited narratives. The narrative above shows how some narrators did creatively alter inherited narratives.

The DNA metaphor also accounts for the "givenness" of many of the historic tellings and retellings of narratives of Wesleyan origins. That is, it accounts for the ways in which communities and interpreters do *not* change the story, the ways in which the story remains tenaciously fixed even in the face of evidence to the contrary of its claims. Historians may have documented certain claims about the Wesleyan narrative, but popular retellings of the narrative, especially in sermons, tended to stick to the script of the heroic traditional versions. I once heard a Methodist bishop proclaim that Elie Halévy had proven that the Wesleys saved England "from a bloody revolution that would have been bloodier than the French Revolution." There may be a small grain of truth in this claim, but Halévy's pro-revolutionary interpretation was that it was perfectly dreadful that the Wesleys had prevented a revolution, whereas the bishop took the Wesleys' stifling of a revolution as a sign of their benevolent conservatism. In the bishop's telling of the story, the memes of the traditional story prevailed even against a radical retelling of it.

And yet elements of creativity and the restructuring of narratives appear in these narratives, especially as they evolved over time. Even telling the same set of words in a very new context alters the meaning of the narrative. Salman Rushdie has described watching *The Wizard of Oz* as a child in a cinema in India, with viewers huddling at the appearance of major characters, trying to come to a consensus as to which traditional Hindu deities were represented by them.[1] Retelling the Wesleyan narrative in North America or in the West Indies in the 1830s may not have been as dramatically different as viewing *The Wizard of Oz* in India, but it would have held very different meanings in those places. The metaphor of computer coding lets us envision both the stubborn persistence of elements of code, like inherited memes, and also the creative work of interpreters whose work allows for an eventual evolution of stories that could be applied to and interpreted in vastly different contexts as Wesleyan communities themselves evolved through time and throughout the world.

What appears most consistently in the creative evolution of these narratives is their reflection of the contemporary issues and crises of the communities (churches) whose identities were encoded in them. In the Wesleyan period, the meaning of the Wesleyan movement itself was encoded as a movement that cultivated holiness and sought the reformation of British society and the Church of England, with evangelism as a means for gathering people into societies for the cultivation of holiness (chapter 1). By the early nineteenth century in North America, the separate ecclesial identity of the Methodist Episcopal Church led to a significant evolution of this earlier identity into a fuller claim to be a denomination (a "sect") alongside others and seeded the narrative module **ChurchFounder** (chapter 2). By the late nineteenth century, with Methodist churches flourishing in Britain and America, with Methodist missions expanding throughout India and China and Africa, and in conflict with the Holiness movement in the

---

1   Salman Rushdie, "Out of Kansas," in the Critic at Large column in *The New Yorker* for May 11, 1992, 93.

United States, the narrative again evolved into the image of John Wesley as primarily concerned with evangelism in the sense of the expansion of Christian communities, and only secondarily (if at all) with the cultivation of holiness (thus code module **WesleyEvangelist** in chapter 3). In the early twentieth century, Methodist narrators emphasized John Wesley's modern tendencies including his emphasis on personal religious experience (Umphrey Lee), his social engagement (Hugh Price Hughes), and his proto-ecumenical tendencies (Herbert Brook Workman, followed by Williams, Outler, and Baker, chapter 4). In the late twentieth century and beyond, narrators reflected the complex and diverse identities of their churches, depicting early Methodism in a commensurately complex fashion (chapter 5).

A great divide in these narratives appeared at the end of the nineteenth century. Up to that point, Wesleyan narrators had presumed or presupposed that the Wesleyan movement was the work of God and that their narratives were an account not only of human events but of a divinely guided enterprise. In the late nineteenth century, Methodist narrators beginning with James Buckley, influenced by Modernism and modern historical scholarship, left the claims of divine guidance to the people they quoted rather than in their own voices as narrators. At the same time, they began to admit more of the fallacies of Methodist leaders including Wesley himself (chapter 4). This typically left the discernment of divine guidance in the Wesleyan movement to their readers without making direct claims to divine guidance in their own voices.

THE ERRORS AND INSIGHTS OF NARRATORS

Because narratives of Wesleyan origins have been told so very frequently and so passionately on the part of Methodist partisans, persistent exaggerations and serious errors have plagued the telling of these narratives. Richard P. Heitzenrater has catalogued typical "myths" and a list of quotations erroneously but consistently attributed to John

Wesley. He even gives a typical narrative, brimming with incorrect and undocumented claims frequently made in Wesleyan narratives. He comments, "The story is *not true*, but it is *traditional*."[2] He makes the point that some of John Wesley's own distortions began building mythical elements that came to characterize Wesleyan narratives.[3]

Narrators often wrote their own experiences and their own contexts into a Wesleyan narrative. John Munsey Turner complained of those who imagined John Wesley "as an eighteenth-century Billy Graham, but always on a horse or at a market cross!" He was likely referring to Arthur Skevington Wood and perhaps other twentieth-century Evangelical interpreters of Wesley.[4] R. Denny Urlin's Victorian-era research seeded the typical Anglican comment that John Wesley was "actually a high churchman," but mistakenly taking "high church" in a nineteenth-century Tractarian sense rather than the eighteenth-century political sense in which Wesley himself used the term, as James H. Rigg pointed out (chapter 3).

But this is not to say that narrators saw only a reflection of themselves "at the bottom of a deep well."[5] Despite the prejudices and errors of narrators, narrators are sometimes gifted with insights into what really happened in the past, and their insights often arise out of their own experiences. Despite James M. Buckley's old-fashioned Methodist conservatism in opposition to the theater and his alliance with the proto-Fundamentalist D. L. Moody, it was Buckley who joined the nascent American Society of Church History and produced the first really modern history of American Methodism. Umphrey Lee had grown up in Sikeston, Missouri and had been hailed as "The Boy Orator of Missouri" for a long, sappy, patriotic speech he gave at age

2   Richard P. Heitzenrater, "The Wesleyan Tradition and the Myths We Love," in *A Living Tradition*, ed. Mary Elizabeth Mullino Moore, (Nashville: Kingswood Books, 2013), 13–44. Heitzenrater's "*not true . . . but traditional*" narrative is on pp. 13–14 and the quotation is on p. 14.

3   Ibid., 15–22.

4   Turner, *John Wesley*, vii.

5   George Tyrrell, *Christianity at the Cross-roads* (London and New York: Longmans, Green and Co, 1909), 44, commenting on Adolph von Harnack and other liberal Protestant "questers" for the historical Jesus. The quotation is often attributed to Albert Schweitzer.

fourteen at an exposition in Jamestown, Virginia.[6] And yet it was Lee
who, twenty-five years later, produced his Columbia University dissertation exploring the modern aspects of John Wesley's thought. Albert
C. Outler had grown up in a Methodist parsonage in Georgia, imbib-
ing the culture of nineteenth-century rural Southern Methodism. But
his exposure to Robert L. Calhoun at Yale University, his immersion in
patristic literature, and his engagement in the Faith and Order movement enabled him to see that John Wesley's own uses of Greek as
well as Latin patristic sources were not incidental or merely academic
interests but stood as formative influences on Wesley's understanding of the centrally Wesleyan conception of Christian holiness. The
insights that arise from the experience of interpreters and narrators
can be hindrances to their historical work, but they can also serve as
grounds for genuine historical insight.

Persistent Wesleyan Icons

What may be more significant than erroneous details and falsely attributed quotations is the persistence of sweeping, iconic impressions
of John Wesley and early Methodism, created through the evolving
coding process described above, iconic impressions that continue to
structure the self-identities of Wesleyan communities today. In what
follows, I will refer to them as "Wesleyan icons." None of these is
strictly false; each is grounded in a selection of material from Wesley's
voluminous literary output. Narrators must always make a selection of
specific material, but the problem with these Wesleyan icons is that
their selections of specific material so overshadows other material as
to give a skewed image of John Wesley and early Methodism. In what
follows, I will consider four specific Wesleyan icons, the typical code
modules that they employ, some of the truths and the exaggerations

---

6   Umphrey Lee, *Oration Delivered at Jamestown Exposition by Umphrey Lee of Sikeston, Missouri,*
     a privately printed pamphlet (date unknown, but probably around 1907 or 1908) reproduced in
     1972 by Bridwell Library.

encoded within them, and how they have been used in defining the identities of Wesleyan communities.

WESLEYAN ICON 1: WESLEY THE CHURCH FOUNDER

It has become a truism since the years of the ecumenical movement in the early twentieth century that John Wesley did not intend to establish a separate church or denomination, and yet the image of Wesley as the founder of "Methodism"—an ambiguous term that could easily be understood as including "Methodist churches"—has persisted. The Wikipedia article on John Wesley, in the most recent moments in which I accessed it, states as John Wesley's most critical accomplishment that he is "credited with the foundation of Methodism," which could be naturally interpreted as meaning the foundation of Methodist churches.[7]

As we have seen (chapter 2), the image of John Wesley as **Church-Founder** was the creation of American Methodists in the mid-1800s, since British Methodists in that period did not acknowledge a formal separation from the Church of England. The icon of Wesley as a Church founder first appeared in Nathan Bangs's *History of the Methodist Episcopal Church* (1839), and Bangs grounded it in his consideration of **AmericanReligion** and then **AmericanOrdinations**, making the case that Methodism was God's providential means of Christianizing the North American continent. Abel Stevens's *Compendious History of Methodism* (1867–68) and Matthew Simpson's *A Hundred Years of Methodism* (1876) followed Bangs in this regard.

By the time of Luke Tyerman, British Methodists had become more comfortable identifying themselves as a church, and Tyerman's 1870 account of the origins of Methodism as "the greatest fact in the history of the church of Christ" built upon the presupposition of **AnglicanDeclension** that had appeared in Coke and Moore's *Life of Wesley* (1792). As Tyerman explained it, Methodist churches came into

---

7   Wikipedia article on "John Wesley," accessed 6 September 2016, https://en.wikipedia.org/wiki/John_Wesley.

existence in response to the need created by the multiple dysfunctions of the Church of England in the eighteenth century.

We must acknowledge at least one truth in the Wesleyan icon of Church founder: John Wesley himself did authorize the establishment of a Methodist church separate from the Church of England in the United States. And more than that, as Frank Baker so carefully documented, Wesley extended his separate Methodist ecclesial provisions—ordinations, an edition of the Prayer Book, and deeds for chapels—to British Methodism, creating by the time of his death a set of Methodist structures in Britain that functioned as a separate church.[8]

WESLEYAN ICON 2: THE HIGH-CHURCH WESLEY

Another persistent Wesleyan icon can be described as the "High Church" Wesley. We can attribute this Wesleyan icon to a single original source: the writings of R. Denny Urlin beginning with *John Wesley's Place in Church History* (1870). Reflecting his own Anglican background, and reacting against the growing sense of Methodist identity in Britain as churches separate from the Church of England, Urlin's works implied a significant challenge: if Methodists wanted to be faithful to Wesley, they should be Anglicans and not members of any other church. His notion has persisted in Anglican circles where the phrase "actually a High Churchman" is often tagged to John Wesley. Americans have much less exposure than British folk to the Evangelical flavors of Anglicanism and thus tend to see all of Anglicanism including Episcopalianism in the United States as "high church."

Although James Harrison Rigg challenged Urlin's particular conclusions about Wesley's "High Church" identification, he did not in any way challenge the claim that Wesley consistently identified himself as an Anglican. Many Victorian-era Methodists were happy with the identification of John Wesley as an Anglican. AME Bishop Henry McNeal Turner offered his own version of a high-church Wesleyanism with an argument

---

8   Baker, *John Wesley and the Church of England*, 283–325.

for the "presbyteral succession" of Methodist clergy from Wesley's time and his own efforts to restore the *Sunday Service* as the ritual of the AME Church (chapter 4). The Methodist Episcopal Church added to the historical statement in its 1892 *Discipline* a phrase identifying John and Charles Wesley as "presbyters of the Church of England."[9] Connecting the Wesleys to their Anglican inheritance suited the growing social and cultural sophistication of many Methodists in the late 1800s.

In the wake of the ecumenical movement in the twentieth century, the identification of the Anglican roots of Methodism became an important theological agendum for Methodists. Whereas earlier twentieth-century interpreters had recognized Wesleyan roots in the Reformation, especially among Lutheran and Reformed theologies, Albert C. Outler focused attention from the 1970s on John Wesley's Anglican and patristic roots (chapter 4). This in turn spawned a generation of scholarly work, including mine, that explored these roots of the Wesleyan movement.

James H. Rigg had pointed out in direct response to R. Denny Urlin that Urlin's identification of John Wesley as "high church" relied on an inappropriate nineteenth-century "ritualising" understanding of the phrase in contrast to the eighteenth-century political context in which Wesley utilized it. More recent scholarship—most notably, that of William Gibson—has shown how strongly Protestant the Church of England was in John Wesley's century.[10] This goes a great way towards explaining, for example, the virtualist understanding of Christ's presence in the Lord's Supper that John and Charles Wesley both expressed,[11] but it also alerts us to the fact that simply identifying the Wesleys as Anglicans does not imply a particularly high-church outlook on their part.

Even if Urlin's claim that John Wesley was "high church" was an

---

9   *Doctrines and Discipline of the Methodist Episcopal Church* (1892), 13.

10   Gibson, *Church of England*, 1688–1832.

11   Campbell, *Wesleyan Beliefs*, 53–57, 105–6; cf. Eric Richard Griffin, "Daniel Brevint and the Eucharistic Calvinism of the Caroline Church of England, 1603—1674" (ThD thesis, University of Toronto, 2000), the conclusion on p. 252.

exaggeration, there remain some important truths in the understanding of Wesley as an Anglican deeply committed to continuity with the Christian church of the first three Christian centuries. John Wesley differed with and violated very specific Anglican articles and canons as well as the Toleration Act of 1689 by

1. preaching within the dioceses of other bishops than his own and in parishes where other priests had been installed as spiritual leaders,[12]

2. authorizing lay preachers,[13] and

3. ordaining clergy in 1784 without being consecrated as a bishop.[14]

Despite these violations, he remained committed to a notably Anglican vision of Christian community, supplying American Methodists in 1784 with his revision of the Book of Common Prayer, prescribing rituals for Morning Prayer, the Lord's Supper, and Evening Prayer for Sunday worship, encouraging the use of the Great Litany on the weekly fast days of Wednesdays and Fridays, offering an annual lectionary and calendar with readings, collects, and proper prefaces for each Sunday in the liturgical cycle, and encouraging elders to celebrate the Lord's Supper every Sunday.[15]

---

12 Council of Nicaea, canons 15–16; in Norman P. Tanner, SJ, ed., *Decrees of the Ecumenical Councils* (London: Sheed and Ward; and Washington, DC: Georgetown University Press, 1990), 1:13; an Anglican canon from 1603 specified: "Ministers Not to Preach or Administer the Communion in Private Houses," in Edmund Gibson, ed., *Codex Juris Ecclesiastici Anglicani: Or, Statutes, Constitutions, Canons, Rubricks and Articles of the Church of England* (London: J. Baskett, 1713), under Title XX on "The Lord's Supper," chapter XV, "The Communion of the Sick," a canon of 1603 identified as lxxi, "Ministers Not to Preach or Administer the Communion in Private Houses," p. 484. Cf. Richard Burn, *The Ecclesiastical Law* (London: S. Sweet, V. and R. Stevens, and G. S. Norton, 9th edition of 1842), 3:442–47; and The Conventicle Acts of 1664 and 1670 that were in many cases invoked against "seditious assemblies."

13 Twenty-third Article of Religion of the Church of England, in *Creeds and Confessions of Faith in the Christian Tradition*, ed. Valerie Hotchkiss and Jaroslav Pelikan (New Haven: Yale University Press, 2003), 2:534.

14 The Anglican Prayer Book stated that bishops ordain other clergy and that three bishops were required to consecrate another bishop: 1662 Book of Common Prayer; in *The Book of Common Prayer: The Texts of 1549, 1559, and 1662*, ed. Brian Cummings (Oxford: Oxford University Press, 2011), 623–32 (deacons), 633–43 (priests), and 644–51 (bishops and archbishops).

15 [John Wesley and the Methodist Episcopal Church], *The Sunday Service of the Methodists in North America* (London: [William Strahan], 1784); and John Wesley, letter to Coke, Asbury, and "Our Brethren in North America," ¶4; in Albert C. Outler, ed., *John Wesley* (A Library of Protestant Thought; New York: Oxford University Press, 1964), 83–84, where Wesley advised elders to administer the Lord's Supper on Sundays.

WESLEYAN ICON 3: WESLEY THE EVANGELIST

Perhaps the most persistent of the Wesleyan icons I identify here is the icon or image of John Wesley as primarily an evangelist in the sense of one whose overriding concern was the expansion of Christian communities by bringing non-Christian persons and persons whose Christian faith was only nominal to active inclusion in a Christian community. Generations of Methodists have been nurtured on narratives implying that John Wesley spent most of his time preaching out-of-doors to the baptized pagans of England whose pitiful national church had long since abandoned any concern for them.

As we have seen, this was neither the way Wesley represented himself (chapter 1) nor the way the earliest Methodists represented him (chapter 2). This image or icon of John Wesley developed in the late 1800s when Methodists were advancing socially, building Gothic sanctuaries, having considerable success attracting people to their churches, relaxing traditional strictures against "worldly" activities, and in the United States were increasingly embarrassed by the emotional excesses of the Holiness movement (chapter 3). The prominence of evangelism in the early Wesleyan movement appeared in historical narratives of Abel Stevens (1867) and Matthew Simpson (1876). The 1892 *Doctrines and Discipline of the Methodist Episcopal Church* claimed that "the only infallible proof of the legitimacy of any branch of the Christian Church is in its ability to seek and save the lost and to disseminate the Pentecostal spirit and life."[16] Old-fashioned Methodists in that era might have recognized "the Pentecostal spirit and life" as a veiled reference to entire sanctification and the sanctified life, but the mission "to seek and save the lost" now took center stage and could be strongly tinctured with American or British nationalism and colonialism.[17]

What is most problematic about the icon of John Wesley as

---

16 *Doctrines and Discipline of the Methodist Episcopal Church* (1892), 16.
17 Mark R. Teasdale, *Methodist Evangelism, American Salvation: The Home Missions of the Methodist Episcopal Church, 1860–1920* (Eugene, OR: Pickwick Publications, 2014), esp. 31–49.

primarily an evangelist is that it downplays or even minimizes Wesley's own stated mission of furthering holiness and reform or, we might say, his focus on depth in contrast to breadth in Christian formation. We have seen (chapters 1 and 2) that John Wesley and the earliest Methodist churches framed the principal mission of Methodists with respect to the cultivation of holiness and reform in society and in the church. The "Large Minutes" raised the issue of where Methodist clergy should attempt to preach. The responses are revealing:

> **Q.** Is it advisable only to preach in as many places as we can, without forming any societies?
>
> **A.** By no means. We have made the trial in various places, and that for a considerable time. And all the seed has fallen as by the way-side. There is scarce any fruit of it remaining.
>
> **Q.** Where should we endeavour to preach most?
>
> **A.** 1. Where we [clergymen] can preach in a Church. 2. Where there is the greatest number of quiet and willing hearers. 3. Where there is most fruit.[18]

If I read these responses correctly, the purpose of Methodist preaching was to gather people into societies. Preaching served the goal of the cultivation of holiness in the early Methodist movement, but the cultivation of holiness was consistently stated as the principal aim of Methodist movement under the Wesleys' leadership—and that applies to Charles Wesley as well as to John Wesley.

The Wesleyan icon of John Wesley as principally an evangelist who called people to Christian communities persisted through the twentieth century and into the present time. A. Skevington Wood's *The Burning Heart* (1967) offered a well-documented version of this image of Wesley, placing the emphasis on evangelism and seeing the cultivation of holiness as "follow-up" (utilizing a term from Billy Graham

---

18 "Large Minutes," following the versions of 1753 and 1763, as given in *The Works of Wesley: The Methodist Societies: The Minutes of Conference*, vol. 10, ed. Rack, 845–46. The word *clergymen* appears in the 1763 version.

revivals) to evangelistic work (chapter 4). Faced with consistent declines in church membership since the 1960s, The United Methodist Church adopted a mission statement in the 1990s focused on evangelistic mission. The mission statement of The United Methodist Church as it appears today can be read as encoding this Wesleyan icon: "The mission of the Church is to make disciples of Jesus Christ for the transformation of the world."[19] The phrase "for the transformation of the world" (added in 2008) can be understood as encoding the concern for reform in the early Wesleyan movement, but the phrase "to make disciples of Jesus Christ" places the emphasis on extending the membership of Christian communities. The mission statement further describes the first element in the process of carrying out this mission, "proclaim the gospel, seek, welcome, and gather persons into the body of Christ."[20] Such an emphasis can allow evangelism to override almost any other concern, for example, to override the commitments that clergy make to form Christians in historic doctrine and liturgy.[21]

Nevertheless, there are historical truths embedded in the image or icon of John Wesley as evangelist: especially John, for John Wesley took up evangelistic practices on which he and his brother came to differ very strongly. John recognized that his goal of cultivating Christian holiness required gathering people into classes, bands, and societies, and he had no parish base to work from. So, for the sake of the cultivation of holiness, John Wesley was willing to invade parishes where other priests of his own church had been installed as spiritual leaders. For the sake of outreach to cultivate holiness, John Wesley

---

19 *The Book of Discipline of The United Methodist Church 2012* (Nashville: United Methodist Publishing House, 2012), ¶120, p. 91. This mission statement has been carried in *Disciplines* of The United Methodist Church since 2008.

20 UMC *Discipline* 2012, ¶122, p. 92. It does go on to describe the importance of Christian nurture in ways that would be consistent with a process of sanctification.

21 It would be hard to reconcile with the form of liturgy that John Wesley sent to American Methodists in his edition of the Prayer Book, and with the Anglican as well as Methodist Article of Religion that claims that one who fails to keep the ritual of one's church, once authorized by the church body, "ought to be rebuked openly (that others may fear to do the like), as one that offendeth against the common order of the Church, and woundeth the consciences of weak brethren": Anglican Article of Religion 34, in Pelikan and Hotchkiss, *Creeds and Confessions of Faith in the Christian Tradition*, 2:537; Methodist Article of Religion 22, in Pelikan and Hotchkiss, *Creeds and Confessions of Faith in the Christian Tradition*, 3:206–207.

was willing to grant lay preachers "license" or permission to preach, in contradiction of an Anglican Article of Religion that stated,

> It is not lawful for any man to take upon him the office of public preaching or ministering the sacraments in the congregation, before he be lawfully called, and sent to execute the same. And those we ought to judge lawfully called and sent, which be chosen and called to this work by men who have public authority given unto them in the congregation to call and send ministers into the Lord's vineyard.[22]

Charles Wesley had preached itinerantly early in the history of the Wesleyan movement, but from about 1756 he quit itinerating, and from around the same time he became increasingly critical of the lay preachers John authorized. He also objected to John's ordinations and kept his own branch of the Wesleyan movement within the bounds of Anglican canonical orthodoxy. John, however, was willing to disregard some very specific aspects of his church's order to serve the goal of cultivating holiness by casting a wide net to gather people into small communities. The image of John Wesley as evangelist does reflect this aspect of his mission.

WESLEYAN ICON 4: WESLEY AS SOCIAL REFORMER

A fourth Wesleyan icon that has persisted since the very first years of the twentieth century is the icon or image of John Wesley as a social reformer. Earlier Methodists had known of the benevolent activities of eighteenth-century Methodist leaders including John and Charles Wesley (code module **MethodistBenevolence**). They were generally aware of John Wesley's objections to slavery and his advocacy of abolition, most famously in the last letter he ever wrote, his letter of late February 1791 to William Wilberforce, encouraging Wilberforce's attempts as a member of Parliament to abolish the slave trade (code module **OppositionToSlavery**).

---

22 Twenty third Article of Religion of the Church of England, in Hotchkiss and Pelikan, *Creeds and Confessions of Faith in the Christian Tradition*, 2:534; cf. Bicknell, *Theological Introduction to the Thirty-Nine Articles of Religion of the Church of England*, 321.

But Hugh Price Hughes recognized around the turn of the twentieth century that Wesley not only practiced benevolence and opposed slavery, but he much more broadly identified with and supported the plight of the poor in early industrial England (thus code module **MinistryWithPoor**). His sense of Wesley's positive contributions to the poor was echoed by George Jackson (1903) and then was taken up by Robert F. Wearmouth (1945), responding to modern social historians who presumed that Methodism, like other forms of traditional religion, only offered palliatives to the poor. It is interesting that, despite American Methodists' involvement with the Social Gospel movement in the early twentieth century, American Methodist leaders seem not to have made the direct connection between Wesley's work on behalf of the poor and their own efforts at social reform in the way in which Hughes and Jackson and Wearmouth did.

The image or icon of Wesley as a social reformer, combining narrative module **SocialDysfunction** as the background to Wesley's work with code modules **OppositionToSlavery** and **MinistryWithPoor**, grew in prominence through the twentieth century as Methodist leaders engaged their church communities in the civil rights movement in the United States and other social reforming movements, and as liberation theologies came to influence Christian communities throughout the world. It would appear in various forms in the narratives of British Methodists Barrie Tabraham (1995) and John Munsey Turner (2002), in the narrative of Nazarene historian Stan Ingersol (2009), and in the work of numerous Wesleyan theologians who have pursued the connections between Wesley's identification with the poor and contemporary efforts for social reform. One twentieth-century Methodist influenced by Liberation theologies could even claim that "Wesley's understanding of stewardship is a frontal attack on the principles of capitalism and the ethos of accumulation and consumption of wealth."[23]

---

23 Theodore W. Jennings, Jr., *Good News to the Poor: John Wesley's Evangelical Economics* (Nashville: Abingdon Press, 1990), 116.

A significant historical problem with some accounts of John Wesley as a social reformer—especially in the more exaggerated form that the previous quotation suggests—is Wesley's well-documented political conservativism, including his opposition to the American Revolution and his consistent advocacy of industry and profit-making among Methodist people. Social historians in the early and mid-twentieth century in fact represented early Methodism under Wesley's leadership as socially repressive and unconcerned about the plight of laboring children and the poor.[24]

The disjuncture between the views of these social historians and those of Methodist interpreters in this period is stark, but careful reconstructions of the political and social conditions of early Methodism in its own context reveal a complex and credible situation. Such interpreters as Theodore Weber, John Munsey Turner, and Jason Vickers have pointed to a newer form of Toryism that prevailed after the Glorious Revolution of 1688. The older Toryism had insisted on an absolute divine right of monarchs. The situation after 1688, when Parliament deposed the reigning monarch and installed another, required a significant revision of Tory political outlooks that Weber describes as "Tory constitutionalism" and Vickers describes as "organic constitutionalism."[25] Wesley did fit this pattern, the newer pattern of political conservatism. In at least one case, John Wesley advocated a Whig candidate for Parliament, fearing that the Tory candidate was a Jacobite—that is, an advocate of the older form of divine right.[26]

Many of John Wesley's reforming activities—his advocacy on

---

24   Examples are J. H. Plumb, *England in the Eighteenth Century*, Pelican History of England series, rev. ed. (1950 Harmondsworth, Middlesex: Penguin Books, 1963), 91–97; and E. P. Thompson, *The Making of the English Working Class* (London: V. Gollancz, 1963).

25   Theodore R. Weber, *Politics in the Order of Salvation: Transforming Wesleyan Political Ethics* (Nashville: Kingswood Books, 2001), and on the specific point about constitutional rights, see chap. 10, pp. 303–52; and Jason E. Vickers, *Wesley: A Guide for the Perplexed* (London and New York: T & T Clark International, 2009); on this matter cf. a summary of research in my article on "The Origins and Early Growth of Methodism, 1730–1791," in Gibson, Forsaith, and Wellings, eds., *Ashgate Research Companion to World Methodism*, 21–24.

26   John Wesley, letter to Ebenezer Blackwell, 4 March 1756; in *The Works of John Wesley: Letters*, vol. 27, ed. Ted A. Campbell, 6–17, and see the notes identifying the candidates involved in this Bristol by-election.

behalf of the abolition of slavery, his careful strictures on the kinds of profit-making appropriate for Christians, his understanding of the plight of the poor, and his pleas for others to understand them—can be understood within a framework of the newer and more moderate forms of political and economic conservatism emerging in his time. And to be fair, it should be noted, contemporary theologians and ethicists may find specific aspects of Wesley's thought and practices relevant as a basis to build contemporary approaches to social reform not grounded in Wesley's own brand of political and economic conservatism.

OTHER WESLEYAN ICONS

We might consider other possible candidates for "Wesleyan icons." The icon or image of Wesley simply as a saint, a holy man, and as an advocate for holiness was perhaps the original way in which Methodist people depicted him before and immediately after his death and consistent with his claim that the principal mission of Methodism was "to spread scriptural holiness over the land."[27]

Since the work of Colin Williams (1960) and Albert C. Outler (1960s and 70s), a new image or icon of John Wesley as a theologian—perhaps a "folk theologian"—has emerged. Though this image has most typically been depicted by way of systematic theological analysis, Martin Schmidt, Robert Tuttle, and Kenneth J. Collins have offered narrative accounts of John Wesley's theological development.[28] A narrative framework seems particularly appropriate when, as Collins's work illustrates, theological development is considered in tandem with spiritual development.

---

27 Heitzenrater, *Elusive Mr. Wesley* (2nd rev. ed., 2003), 329–49; and *"Faithful Unto Death": Last Years and Legacy of John Wesley* (Bridwell Publications, New Series, no. 4; Dallas: Bridwell Library: 1991), 15–25.

28 Schmidt, *John Wesley* (1953–1966); Tuttle, *John Wesley: His Life and Theology* (1978); and Kenneth J. Collins, *A Real Christian: The Life of John Wesley* (1999). Schmidt's work considered John Wesley's theological development only to 1738, from which point he presupposed that Wesley's theological views remained consistent.

ENCODING WESLEYAN TRADITIONS

A scene in the film *Annie Hall* has a blowhard professor standing in line at a cinema trying to impress his girlfriend with his knowledge of Marshall McLuhan's theory of media. The Woody Allen character miraculously produces the real Marshall McLuhan who informs the arrogant professor how utterly mistaken he is. Woody Allen then looks in the camera and says, "Boy, if life were only like this!" At the end of a survey of narratives about John Wesley and the early Methodist movement, we might wish that the real John Wesley would show up and clarify some of the conflicting claims that have been made about him.

If there is a consistent thread in the narrative that runs through the pages above, it is that the telling and the retelling of narratives of Wesleyan origins have persisted and will persist into the future. This means that the false stories and misattributed quotations will probably persist, as evidenced in the plethora of Facebook memes that rebroadcast such quotations. The Wesleyan icons described above will continue to be transmitted, creative new retellings and reappropriations of the narratives will appear, and new scholarly discoveries will continue to be made. Interpreters will continue to make historical judgments based on available evidence amid conflicting claims about John Wesley and early Methodism and amid seriously conflicting claims about the contemporary identities of Wesleyan and Methodist communities.

Handing on narratives of Wesleyan origins is part of a larger process of encoding and transmitting the identity of Wesleyan communities that evolve and adapt and in other ways change over time. Other parts of this traditioning process are the transmission of teachings characteristic of Wesleyan communities and practices that have characterized these communities.

Creative contemporary efforts to identify and rethink particular aspects of a historic tradition relevant to contemporary issues are a sign of the vitality of a tradition. The Oxford Institute of Methodist Theological Studies has sponsored consistently creative attempts to relate the resources of the Wesleyan past to contemporary issues facing Wesleyan communities, especially in its systematic theology sessions.[29] Another contemporary example of this process is the collection of essays edited by Mary Elizabeth Mullino Moore published under the title *A Living Tradition: Critical Recovery and Reconstruction of Wesleyan Heritage* (see chapter 5).[30]

The present work also seeks the revitalization of a Wesleyan tradition but in a different way than in the work of contemporary systematic theology or moral theology. I have attempted in this volume, in a parallel study of *Wesleyan Beliefs,* and in a projected parallel volume on Wesleyan practices, to identify a persistent core of beliefs, narratives, and practices that have characterized Wesleyan communities through their histories from the beginnings of the Wesleyan movement to the present time. I have attempted to describe something like the fullness or integrity of this tradition through time. This kind of scholarship may not carry the vibrancy of creative, contemporary individuals engaging utterly pressing contemporary theological and ethical and social issues. For one thing, the scholarship represented in this volume is concerned with the teachings and practices and narratives transmitted by and through communities, and by their very natures, communities evolve more slowly than creative individuals might hope.

But communities do adapt and change and they do transmit identities encoded in stories and teachings and practices across generations, as the previous chapters show. Gifted leaders in communities not only transmit but also transform the cultures of communities and sometimes even the cultures of broader communities around them. We need to pay attention to the fullness or integrity of the tradition, not just in response to pressing contemporary needs, but because there are elements of the tradition whose relevance may only be appreciated in the future.

---

29 Cf. Brian E. Beck, *Exploring Methodism's Heritage: The Oxford Institute of Methodist Theological Studies* (Nashville: General Board of Higher Education and Ministry of The United Methodist Church, 2004).

30 See especially the introductory and concluding essays by Moore, 1–12 and 203–23.

Handing on a Deep Christian Tradition

On a Sunday morning in Seoul I attended the Yoido Full Gospel Church, perhaps the largest Christian congregation in the world with about a half million members. The phrase *Full Gospel* signifies that the congregation is part of the Pentecostal tradition. But it didn't look or sound like the Pentecostal congregations I knew growing up in Texas. I heard the congregation singing in Korean the Thomas Ken doxology ("Praise God from whom all blessings flow . . .") to the Reformation-age tune "Old 100th" played on a pipe organ, and then I heard the congregation reciting together the Apostles' Creed. I saw an altar table with candles and clergy wearing traditional (Western-style) clergy gowns with stoles.

The Yoido Full Gospel Church has thrived beyond its critical transition from its founding pastor, David Yonggi Cho. It is surviving when other mega-churches like the famed Crystal Cathedral in Orange County, California, have scaled back hugely or ceased operations altogether after the transition from their founding pastor. The Yoido Church has built not a single-generation congregation, but it has found ways to transmit its church culture to subsequent generations. Part of this is its extensive use of small, home-based groups that parallel early Methodist classes and bands. Another part of their ability to transmit their culture is their use of older Christian traditions mentioned above—in their case, western Protestant traditions that have come by way of Presbyterian as well as Methodist influences on Korean Protestant culture.

Tradition is what survives beyond a generation. It literally denotes that which is "handed on" from one group to another, from one generation to another.[31] Narratives are one of the prominent ways in which one generation hands on its culture and the identity of its community to future generations. This work has shown how, since the time of John Wesley himself, Wesleyan communities have consistently

---

31   The English word "tradition" comes from the Latin *tradere*, "to hand on." The New Testament Greek equivalent is "παραδοῦναι," with the same meaning, utilized in 1 Corinthians 11:23 and 15:1, 3.

used narratives of their Wesleyan origins to encode who they are and what they stand for.

At the heart of the Wesleyan tradition is the deep mystery of Christian faith, and what Wesleyan Christians "hand on" today is a distinctive way of being Christian.

> Since many have undertaken to set down an orderly account of the events that have been fulfilled among us, just as they were handed on to us. . . . (Luke 1:1–2a)

> For I received from the Lord what I also handed on to you. . . . (I Corinthians 11:23)

> For I handed on to you as of first importance what I in turn had received: that Christ died for our sins in accordance with the scriptures, and that he was buried, and that he was raised on the third day in accordance with the scriptures. (I Corinthians 15:3–4)

Bibliography

African Methodist Episcopal Church. *The Catechism (Formerly "The Turner Catechism") of the A.M.E. Church.* Nashville: A.M.E.C. Sunday School Union; repr. ed. of 2000.

———. *The Doctrines and Discipline of the African Methodist Episcopal Church.* Philadelphia: Richard Allen and Jacob Tapisco for the African Methodist Connection in the United States. John H. Cunningham, Printer, 1817.

African Methodist Episcopal Zion Church. *The Doctrines and Discipline of the African Methodist Episcopal Zion Church, Revised by the General Conference, Indianapolis, Indiana, 1924.* Charlotte, NC: A.M.E. Zion Publication House, 1925.

[Anonymous] *A Catechism for Wesleyan Methodists: Particularly for Methodist Class Leaders and Local Preachers, Wherein the Various Points at Issue between the Conference and the People are Taken Up and Discussed in Familiar Dialogue.* Liverpool: E. Smith and Co., 1834.

Ayling, Stanley Edward. *John Wesley.* Cleveland and New York: William Collins, 1979.

Baker, Frank. *John Wesley and the Church of England.* Nashville: Abingdon Press, 1970.

———. *Union Catalogue of the Publications of John and Charles Wesley.* 2nd ed. Stone Mountain, GA: George Zimmerman, 1991.

Bangs, Nathan. *A History of the Methodist Episcopal Church.* 4 vols. New York: T. Mason and G. Lane, 1839.

Beard, George. *The History of Methodism, or the Wesleyan Centenary: A Poem in Twelve Books.* London: Simpkin, Marshall, and Co., and Southwark: J. C. Beard, n.d., (ca. 1840).

Beck, Brian E. *Exploring Methodism's Heritage: The Oxford Institute of Methodist Theological Studies.* Nashville: General Board of Higher Education and Ministry of The United Methodist Church, 2004.

Berger, Peter L., and Thomas Luckmann. *The Social Construction of Reality.* 2nd ed. Garden City, New York: Anchor Books, 1967.

Berman, Art. *Preface to Modernism.* Urbana and Chicago University of Illinois Press, 1994.

Bicknell, E. J. *A Theological Introduction to the Thirty-Nine Articles of Religion of the Church of England.* 3rd ed. London: Longmans, Green, and Co., 1955.

Bondi, Roberta C. "The Meeting of Oriental Orthodoxy and United Methodism." In Paul Fries and Tiran Nersoyan, eds. *Christ in East and West.* Macon GA: Mercer University Press, 1987, 171–84.

———. "The Role of the Holy Spirit from a United Methodist Perspective." *Greek Orthodox Theological Review* 31:3–4 (1986): 351–60.

Book of Common Prayer: see entries under Cummings, Brian, and Episcopal Church in the USA.

Bowen, Marjorie. *Wrestling Jacob: A Study in the Life of John Wesley and Some Members of the Family.* London: Religious Book Club, 1938.

Brantley, Richard E. Locke. *Wesley, and the Method of English Romanticism.* Gainesville: University Press of Florida, 1984.

Bresee, Phineas F. *Twenty-Nine Sermons.* Los Angeles: Nazarene Publishing Co., 1903.

Bucke, Emory S., ed. *History of American Methodism.* 3 vols. New York and Nashville: Abingdon Press, 1964.

Buckley, James M. *Christians and the Theater.* New York: Phillips and Hunt; and Cincinnati: Cranston and Stowe, 1886, but copyrighted 1875.

———. *History of Methodists in the United States.* New York: Christian Literature Co., 1896.

———. *The Fundamentals and Their Contrasts.* New York: Eaton and Mains; and Cincinnati: Jennings and Graham, 1906.

Burn, Richard. *The Ecclesiastical Law.* 4 vols. 9th ed. London: S. Sweet, V. and R. Stevens, and G. S. Norton, 1842.

Campbell, Ted A. "Christian Tradition, John Wesley, and Evangelicalism"; in *Anglican Theological Review* 74:1 (Winter 1992): 62–63.

———. "The Image of Christ in the Poor: On the Medieval Roots of the Wesleys' Ministry with the Poor"; in Richard P. Heitzenrater, ed., *The Poor and the People Called Methodists.* Nashville: Kingswood, 2002.

———. "Is It Just Nostalgia? The Renewal of Wesleyan Studies." *Christian Century* 107:13 (18 April 1990): 396–98.

———. *John Wesley and Christian Antiquity: Religious Vision and Cultural Change.* Nashville: Kingswood Books imprint of the Abingdon Press, 1991.

———. "John Wesley's Conceptions and Uses of Christian Antiquity." PhD dissertation, Southern Methodist University, 1984.

———. "The Origins and Early Growth of Methodism, 1730–1791," in Gibson, Forsaith, and Wellings, eds., *Ashgate Research Companion to World Methodism,* 21–24.

———. *The Sky Is Falling, the Church Is Dying, and Other False Alarms.* Nashville: Abingdon Press, 2015.

———. *Wesleyan Beliefs: Formal and Popular Expressions of Core Teachings of Wesleyan Communities.* Nashville: Kingswood Books, 2010.

Cannon, William R. *The Theology of John Wesley, with Special Reference to the Doctrine of Justification.* Nashville and New York: Abingdon-Cokesbury Press, 1946.

Chalmers, Thomas. *Sermons and Discourses.* 2 vols. New York: Robert Carter, 1844.

Chiles, Robert E. *Theological Transition in American Methodism, 1790–1935.* New York and Nashville: Abingdon Press, 1965.

Church of the Nazarene [Pentecostal Church of the Nazarene]. *Manual of the Pentecostal Church of the Nazarene: Published by Authority of the General Assembly Held at Pilot Point, Texas, 1908.* Los Angeles: Nazarene Publishing Co., 1908.

Clapper, Gregory S. *John Wesley on Religious Affections: His Views on Experience and Emotion and Their Role in the Christian Life and Theology.* Metuchen, New Jersey: The Scarecrow Press, 1989.

Clark, Elmer T. "What Happened at Aldersgate," in Clark, ed. *What Happened at Aldersgate*, 11–42.

———. ed. *What Happened at Aldersgate.* Nashville: Methodist Publishing Corporation, 1938.

Clark, J. C. D. *English Society, 1688-1832.* Cambridge: Cambridge University Press, 1985.

Coke, [Thomas] and [Henry] Moore. *The Life of the Rev. John Wesley, A.M.: Including an Account of the Great Revival of Religion, in Europe and America, of which He was the First and Chief Instrument.* London: G. Paramore, 1792.

Collins, Kenneth J. *A Real Christian: The Life of John Wesley.* Nashville: Abingdon Press, 1999.

Connor, Steven. *Postmodernist Culture: An Introduction to Theories of the Contemporary.* Oxford: Basil Blackwell, 1989.

Crutcher, Timothy J. *John Wesley: His Life and Thought.* Kansas City: Beacon Hill Press, 2015.

Cummings, Brian, ed., *The Book of Common Prayer: The Texts of 1549, 1559, and 1662.* Oxford: Oxford University Press, 2011.

Davies, Rupert E., and E. Gordon Rupp, eds., *A History of the Methodist Church in Great Britain.* 4 vols. London: Epworth Press, 1965–1988.

Dawkins, Richard. *The Selfish Gene.* New York and Oxford: Oxford University Press, 1976.

Deschner, John. *Wesley's Christology: An Interpretation.* rev. ed. Dallas: Southern Methodist University Press, 1985.

Dickerson, Dennis C. *African Methodism and Its Wesleyan Heritage: Reflections on AME Church History.* Nashville: AMEC Sunday School Union, 2009.

Dockery, David S.: see entry under "George, Timothy."

Drabble, Margaret, ed. *The Oxford Companion to English Literature.* 6th ed. Oxford: Oxford University Press, 2000.

Dreyer, Frederick. "Faith and Experience in the Thought of John Wesley." *American Historical Review* 88 (1983): 12–30.

Drinkhouse, Edward J. *History of Methodist Reform: Synoptical of General Methodism, with Special and Comprehensive Reference to Its Most Salient Exhibition in the History of the Methodist Protestant Church.* Baltimore and Pittsburgh: Board of Publication of the Methodist Protestant Church, 1899.

Dunlap, E. Dale. "Methodist Theology in Great Britain in the Nineteenth Century: With Special Reference to the Theology of Adam Clarke, Richard Watson, and William Burt Pope." PhD dissertation, Yale University, 1956. Repr. ed. Ann Arbor, MI: University Microfilms International.

Edwards, Maldwyn. "John Wesley." In Davies and Rupp, eds., *A History of the Methodist Church in Great Britain*, 37–79.

———. *John Wesley and the Eighteenth Century*. London: Epworth Press, 1933.

Episcopal Church in the USA. *The Book of Common Prayer*. New York: Oxford University Press, 1990.

Ferguson, Charles W. *Organizing to Beat the Devil: Methodists and the Making of America*. Garden City, New York: Doubleday and Co., 1971.

Foster, Douglas A. "The Nature of the Apostolicity of the Church: Perspectives from the Churches of Christ." In Ted A. Campbell, Ann K. Riggs, and Gilbert W. Stafford, eds., *Ancient Faith and American-Born Churches*. New York, NY and Mahwah, NJ: Paulist Press, 2006.

George, Timothy, and David S. Dockery. *Theologians of the Baptist Tradition*. Nashville: Broadman and Holman, 2001.

Gibson, Edmund, ed. *Codex Juris Ecclesiastici Anglicani: Or, Statutes, Constitutions, Canons, Rubricks and Articles of the Church of England*. London: J. Baskett, 1713.

Gibson, William. *The Church of England, 1688-1832: Unity and Accord*. London: Routledge, 2001.

———. Peter Forsaith, and Martin Wellings, eds., *The Ashgate Research Companion to World Methodism*. Farnham, Surrey: Ashgate, 2013.

Goodloe, Robert W.: see entry under "Luccock, Halford E."

Gregory, Jeremy. *Restoration, Reformation, and Reform, 1660–1828: The Archbishops of Canterbury and Their Diocese*. Oxford: Oxford University Press, 2000.

Griffin, Eric Richard. "Daniel Brevint and the Eucharistic Calvinism of the Caroline Church of England, 1603–1674." ThD thesis, University of Toronto, 2000.

Haggadah: See entry under "Tabory, Joseph."

Hampson, John. *Memoirs of the Late Rev. John Wesley, A.M., with a Review of His Life and Writings, and a History of Methodism from It's Commencement in 1729 to the Present Time*. 3 vols. London: James Graham, 1791.

Harmon, Nolan B., ed. *Encyclopedia of World Methodism*. 2 vols. Nashville: United Methodist Publishing House, 1976.

Harmon, Steven R. *Towards Baptist Catholicity: Essays on Tradition and the Baptist Vision*. Studies in Baptist History and Thought series. Waynesboro, GA: Paternoster Press, 2006.

Harrison, G. Elsie. *Son to Susanna: The Private Life of John Wesley*. Nashville: Cokesbury Press, 1938.

Hattersley, Roy. *The Life of John Wesley: A Brand from the Burning*. New York: Doubleday, 2003.

Haydon, Colin: see entry under "Walsh, John."

Heitzenrater, Richard P. *The Elusive Mr. Wesley*. 2nd ed. Nashville: Abingdon Press, 2003.

———. *"Faithful Unto Death": Last Years and Legacy of John Wesley*. The Bridwell Publications, New Series, no. 4. Dallas: Bridwell Library: 1991.

———. *Wesley and the People Called Methodists*. Nashville: Abingdon Press, 1995.

———. "The Wesleyan Tradition and the Myths We Love," in Mary Elizabeth Mullino Moore, ed., *A Living Tradition*. Nashville: Kingswood Books, 2013, 13–44.

———. See entry under "Wesley, John."

Hempton, David. *Methodism: Empire of the Spirit*. New Haven and London: Yale University Press, 2005.

Hobsbawm, Eric, "Introduction: Inventing Traditions." In Eric Hobsbawm and Terence Ranger, eds., *The Invention of Tradition*. Cambridge: Cambridge University Press, 1983, 1–14.

Hotchkiss, Valerie, and Jaroslav Pelikan, eds., *Creeds and Confessions of Faith in the Christian Tradition*. 3 vols. New Haven: Yale University Press, 2003.

Hughes, Hugh Price. Introduction to *The Journal of John Wesley*. repr. ed. Chicago: Moody Press, 1974.

———. *Social Christianity: Sermons Delivered in St. James Hall, London*. London: Hodder and Stoughton, 1890.

Hutchinson, Paul: see entry under "Luccock, Halford E."

Hyatt, Eddie. *2000 Years of Charismatic Christianity: A 21st Century Look at Church History from a Pentecostal, Charismatic Perspective*. Dallas, Texas: Hyatt International Ministries, 1998.

Ingersol, Stan. *Nazarene Roots: Pastors, Prophets, Revivalists, and Reformers*. Kansas City: Stan Ingersol and the Beacon Hill Press, 2009.

Inskip, John S., ed. *Holiness Miscellany*. Philadelphia: National Publishing Association for the Promotion of Holiness, 1882.

Jackson, George. *The Old Methodism and the New*. London: Hodder and Stoughton, 1903.

Jackson, Thomas. *The Centenary of Wesleyan Methodism: A Brief Sketch of the Rise, Progress, and Present State of the Wesleyan-Methodist Societies Throughout the World*. London: John Mason, 1839.

James, William. *The Varieties of Religious Experience: A Study in Human Nature*. New York: The Modern Library, 1902.

Jennings, Theodore W. Jr. *Good News to the Poor: John Wesley's Evangelical Economics*. Nashville: Abingdon Press, 1990.

Jonas, W. Glenn Jr. *The Baptist River: Essays on Many Tributaries of a Diverse Tradition*. Macon, GA: Mercer University Press, 2006.

Kelley, Dean M. *Why Conservative Churches are Growing: A Study in Sociology of Religion*. New York: Harper and Row, 1972.

Langford, Thomas A. *Practical Divinity: Theology in the Wesleyan Tradition*. 2 vols. rev. ed. Nashville: Abingdon Press, 1998.

Lash, Ephrem. "The Greek Writings Attributed to St. Ephrem the Syrian." In John Behr, Andrew Louth, and Dimitri Conomos, eds. *Abba: The Tradition of Orthodoxy in the West*. Crestwood, New York: St. Vladimir's Seminary Press, 2003.

Lee, Hoo-Jung. "The Doctrine of New Creation in the Theology of John Wesley." PhD dissertation, Emory University, 1991.

Lee, Jesse. *A Short History of the Methodists in the United States of America: Beginning at 1766, and Continued to 1809, to Which is Prefixed a Brief Account of Their Rise in England in the year 1729.* Baltimore: Magill and Clime, 1810.

Lee, Umphrey. *John Wesley and Modern Religion.* Nashville: Cokesbury Press, 1936.

———. "Oration Delivered at Jamestown Exposition by Umphrey Lee of Sikeston, Missouri." A privately printed pamphlet (date unknown, but probably around 1907 or 1908) reproduced in 1972 by Bridwell Library.

Lindsay, James Gordon. "John Wesley and William Carey," vol. 4 of *Men Who Changed the World.* Dallas, Texas: Christ for the Nations, ca. 1972.

Lloyd, Gareth, *Charles Wesley and the Struggle for Methodist Identity.* Oxford: Oxford University Press, 2007.

Long, D. Stephen. *John Wesley's Moral Theology: The Quest for God and Goodness.* Nashville: Abingdon Press, 2005.

Luccock, Halford E., Paul Hutchinson, and Robert W. Goodloe. *The Story of Methodism.* New York and Nashville: Abingdon-Cokesbury Press, 1949.

Luckmann, Thomas: see entry under "Berger, Peter."

Maddox, Randy L. "Aldersgate: A Tradition History." In Maddox, ed. *Aldersgate Reconsidered*, 133–146.

———. ed. *Aldersgate Reconsidered.* Nashville: Kingswood Books, 1990.

Matthews, Rex Dale. "'Religion and Reason Joined': A Study in the Theology of John Wesley." PhD dissertation, Harvard University, 1986.

McCaine, Alexander. *Letters on the Organization and Early History of the Methodist Episcopal Church.* Boston: Thomas F. Norris, Olive Branch Office, 1850.

———. *The History and Mystery of Methodist Episcopacy, Or, A Glance at "The Institutions of the Church As We Received Them From Our Fathers."* Baltimore: Richard J. Matchett, 1827.

McCormick, Kelley Steve. "John Wesley's Use of John Chrysostom on the Christian Life." PhD dissertation, Drew University, 1983.

McPherson, Aimee Semple. *This is That: Personal Experiences, Sermons and Writings.* Los Angeles: Bridal Call Publishing House, 1919. Repr. ed. in the series "'The Higher Christian Life': Sources for the Study of the Holiness, Pentecostal, and Keswick Movements." New York and London: Garland Publishing, 1985.

Meeks, M. Douglas, ed. *The Future of the Methodist Theological Traditions.* Conference papers, Seventh Oxford Institute of Methodist Theological Studies, Oxford, England, 1982. Nashville: Abingdon Press, 1985.

Megill, Allan, ed., *Rethinking Objectivity.* Durham, NC and London: Duke University Press, 1994.

Meredith, Lawrence. "Essential Doctrine in the Theology of John Wesley with Special Attention to the Methodist Standards of Doctrine." PhD dissertation, Harvard University, 1962.

Methodist Episcopal Church. *A Form of Discipline for the Ministers, Preachers, and Members of the Methodist Episcopal Church in America, Considered and Approved at a Conference held at Baltimore, in the State of Maryland, On Monday the 27th of December, 1784.* New York: W. Ross, 1787.

———. *The Doctrines and Discipline of the Methodist Episcopal Church*. New York: Hunt and Eaton, and Cincinnati: Cranston and Curts, 1892.

———. *The Doctrines and Discipline of the Methodist Episcopal Church*. New York: Eaton and Mains, and Cincinnati: Curts and Jennings, 1896.

———. *Journal of the General Conference of the Methodist Episcopal Church*. New York: Eaton and Mains, and Cincinnati: Cuts and Jennings, 1896.

Methodist Episcopal Church, South. *Journal of the General Conference of the Methodist Episcopal Church, South*. Nashville: Publishing House of the Methodist Episcopal Church, South, 1894.

Monk, Robert C. *John Wesley: His Puritan Heritage: A Study of the Christian Life*. Nashville: Abingdon Press, 1966.

Moore, Henry: see entry under "Coke, Thomas."

Moore, Mary Elizabeth Mullino, ed. *A Living Tradition: Critical Recovery and Reconstruction of Wesleyan Heritage*. Nashville: Kingswood Books, 2013.

Norwood, Frederick A. *The Story of American Methodism: A History of the United Methodists and Their Relations*. Nashville: Abingdon Press, 1974.

Outler, Albert C. "A New Future for Wesley Studies: An Agenda for 'Phase III.'" In Meeks, ed., *Future of the Methodist Theological Traditions*, 34–52.

———. *Theology in the Wesleyan Spirit*. Nashville: Tidings, 1975.

———. See entries under "Wesley, John."

Palmer, Phoebe. *The Way of Holiness*. New York: Lane and Scott, 1849.

Parham, Charles F. *A Voice Crying in the Wilderness*. Charleston, SC: privately published by Charles F. Parham, 4th ed. of 1944. Repr. 1985; originally published 1901.

Pascoe, Louis B. *Jean Gerson: Principles of Church Reform*. Leiden: E. J. Brill, 1973.

Peck, Jesse T. *The Central Idea of Christianity*. Louisville, KY: Pentecostal Publishing Co., n.d. (thought to have been written around 1856).

Pelikan, Jaroslav: see entry under "Hotchkiss, Valerie."

Plumb, J. H. *England in the Eighteenth Century*. Pelican History of England series. Harmondsworth, Middlesex: Penguin Books, 1950; rev.ed. of 1963.

Pree, Wolfgang. *Design Patterns for Object-Oriented Software Development*. Workingham: Addison-Wesley Publishing Company, 1995.

Rack, Henry D. *Reasonable Enthusiast: John Wesley and the Rise of Methodism*. Philadelphia: Trinity Press International, 1989.

———. See entry under "Wesley, John."

Rall, Harris Franklin. *Modern Premillennialism and the Christian Hope*. New York and Cincinnati: Abingdon Press, 1920.

———. *Was John Wesley a Premillennialist?* The Ryerson Essays, no. 1. Toronto: Methodist Book & Publishing House, 1921.

Richey, Russell E. *Early American Methodism*. Bloomington: Indiana University Press, 1991.

———. "History as a Bearer of Denominational Identity: Methodism as a Case Study." In Jackson Carroll and Wade Clark Roof, eds. *Beyond Establishment: Protestant Identity in a Post-Protestant Age*. Louisville: Westminster/John Knox, 1993., 270–95.

———. "History in the Discipline." In Langford, *Doctrine and Theology in The United Methodist Church*, 190–202.

Richey, Russell E., Kenneth E. Rowe, and Jean Miller Schmidt. *The Methodist Experience in America, A History*, vol. 1. Nashville: Abingdon Press, 2010.

Rigg, James H. *The Churchmanship of John Wesley: And the Relations of Wesleyan Methodism to the Church of England*. London: Wesleyan-Methodist Book-Room, rev. ed., 1886.

———. *The Living Wesley*. London: Charles H. Kelley, 3rd ed., 1905; the 1st ed. was 1874.

———. *Was John Wesley A High Churchman? A Dialogue for the Times*. London: The Wesleyan Methodist Book Room, 1882.

Robeck, Cecil M. Jr. "When Being a 'Martyr' Is Not Enough: Catholics and Pentecostals." In *Pneuma: Journal of the Society for Pentecostal Studies* 21:1 (Spring 1999): 3–10.

Rupp, E. Gordon: see entry under "Davies, Rupert E."

Rushdie, Salman. "Out of Kansas." In the Critic at Large column in *The New Yorker* (11 May 1992), 93.

Schmidt, Jean Miller. "'Strangely Warmed': The Place of Aldersgate in the Methodist Canon." In Maddox, ed. *Aldersgate Reconsidered*, 109–19.

Schmidt, Martin. *John Wesley*. 2 vols. Zürich and Frankfurt am Main: Gotthelf-Verlag, 1953–1966.

Shipley, David C. "The European Heritage." In Bucke, ed., *History of American Methodism*, vol. 1, 9–42.

Simpson, Mathew. *A Hundred Years of Methodism*. New York: Nelson and Phillips; Cincinnati: Hitchcock and Walden, 1876.

Stapleton, Michael, consultant editor. *The Cambridge Guide to English Literature*. Cambridge: Cambridge University Press, 1983.

Starkey, Lycurgus M. *The Work of the Holy Spirit: A Study in Wesleyan Theology*. New York: Abingdon Press, 1962.

Stevens, Abel. *A Compendious History of American Methodism: Abridged from the Author's "History of the Methodist Episcopal Church."* New York: Phillips and Hunt, and Cincinnati: Walden and Stowe, 1867, although a preface printed in the book carries the date 1868.

Stone, Ronald H. *John Wesley's Life and Ethics*. Nashville: Abingdon Press, 2001.

Stout, Harry S. *The Divine Dramatist: George Whitefield and the Rise of Modern Evangelicalism*. Grand Rapids: Eerdmans, 1991.

Sweet, William Warren. *Methodism in American History*. Nashville: Abingdon Press, 1954.

Tabory, Joseph, ed. *JPS Commentary on the Haggadah*. Philadelphia: Jewish Publication Society, 2008/5768.

Tanner, Norman P., SJ, ed., *Decrees of the Ecumenical Councils*. 2 vols. London: Sheed and Ward; and Washington, DC: Georgetown University Press, 1990.

Taylor, George Lansing. *The Gospel River: Or, The Evolution of Christianity*. New York: Hunt & Eaton; and Cincinnati: Cranston and Stowe, 1889.

Taylor, Stephen: see entry under "Walsh, John."

Thompson, E. P. *The Making of the English Working Class*. London: V. Gollancz, 1963.

Tomkins, Stephen. *John Wesley: A Biography*. Grand Rapids: Eerdmans, 2003.

Tuck, William Powell. *Our Baptist Tradition*. Macon, GA: Smith and Helwys, 2005.

Tucker, Karen B. Westerfield. *American Methodist Worship*. New York: Oxford University Press, 2001.

Turner, Henry McNeal. *The Genius and Theory of Methodist Polity, or the Machinery of Methodism: Practically Illustrated through a Series of Questions and Answers*. Philadelphia: Publication Department, A.M.E. Church, 1885.

Turner, John Munsey. *John Wesley: The Evangelical Revival and the Rise of Methodism in England*. Peterborough: Epworth Press, 2002.

Tuttle, Robert G. Jr. *John Wesley: His Life and Theology*. Grand Rapids: Zondervan, 1978.

Tyerman, Luke. *The Life and Times of the Reverend John Wesley, M.A., Founder of the Methodists*. 3 vols. New York: Harper and Brothers, Publishers, 1872.

Tyrrell, George. *Christianity at the Cross-roads*. London and New York: Longmans, Green and Co., 1909.

United Methodist Church. *The Book of Discipline of The United Methodist Church 2012*. Nashville: United Methodist Publishing House, 2012.

Urlin, Richard Denny. *The Churchman's Life of Wesley*. London: Society for Promoting Christian Knowledge, 1880.

———. *John Wesley's Place in Church History: Determined with the Aid of Facts and Documents Unknown to, Or Unnoticed by, His Biographers*. London, Oxford, and Cambridge: Rivingtons, 1870.

Vedder, Henry C. Review of J. M. Buckley, *History of Methodists in the United States* [1899 edition]. In *American Journal of Theology*, 1900: 200–203.

Vickers, Jason E. *Wesley: A Guide for the Perplexed*. London and New York: T & T Clark International, 2009.

Walsh, John. "Methodism and the Mob." In *Studies in Church History* 8 (1977): 213–27.

———, Colin Haydon, and Stephen Taylor, eds. *The Church of England, c. 1689–c. 1833: From Toleration to Tractarianism*. Cambridge: Cambridge University Press, 1993.

Ward, W. Reginald: see entry under "Wesley, John."

Wearmouth, Robert F. *Methodism and the Common People of the Eighteenth Century*. London; Epworth Press, 1945.

Weber, Theodore R. *Politics in the Order of Salvation: Transforming Wesleyan Political Ethics*. Nashville: Kingswood Books, 2001.

Wesley, John. *John Wesley: A Representative Collection of His Writings*. Albert C. Outler, ed. A Library of Protestant Thought. New York: Oxford University Press, 1964.

———. *Journal and Diaries*. W. Reginald Ward and Richard P. Heitzenrater, eds. Bicentennial Edition of *The Works of John Wesley*, vols. 18–24. Nashville: Abingdon Press, 1988ff.

———. *Letters*. Frank Baker and Ted A. Campbell, eds. Bicentennial Edition of *The Works of John Wesley*, vols. 25–27. Nashville: Abingdon Press, 2015.

———. *The Methodist Societies: History, Nature, and Design.* Rupert E. Davies, ed. Bicentennial Edition of *The Works of John Wesley*, vol. 9. Nashville: Abingdon Press, 1989.

———. *The Methodist Societies: The Minutes of Conference.* Henry D. Rack, ed. Bicentennial Edition of *The Works of John Wesley*, vol. 10. Nashville: Abingdon Press, 2011.

———. *Sermons.* Albert C. Outler, ed. Bicentennial Edition of *The Works of John Wesley*. 4 vols. Nashville: Abingdon Press, 1984-1987.

[——— and the Methodist Episcopal Church. *The Sunday Service of the Methodists in North America.* London: [William Strahan], 1784.

Whitehead, John, *The Life of the Rev. John Wesley, M.A., Sometime Fellows of Lincoln College, Oxford.* 2 vols. London: Stephen Couchman, 1793 and 1796.

Wigger, John. *Taking Heaven by Storm: Methodism and the Rise of Popular Religion in America.* Urbana and Chicago: University of Illinois Press, 1998.

Williams, Colin W. *John Wesley's Theology Today.* Nashville: Abingdon Press, 1960.

Wood, A. Skevington. *The Burning Heart: John Wesley: Evangelist.* Exeter: Paternoster Press, 1967.

Workman, Herbert Brook. *The Place of Methodism in the Catholic Church.* London: Epworth Press, rev. ed. of 1921; first edition was 1909.

INDEX

CPSIA information can be obtained
at www.ICGtesting.com
Printed in the USA
LVHW031157230520
656342LV00007B/183

9 780938 162445